JCMS Annual Review of the European Union in 2018

Edited by

Theofanis Exadaktylos, Roberta Guerrina and Emanuele Massetti

General Editors: Toni Haastrup and Richard Whitman

WILEY

This edition first published 2019

© 2019 John Wiley & Sons Ltd except for editorial material and organization

Registered Office

John Wiley & Sons Ltd, The Atrium, Southern Gate, Chichester, West Sussex, PO19 8SQ, UK

Editorial Offices

350 Main Street, Malden, MA 02148--5020, USA

9600 Garsington Road, Oxford, OX4 2DQ, UK

The Atrium, Southern Gate, Chichester, West Sussex, PO19 8SQ, UK

For details of our global editorial offices, for customer services, and for information about how to apply for permission to reuse the copyright material in this book please see our website at www.wiley.com/wiley-blackwell.

Library of Congress Cataloging-in-Publication Data

Library of Congress Cataloging-in-Publication data is available for this book

ISBN 978-1-119-57208-4

ISSN 0021-9886 (print) 1468-5965 (online)

A catalogue record for this book is available from the British Library.

Set in 11/12.5 pt Times by Toppan Best-set Premedia Limited

Printed in Singapore

1   2019

CONTENTS

JCMS 2019 Volume 57. Annual Review pp. 5–12   DOI: 10.1111/jcms.12954

Sailing through Troubled Waters and towards 'Someplace …'

THEOFANIS EXADAKTYLOS,[1] ROBERTA GUERRINA[1] and EMANUELE MASSETTI[2]
[1] University of Surrey, Guildford, United Kingdom [2] University of Trento, Trento, Italy

In his very critical book on the European economic and monetary union (EMU), Ashoka Mody uses one of the adages created by the famous American baseball player Yogi Berra: 'If you don't know where you're going […] you'll end up someplace else' (Mody, 2018). While the Indian-born economist sees this adage as appropriate for the EU in a long-term perspective, it can easily apply to the latest developments in the process of European integration.

2017 brought about some new hope, such as the election of Macron and the possible formation of a new Franco-German progressive agenda (Kriesi, 2018; Verdun, 2018), incremental progresses on the regulation strategy (Radaelli, 2018) and some steps towards the development of a common defence policy (Tocci, 2018). The year 2018 can be seen as one of transition. It is clear that Europe is now moving through very troubled waters, where the final destination remains unclear. In anticipation of the renewal of several top EU positions (including those resulting from the European Parliament elections) in 2019, we argue that 2018 was a bridge year, looking forward to better leadership and a more grounded understanding of the EU's problems, possibly with a clearer vision.

In our view, four main challenges have maintained or acquired high salience during 2018: firstly, the effects and legacy of the economic crisis (inequality, unemployment and poverty); secondly, a more turbulent and threatening international scenario, especially (but not exclusively) in terms of EU–US relations; thirdly, the electoral rise of populist and eurosceptic political forces, particularly those that use illiberal discourse and, last but not least, the delays in the Brexit process. These challenges pertain to different domains and are very different in nature. Yet it is clear that there are also important links between them, and they are best understood as part of a single phenomenon of contestation in which the very identity and purpose of the European project are in the balance. A new EU leadership, grounded in and mindful of the roots of these challenges, as well as the linkages between them, could bring the EU to a 'someplace else' that will be better, rather than worse, than where we are now.

We start from the EU policy failures related to the economic crisis because of the scale of the immediate social costs associated with it – inequality, poverty and social exclusion – and of the far-reaching implications for both EU politics and international politics. Inequality, poverty and social exclusion are long-standing and global challenges that go far beyond Europe (Grusky and Kanbur, 2006). Compared with the USA, the rise of inequality in the EU has been partially mitigated by the redistributive effects of the European social model (Blanchet et al., 2019a). However, the reaction of the EU at the onset of the Euro crisis in 2010 has primarily resulted in the imposition of austerity measures on several eurozone members (Kitromilides, 2011). These measures have been perceived by many as unnecessarily draconian and antithetical to the values embedded in the European project. The inevitable negative effects that these measures would have had on national welfare systems were not given due consideration, as in the minds of top EU officials the European social model was already 'gone' and not worth being properly protected, let alone restored.[1] A consensual view that has emerged among economists considered that the EU's handling of the Euro crisis was a massive and multistage policy failure (Baldwin and Giavazzi, 2015) with an asymmetrical impact in terms of the demographic groups worst affected at the national level (Cavanagh and O'Dwyer, 2018). In addition, the imposed fiscal discipline curtailed the capacity of the same states to maintain what was left of their respective versions of the European social model at a time in which this was most needed (Blanchet *et al.*, 2019b). Indeed, the countries that were forced to implement the harsher austerity measures and structural reforms were the ones that experienced substantive increases in unemployment, poverty and inequality (Herman, 2017), particularly among the groups traditionally seen as marginal (O'Dwyer, 2018). Austerity policies have not only been applied in compliance with the pre-existing Maastricht criteria, they have been further institutionalized with even stricter criteria and procedures, such as the so-called fiscal compact and the European semester (Bird and Mandilares, 2013). As a consequence, the current EMU system has kept inflicting scars in the social fabric of several EU countries, starting from those that are caught in the austerity-stagnation trap. This mechanism de facto polarizes the structural asymmetries that are at the root of the problem both at the national and European level (O'Dwyer, 2018; Heimberger and Kapeller, 2017). In the absence of any substantive and far-reaching reform there are strong indications of path-dependency, as signs of a new global economic slow-down accumulated in the final months of 2018.

Possible solutions to the structural economic issues of the EMU and to the social and political problems that they entail are briefly discussed below, when we present De Grauwe and Ji's contribution in this issue. The political initiatives that sought to address the inconsistencies of the EMU or to alleviate their consequences have produced negligible results. Indeed, the Juncker Commission's strategic investment fund, launched in mid-2015 with the view of boosting economic growth, and the proclamation of a European pillar of social rights in autumn 2017, while representing positive signals, have not yet produced significant improvements, nor are they likely to provide any game-changing result in the near future. More crucially, the reformist agenda launched by the new French President Emmanuel Macron for the EU in 2017 came up against German resistance to any step in the direction of risk-sharing. Some key events of 2018, such as the start of the Yellow Vest populist and protest movement, as well as the victory of populist and eurosceptic parties in the Italian general election, suggest that the EU status quo is fragile.

EMU structural issues and the ensuing economic crisis have contributed to the recent rise of populist and eurosceptic parties (Algan *et al.*, 2017; Braun and Tausendpfund, 2014; Hernandez and Kriesi, 2016; Hobolt and de Vries, 2016). They also have had important consequences on international politics, particularly for EU–US relations. In a way, given the fact that the USA has been governed since 2017 by a populist leader, President

---

[1]See the February 2012 interview by *The Wall Street Journal* with the President of the European Central Bank, Mario Draghi (https://www.ecb.europa.eu/press/key/date/2012/html/sp120224.en.html).

Donald Trump, the two themes overlap to some extent. However, it is important to note that the Trump administration's criticisms of the EMU imbalances and the macroeconomic policies of the dominant economy (Germany), which are deemed to be responsible for the deflationary trends within the eurozone, are nothing new. The main bone of contention has been exporting these dynamics in the international economy by skewing trade relations. In particular, the USA appears to be deeply troubled by Germany's large and continuous trade account surpluses. In January 2017 the Head of the National Trade Council Peter Navarro staged a frontal attack on Germany, accusing it of manipulating currency.[2] Indeed, moving to 2018, things appear to have taken a risky course, with the USA starting a trade war (a retaliation, in their view) against several trading partners, including the EU. This war did not consist only of filing disputes before the World Trade Organization but entailed introducing or increasing trade tariffs on specific goods. However, things may get worse in the years to come, as 2019 started with US threats to impose tariffs on imported automobiles, including those from Germany.

In addition to the ever more strained relations with the USA, the EU also had to face up Chinese assertiveness, particularly its belt and road initiative (BRI), which threatens to weaken the relative weight of the EU in global economic partnerships and even to penetrate deep into Europe, dividing EU member states. Indeed, the EU has tried to counter the Chinese initiative by launching an alternative EU–Asia connectivity strategy in September 2018 (European Commission, 2018), while Germany and France have demanded that BRI negotiations in Europe may occur only between China and the EU as a united actor. However, the year 2018 has seen the first EU member state, Greece, sign a separate BRI agreement with China. In early 2019 two more member states, Italy and Luxemburg, followed suit. Clearly, an economically ever more divided EU is increasingly exposed to political divisions in internal and international politics alike. These internal weaknesses also affect relationships with external partners that are themselves increasingly haunted by their domestic problems, such as Russia (see David and Romanova, 2019 in this issue).

These intersecting political and economic dynamics help us to make sense, in part, of the rise of populist and eurosceptic parties. This is a complex challenge that can be understood only by recognizing the heterogeneous nature of the ideological and political motivation of different groups. Indeed, populism characterizes itself primarily as an anti-elitist view (Canovan, 2002). It is also crucial to note that an excessive emphasis on the homogeneity of the people and/or on a monolithic understanding of the 'general will' is creating tensions with the liberal and pluralist pillar of contemporary democracies (Meny and Surel, 2002). The importance of the differentiation between left-wing (and pluralist) populism and right-wing (and anti-pluralist) populism emerges clearly, for instance, in the contribution by Lombardo and Kantola (2019, in this issue), whereby alliances between feminist and left-wing populist movements, such as the Indignados, are contrasted with the anti-gender rhetoric and initiatives of right-wing populist parties.

Given the persistence of a 'democratic deficit' (Follesdal and Hix, 2006), and of a mismatch between an optimistic theory and a gloomier reality of liberal intergovernmentalism (Hix, 2018), or, at the very least, of a 'credibility crisis' (Majone, 2000), the EU seems to have become a potent generator of populist politics. Under these conditions of dubious 'input legitimacy' and falling 'output legitimacy', populism and

---

[2]Navarro, P. (2017) 'Trump's top Adviser Accused Germany of Currency Exploitation'. *Financial Times*, 31 January.

euroscepticism have become inherently linked, both conceptually and empirically (Heinisch *et al.,* 2018). However, distinguishing between left-wing and right-wing populism appears to bear non-trivial consequences on the positioning of populist forces vis-à-vis the EU and European integration. Although the imposition of austerity policies has pushed left-wing populist parties to adopt a more radical criticism of the EU, these political forces remain overwhelmingly within the category of soft euroscepticism (Conti and Memoli, 2012; Della Porta *et al.,* 2017; March and Rommerskirchen, 2012;). In contrast, right-wing populist parties, on average, appear to stage a more principled and radical opposition to both the EU and European integration than their left-wing counterparts (De Vries and Edwards, 2009; Hooghe *et al.,* 2002; Van Elsas and van der Brug, 2014). More importantly, governing right-wing populist parties, particularly in central and eastern Europe, are implementing domestic institutional reforms that threat to disturb the due division of powers that underpins the rule of law in their respective states (Bugaric, 2008; Bustikova and Guasti, 2017). The EU has shown its de facto ineffectiveness in 2018 (and in previous years) in the face of such violations of liberal democratic standards. The implicit legitimation given to some of these political forces by their membership of the European People's Party (EPP), constitutes a further source of reputational and substantive damage, both internally and on the international scene.

In 2018 there were four presidential elections within the EU – the Czech Republic, Cyprus, Finland and Ireland; seven parliamentary elections – Italy, Hungary, Slovenia, Sweden, the Czech Republic (Senate), Latvia and Luxemburg; and three notable regional elections – Bavaria, Hessen and Andalusia. Three of the four elected (or re-elected) presidents – Cyprus, Finland and Ireland – are clearly europhile political figures, whereas the reconfirmed President of the Czech Republic, Milos Zeman, can be considered a left-wing populist and a soft eurosceptic. The parliamentary elections confirm the rising course of populist and eurosceptic parties that was noted in 2017 (Halikiopoulou, 2018). The Italian general election sanctioned the establishment of the second populist and eurosceptic government, after Greece, in western Europe. As Maggini and Chiaramonte (2019) report in this issue, the populist Five Star Movement increased its vote share from 25 to 32 per cent, while the radical-right populist Northern League increased its vote share from 4 to well over 17 per cent. The two populist and eurosceptic forces went on to form a government that promised to take an antagonistic stance vis-à-vis the EU. In Hungary, not only did the populist and eurosceptic (and EPP member) Hungarian Civic Alliance (Fidesz) strengthen its already dominant position, returning Viktor Orbán as the undisputed prime minister, but the far-right populist Movement for a Better Hungary (Jobbik) became the second party in parliament. In Slovenia the right-wing populist and eurosceptic (and EPP member) Social Democratic Party emerged as the first party, although eventually the government was formed by europhile coalition. In Sweden, the right-wing populist and hard eurosceptic Swedish Democrats increased their vote share from below 13 to well over 17 per cent, while the soft-eurosceptic Left Party also increased their vote share. Finally, the eurosceptic Civic Democratic Party was the main winner of the Senate elections in the Czech Republic; while the newly formed and eurosceptic Who Owns the State? (KPV) party obtained more than 14 per cent of the votes in Latvia. Moving to regional elections, the right-wing populist and eurosceptic Alternative for Germany (AfD) entered two more regional assemblies in Germany, with 13 per cent of the votes in Hessen and 10 per cent in Bavaria (see Arzheimer, 2019, in this issue); while the Andalusian election witnessed the first breakthrough of a far-right populist and eurosceptic party (Vox) with 11 per cent of votes since Spain's transition to democracy.

Last but not least, Brexit negotiations kept on absorbing a considerable amount of time and energy during 2018, without having yet produced either an orderly or a certain outcome. Indeed, the initial deadline for signing and ratifying a deal (the end of March) was postponed by six months (to the end of October) after multiple dramas were staged in votes in Westminster between late 2018 and early 2019. So far, the issue of the Irish border has emerged as the hard rock against which the goodwill for finding an internally acceptable compromise by both sides has been smashed. Clearly, the exit of a member state like the UK – a political and economic heavyweight in Europe with strong relationships with the Commonwealth – represents a terrible blow for the EU, not only in terms of domestic but also international politics (see Meunier and Nicolaidis, 2019, in this issue).

While the causes of Brexit are multifold and include UK-specific factors, Simon Hix has offered a compelling analytical perspective that links Brexit with the populist backlash that EU and national elites have contributed to creating. What we can observe is 'that many voters across Europe no longer trust their governments to represent their interests in EU politics, and that voters are deeply suspicious of the pro-European instincts of mainstream party elites' (Hix, 2018, p. 1596). However, so far, no other member state, including those governed by populist and eurosceptic parties, appears to consider seriously following in the British footsteps. Therefore, the feared domino effect appears to have been averted, for the time being. In addition, the negotiation process has shown there is considerable unity on the EU side. Obviously, there is no guarantee that this unity can be built upon and transferred to other issues or policy areas; nor even that it can be maintained up to the end of the Brexit negotiation or in the various post-Brexit scenarios. Yet, this unity in the face of the first defection from the EU club represents one of the very few positive signals of the year 2018.

This Annual Review tries to capture these complex political and economic dynamics in order to synthesize the state of play of the EU, as well as the new and ongoing challenges to the process of European integration. For this reason, it kicks off with two contributions that analyse the Brexit challenge from the point of view of the emerging EU27. Brigid Laffan's annual lecture in this issue provides a structured analysis of the overall strategy, the discourse frames and the organizational resources deployed by the EU in order to maintain a common front vis-à-vis the UK. It shows how Theresa May's mantra; 'Brexit means Brexit', was turned against British cherry-picking ambitions, and internal solidarity amongst the remaining 27 members was fed by immediately isolating the defector. In contrast, Jensen and Kelstrup (2019) analyse the puzzle of EU27 unity in Brexit negotiations in the light of different and competing theoretical approaches. While they remain agnostic about the durability of this unity in the unfolding process of Brexit, these authors propose the use of their analytical framework for analysing EU unity in other cases.

Coming to what has been earlier presented as the most structural challenge for the EU, namely fixing the EMU, De Grauwe and Ji (2019, in this issue) point out how the current EU leadership are still entertaining themselves with proposals that do not address the root of the problem. The contribution depicts a sort of paradox, whereby fiscal and political integration is presented as the only resolutive solution, albeit one currently ignored by EU policy-makers; while proposals advanced for 'market' solutions are dismissed. At the same time, De Grauwe and Ji seem to acknowledge that the political conditions that have determined the adoption of such palliative proposals and the rejection of even small steps in the direction of a political solution (that is, German dominance in the EU) will not be easily circumvented.

The rise of populist and eurosceptic parties is discussed in two contributions. Maggini and Chiaramonte (2019, this issue) present a detailed analysis of the 2018 Italian election, which saw the victory of the populist and eurosceptic parties, the Five Star Movement and the Northern League. Interestingly, their analysis of the twitter electoral campaign shows that euroscepticism was not a salient issue both on the demand and the supply side of the electoral market. Yet it remains to be clarified whether these findings anticipate a reversal of the growth of euroscepticism in Italian public opinion or, rather, whether there might be some disalignment in issue salience and positions between the twitter public and the whole public (and the respective parties' campaigns). Arzheimer (2019) provides a longitudinal analysis of AfD's breakthrough in German politics. Focusing on the 2018 regional elections in Bavaria and Hessen, the contribution discusses the electoral consolidation of the new right-wing populist parties and the ensuing acceptance of its presence in the increasingly fragmented German party system.

Lombardo and Kantola's (2019, in this issue) contribution builds on last year's reflections in the Annual Review by Cavaghan and O'Dwyer (2018) and Emejulu and Basu (2018), thus encouraging us to broaden our analytical frames to understand the impact of these complex trends on different groups. A feminist analysis of European integration and disintegration provides an important entry point for challenging mainstream narratives about crisis and recovery. Moreover, it also draws attention to the different ways in which both European governance and its more vocal critics, reproduce highly gendered and racialized structures and discourses.

Finally, EU external relations are dealt with in the contributions by Meunier and Nicolaidis (2019, in this issue), who take a comprehensive view; Aggestam and Hyde-Price (2019), who focus on EU–US relations; David and Romanova (2019), who analyse EU-Russia relations; and, finally, Carbone (2019, in this issue), on the relationship between the EU and trade partners in Africa, the Caribbean and the Pacific region (ACP).

Meunier and Nicolaidis offer a particularly sharp view on the linkages between the different challenges that the EU has to face and EU's international relations. They discuss, among other important issues, how the EU capacity to impose political conditionality on external trade partners has been badly affected by the internal weaknesses that undermined the EU normative credentials – for example, the imposition of economic hardship on growing sections of the population; the deepening and expansion of illiberal reforms in some member states (see also David and Romanova, this issue) – and external factors, like the emergence of credible alternatives to the EU as a major economic partner, such as China's BRI. David and Romanova (2019) show how the incapacity of the EU and Russia to emerge from the depth of very strained relationship, with all the ensuing reciprocal costs, appears to be determined not only by their diverging views on specific geopolitical issues and on the rule of law but also by the perceived weakening of the EU (and the West in general) in the eyes of Russia and the tutelage that US-dominated Nato still exercises on the EU's foreign and security policy. Carbone's contribution closes the Annual Review with an analysis of the key phases and issues in the renegotiation of a comprehensive trade agreement between the EU and ACP countries. This analysis shows important divisions emerging both within the EU (particularly on the issue of migration) and between ACP countries, particularly as consequence of the pressure exercised by the African Union on African partners. Finally, as in every year, the Chronology, available online only, is a thorough reference point highlighting some of the most important dates and key events in 2018.

Conclusion

Our aim again this year has been to highlight areas in European politics that merit attention from both an academic and a practitioner point of view. We argue that 2018 was a bridge year between the culmination of European challenges and a critical juncture in 2019, marking not only ten years since the European financial crisis began but also the challenges of integration and disintegration with Brexit and the change of guard in the leadership of the EU. In the same spirit as the Annual Review of 2017, this issue presents diverging views and critical opinions not only in the context of EU institutions but also in the realm of domestic European politics and international relations. In our preparation of the Annual Review of 2018, we have noted the continuation of the issues and trends identified in this year's issue.

References

Algan, Y., Guriev, S., Papaioannou, E. and Passari, E. (2017) 'The European Trust Crisis and the Rise of Populism'. *Brookings Papers on Economic Activity*, Vol. 2017, pp. 309–400.

Baldwin, R. and Giavazzi, F. (2015) *The Eurozone Crisis: A Consensus View of the Causes and a Few Possible Solutions* (London: Centre for Economic Research Policy).

Bird, G. and Mandilares, A. (2013) 'Fiscal Imbalances and Output Crises in Europe: Will the Fiscal Compact Help or Hinder?' *Journal of Economic Policy Reform*, Vol. 16, No. 1, pp. 1–16.

Blanchet, T., Chancel, L. and Gethin, A. (2019a) 'Forty Years of Inequality in Europe: Evidence from Distributional National Accounts', VOX CEPR Policy Portal. Available online at: https://voxeu.org/article/forty-years-inequality-europe. Last accessed 30 July 2019.

Blanchet, T., Chancel L., and Gethin, A. (2019b) 'How Unequal is Europe? Evidence from Distributional National Accounts', WID.world Working Paper 2019/6. Available online at: https://wid.world/document/bcg2019-full-paper/. Last accessed 30 July 2019.

Braun, D. and Tausendpfund, M. (2014) 'The Impact of the Euro Crisis on Citizens' Support for the European Union'. *Journal of European Integration*, Vol. 36, No. 3, pp. 231–45.

Bugaric, B. (2008) 'Populism, Liberal Democracy, and the Rule of Law in Central and Eastern Europe'. *Communist and Post-Communist Studies*, Vol. 41, No. 2, pp. 191–203.

Bustikova, L. and Guasti, P. (2017) 'The Illiberal Turn or Swerve in Central Europe?' *Politics and Governance*, Vol. 5, No. 4, pp. 166–76.

Canovan, M. (2002). The people, the masses, and the mobilization of power: the paradox of Hannah Arendt's" populism". *Social Research: An International Quarterly*, 69(2), 403–22.

Conti, N. and Memoli, V. (2012) 'The Multi-faceted Nature of Party-Based Euroscepticism'. *Acta Politica*, Vol. 47, No. 2, pp. 91–112.

De Vries, C.E. and Edwards, E.E. (2009) 'Taking Europe to its Extremes. Extremist Parties and Public Euroscepticism'. *Party Politics*, Vol. 15, No. 1, pp. 5–28.

Della Porta, D., Kouki, H. and Fernandez, J. (2017) 'Left's Love and Hate for Europe: Syriza, Podemos and Critical Visions of Europe During the Crisis'. In Caiani, M. and Guerra, S. (eds) *Euroscepticism, Democracy and the Media: Communicating Europe, Contesting Europe* (Basingstoke: Palgrave).

European Commission (2018) 'EU Steps up its Strategy for Connecting Europe and Asia', 19/09/2018. Available at: http://europa.eu/rapid/press-release_IP-18-5803_en.htm. Last accessed 30 July 2019.

Follesdal, A. and Hix, S. (2006) 'Why There is a Democratic Deficit in the EU: A Response to Majone and Moravcsik'. *Journal of Common Market Studies*, Vol. 44, No. 3, pp. 533–62.

Grusky, D.B. and Kanbur, R. (eds) (2006) *Poverty and Inequality* (Stanford, CA: Stanford University Press).

Halikiopoulou, D. (2018). A right-wing populist momentum? A review of 2017 elections across Europe. *Journal of Common Market Studies*, 56(S1), 63–73.

Heimberger, P. and Kapeller, J. (2017) 'The Performativity of Potential Output: Pro-cyclicality and Path Dependency in Coordinating European Fiscal Policies'. *Review of International Political Economy*, Vol. 24, No. 5, pp. 904–28.

Heinisch, R., Massetti, E. and Mazzoleni, O. (2018) 'Populism and Ethno-territorial Politics in European Multi-level Systems'. *Comparative European Politics*, Vol. 16, No. 6, pp. 923–36.

Herman, C. (2017) 'Crisis, Structural Reform and the Dismantling of the European Social Model(s)'. *Economic and Industrial Democracy*, Vol. 38, No. 1, pp. 51–68.

Hernández, E. and Kriesi, H. (2016) 'The Electoral Consequences of the Financial and Economic Crisis in Europe'. *European Journal of Political Research*, Vol. 55, No. 2, pp. 203–24.

Hix, S. (2018) 'When Optimism Fails: Liberal Intergovernmentalism and Citizen Representation'. *JCMS*, Vol. 56, No. 7, pp. 1595–613.

Hobolt, S.B. and De Vries, C. (2016) 'Turning against the Union? The Impact of the Crisis on the Eurosceptic Vote in the 2014 European Parliament Elections'. *Electoral Studies*, Vol. 44, pp. 504–14.

Hooghe, L., Marks, G. and Wilson, C.J. (2002) 'Does Left/Right Structure Party Positions on European Integration?' *Comparative Political Studies*, Vol. 35, No. 8, pp. 965–89.

Kitromilides, Y. (2011) 'Deficit Reduction, the Age of Austerity, and the Paradox of Insolvency'. *Journal of Post Keynesian Economics*, Vol. 33, No. 3, pp. 517–36.

Kriesi, H. (2018). The 2017 French and German Elections. *Journal of Common Market Studies*, 56(S1), 51–62.

Majone, G. (2000) 'The Credibility Crisis of Community Regulation'. *Journal of Common Market Studies*, Vol. 38, No. 2, pp. 273–302.

March, L. and Rommerskirchen, C. (2012) 'Out of Left Field? Explaining the Variable Electoral Success of European Radical Left Parties'. *Party Politics*, Vol. 21, No. 1, pp. 40–53.

Mény, Y., & Surel, Y. (2002). The constitutive ambiguity of populism. In Mény, Y., & Surel, Y. (eds). *Democracies and the populist challenge* (pp. 1–21). Palgrave Macmillan, London.

Mody, Ashoka (2018) *EuroTragedy: A Drama in Nine Acts*, New York: Oxford University Press

O'Dwyer, M. (2018) 'Making Sense of Austerity: The Gendered Ideas of European Economic Policy'. *Comparative European Politics*, Vol. 16, No. 5, pp. 745–61.

Radaelli, C. M. (2018). Halfway through the better regulation strategy of the Juncker Commission: what does the evidence say?. *Journal of Common Market Studies*, 56(S1), 85–95.

Tocci, N. (2018). Towards a European security and defence union: Was 2017 a watershed?. *Journal of Common Market Studies*, 56(S1), 131–41.

Van Elsas, E.J. and van der Brug, W. (2014) 'The Changing Relationship Between Left–Right Ideology and Euroscepticism, 1973–2010'. *European Union Politics*, Vol. 16, No. 2, pp. 194–215.

Verdun, A. (2018). Institutional Architecture of the Euro Area. *Journal of Common Market Studies*, 56(S1), 74–84.

JCMS 2019 Volume 57. Annual Review pp. 13–27   DOI: 10.1111/jcms.12917

How the EU27 Came to Be*

BRIGID LAFFAN
Robert Schuman Centre for Advanced Studies, European University Institute, Florence

Introduction

The evening of 23 June 2016 was a momentous one in the history of European integration. In an 'in-out' referendum, the UK opted for 'exit' over 'voice' when voting by 52 per cent to leave the EU.[1] On that narrow margin, the first member state in the history of the EU was heading for the exit. The Brexit shock came at a time when the EU had endured a series of crises beginning with acute turbulence in the Eurozone, followed by the refugee crisis in 2015 and a deteriorating geopolitical environment. The immediate reaction from the media was that this shock might lead to the disintegration of the EU as the final straw that broke the camel's back. It seemed more than a weakened Union could bear. In fact, the EU responded to Brexit with resolve and a determination to protect the polity. The reflex was almost biological in character and the intent was to preserve the genus.

In this lecture, I explore what the EU response reveals about the Union, about what membership means and how the EU behaved as a strategic actor in the aftermath of the referendum. My objective is to understand and explain how the Union framed Brexit, created a Brexit toolkit and defended its interests. The reaction to Brexit, I will argue, reveals the DNA of the EU as a maturing polity exemplified by the Union's determination to use its full capacity when faced with an existential threat. By June 2016, the Union's capacity to absorb shocks had strengthened as Europe's Union had been tested and contested through crises (Laffan, 2018). The context in which the UK embarked on a referendum and its subsequent outcome is important to understanding the Union's reflex when the result became apparent.

I. Context

In January 2013 the UK Prime Minister David Cameron made a commitment to holding an 'in-out' referendum on EU membership if he returned to power. His strategy was to renegotiate the terms of membership, which would subsequently form the basis of a popular vote. In 2015 Prime Minister Cameron won the May election and embarked on his renegotiation plan. For the other member states, the Cameron renegotiation was a distraction, a form of British self-indulgence. Despite this, the UK's partners agreed a settlement in February 2016 that many felt was far too generous to London.[2] The other member states watched on as the polarized debate in the UK led to a vote to exit in the referendum.

* JCMS Annual Review Lecture, delivered 4 April 2019 at the European Parliament, Brussels.
[1] I would like to thank officials at the Council, members of President Tusk's Cabinet and members of Task Force 50 in the EU Commission for agreeing to be interviewed for this lecture.
[2] This was a recurrent theme in interviews for this lecture.

Brexit was perceived as an existential threat in the immediate aftermath of the vote. The remaining 27 member states and European institutions were determined that Brexit would not have a domino effect leading to the disintegration of the Union. Brexit would have to be weathered and the EU would continue and prosper without the UK. An urgent response came in the form of two statements on 24 June, the first from President Tusk of the European Council, followed by a joint statement from the presidents of the European Council, the Council Presidency, and the European Commission and Parliament. This was the first European framing of the UK's decision to leave. The key elements of the Union's reflex narrative were:

- *The survival of the Union*: Speaking on behalf of the 27 member states, President Tusk asserted that '[f]or all of us, the Union is the framework of our common future' (Tusk, 2016a). The EU Joint Statement was a projection of strength: 'We will stand strong and uphold the EU's core values of promoting peace and the well-being of its peoples. The Union of 27 member states will continue' (EU, 2016). The protection of the polity and the will to survive was paramount.
- *Unity*: President Tusk declared: 'Today on behalf of the 27 leaders I can say that we are determined to keep our unity as twenty seven' (Tusk, 2016a). This pledge of unity was reinforced in the statement from the EU institutions, affirming that '[t]his is an unprecedented situation but we are united in our response' (EU, 2016).
- *Process and orderly withdrawal*. The statements pointed to the Treaty of Lisbon Art. 50, the legal roadmap to an orderly exit.
- *The UK as an embryonic other*. The future relationship would be negotiated with the UK as a third country and would involve a balance of rights and obligations. The departure, an endogenous shock, was framed as an exogenous one. While expressing genuine regret at the outcome of the referendum, the Union swiftly moved to control and contain Brexit. President Tusk immediately offered the European Council of 27 an informal discussion within a week of the referendum, where he proposed that the heads of state and government (HoSG 27) should engage in reflection on the future of the Union. The Union of 27 was in the process of becoming a reality, just as the UK was becoming a third country.

II. Framework of Analysis

The EU is a polity consisting of its member states and the collective, the whole and the parts, held together by treaties, institutions, law, a commitment to the pooling of sovereignty and deep interdependence. The analytical framework for the first part of the article is derived from three core concepts in political science: ideas, institutions and interests. These core concepts are translated into three interrelated elements: framing, deploying capacity and building method and interests[3] (see Figure 1).

[3]The empirical data for this lecture are based on a content analysis of over 60 documents, involving 1000 codes and including official negotiating documents, speeches, press releases and interviews. The documents were analysed using MaxQDA. I would like to acknowledge and thank Valentina Petrovic, researcher at the European University Institute for her invaluable assistance with this.

Figure 1: Analytical Framework. [Colour figure can be viewed at wileyonlinelibrary.com]

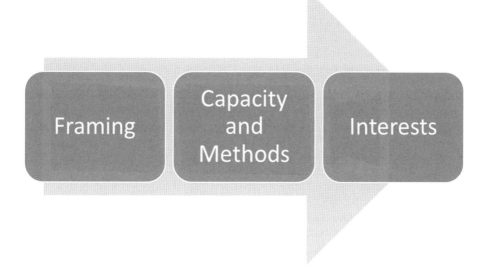

Framing. Framing is a key component of any political process, particularly in the context of a big political event. Political actors are forced to develop understandings of the event and the challenges associated with it. These challenges are not simply givens but are matters of interpretation and decoding. Snow and Benford define a frame 'as an interpretive schemata that signifies and condenses the "world out there"' (Snow and Benford, 1992, p. 137). The process of framing is highly political. According to Kingdon, there are 'great political stakes in problem definition' (Kingdon, 2011, p. 110). Crucial for Stone is the use of language whereby political actors use 'different methods, or languages' of problem definition (Stone, 2002, p. 134). Framing is designed to produce a persuasive and compelling story of what the situation is. This analysis seeks to map the framing of Brexit by the EU27 and the core ideas deployed by the Union to make sense of Brexit and respond to it. The Union's framing of Brexit had a dual purpose: firstly, it provided the EU, a political system involving 27 states, with an internal frame of reference and a master narrative; and secondly, it prepared the Union for negotiating with the member state that had opted to exit.

Deploying capacity and building method. The EU does not have the infrastructural power and financial clout of a mature nation-state. However, since its inception it has developed a formidable governing capacity through its supranational institutions, with high quality multinational and multicultural staff, established rules of the game, shared norms and various repertoires of how to do business. The supranational institutions are complemented by the Council in all of its formations, with political authority and direction radiating from the European Council. The complex ecology of the EU is characterized by dense institutional networks and designated roles designed to deliver collective agreement and action in an environment of heterogeneity. As a formidable negotiating machine, which has the capacity and resources to disaggregate complex problems and forge shared understandings across the member states, the Union drew on its experience, expertise and resources to build a Brexit toolkit. The institutions organized, orchestrated and nurtured the collective capacity of the Union.

Interests. Interests and preferences are as pervasive in the EU as they are in all political systems. In the Union, much of its politics and policy-making is designed to forge agreement from the many and varied preferences, evolving from their material and ideational interests, of the member states. Grand theories of European integration treat interests very differently. Liberal intergovernmentalism accords primacy to domestic preference formation shaped especially by economic interests (Moravcsik, 1998). In liberal intergovernmentalism, the interests that gain traction in domestic politics are transformed into national interests and taken to Brussels. The neo-functionalist tradition, on the other hand, proffers a much more pluralist view of how interests work in the EU by according greater weight to supranational institutions and to the emergence of organized interests in the Brussels arena (Jensen, 2016). Undoubtedly, Brexit has a significant material dimension as the UK is the fifth largest economy in the world, a major net contributor to the EU budget and a net importer of goods from the rest of the EU. However, Brexit was primarily perceived as central to the *raison d'état* of the EU. This meant that material interests were interwoven with the preservation of the polity.

Framing Brexit

'Brexit means Brexit' was an early and frequently restated slogan deployed by Theresa May after she became prime minister in July 2016. This was not particularly enlightening on what kind of relationship the UK envisaged with the EU after exiting or how that relationship might be secured. The EU proactively framed what Brexit might mean and what future relationship it sought to build with the departing UK. The tone from the outset was one of sadness that a member state was leaving but also respect for the political outcome: the HoSG captured this by saying: 'deeply regret the outcome of the referendum in the UK but we respect the will expressed by a majority of the British people' in their first statement (HoSG, 2016). European leaders consistently presented Brexit as an exercise in damage limitation or 'lose-lose', a formulation used repeatedly by presidents' Tusk and Juncker and by the chief negotiator Michel Barnier. Speaking in October 2016, just months after the referendum, President Tusk, in addressing the 'cake and eat it' narrative, asserted that '[t]he brutal truth is that Brexit will be a loss for all of us. There will be no cakes on the table. For anyone. There will be only salt and vinegar' (Tusk, 2016b). Looking to the future, the Union emphasized that it wished 'to have the United Kingdom as a close partner in the future' and never diverged from this (European Council, 2017).

The dominant EU framing of Brexit that runs through all official documents is unity. In an analysis of more than 60 of the most significant negotiating documents and speeches, references to unity were present in 67 per cent of the texts analysed for this lecture (see Table 1). At the first opportunity the HoSG emphasized the goal of unity:

> The outcome of the UK referendum creates a new situation for the European Union. *We are determined to remain united and work in the framework of the EU* to deal with the challenges of the 21st century and find solutions in the interest of our nations and peoples. (HoSG 27, 2016)

Table 1: EU27 Narrative on Brexit Negotiations

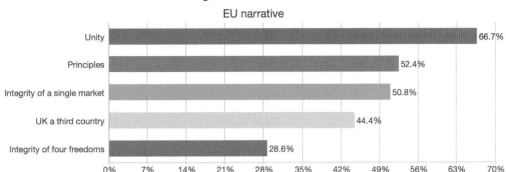

The commitment to unity was repeated by the EU throughout the negotiations, for example, at the March 2017 European Council (Art. 50): 'Throughout these negotiations the Union will maintain its unity and act as one with the aim of reaching a result that is fair and equitable for all Member States and in the interest of its citizens' (European Council, 2017). In Salzburg President Tusk 'reconfirmed our full unity' (Tusk, 2018). The commitment to unity began as a rhetorical device in the aftermath of the referendum but morphed into practice, a norm, that proved enduring, much to the surprise of many observers. Unity, initially a signalling device, was continuously demonstrated by the EU27.

The second theme that dominated the EU framing was adherence to the fundamental principles of the Union. In its March 2018 resolution on the future relationship the European Parliament recorded nine fundamental principles, which included

- the obligations, rights and benefits of membership
- the autonomy of EU decision-making and safeguarding the Union's legal order
- the maintenance of democratic principles
- the integrity of the single market and the customs union and the indivisibility of the four freedoms (European Parliament, 2018). Over 50 per cent of the official documents that were analysed made reference to principles (see Table 1). These principles, which were both substantive and procedural, represented core EU red lines and were a crucial guide to the negotiations. Substantive principles in the official texts addressed primarily but not only the 'integrity of the single market' (50.8 per cent of documents) and the 'integrity of the four freedoms' (28.6 per cent of documents). The sustained emphasis on the single market and the four freedoms reflected the UK's embeddedness in the market and the fact that maintaining market access was a key UK negotiating goal. The Union's persistent opposition to cherry-picking was expressed as follows: 'Preserving the integrity of the Single Market excludes participation based on a sector-by-sector approach' (European Council, 2017). This was translated from official language into political communication in the following way by Prime Minister of Luxemburg, Xavier Bettels when he said: 'Before they were in with a lot of opt-outs, now they are out and they want a lot of opt-ins' (Bettel, 2018).

The third significant theme was linked to the UK as a third country. Approximately 44.4 per cent of the documents analysed referred to the UK becoming a third country or non-member state (see Table 1). The fundamental issue of the balance of rights and obligations was presented as follows:

> 'A non-member of the Union, that does not live up to the same obligations as a member, cannot have the same rights and enjoy the same benefits as a member', and any future agreement would have to be 'be based on a balance of rights and obligations, and ensure a level playing field' (European Council, 2017).

Concerns about a level playing field informed the positions of the Article 50 Task Force and the member states, especially the most economically open ones, from the outset. The deep unease that the UK might undercut EU27 economies by lowering standards was crucial to defining the EU position.

The terse language of European Council statements and official documents was translated into compelling storylines by the key institutional players. For example, when meeting the press after the June 2016 informal council, President Tusk said that there could be 'no single market a la carte' (Tusk, 2016c). This was reiterated by President Juncker at the same press conference: 'those who want free access to our internal market, they have to implement the four freedoms without exception, and I have to add without nuances' (Juncker, 2016a).

Brexit was not of the EU's making, but once the referendum was over the EU acted with speed to frame the event. Official documents and related press conferences displayed a remarkable consistency and coherence that began in the immediate aftermath of the referendum and remained throughout the process.

Deploying Capacity and Building Method

The EU27 had to translate the collective framing of the UK's exit into a process that would strengthen, not weaken the Union. The EU's approach was shaped by three objectives: to protect the foundational principles of the EU, to maximize EU influence in the negotiations and to maintain the unity of the 27. The commitment to unity had to be sustained by nurturing an environment of trust among the member states and institutions. Article 50 of the Treaty of Lisbon was the bible for the Brexit negotiations because it provided the necessary legal framework in which to organize the process. According to Hillion, 'the withdrawal procedure is firmly embedded in the constitutional order of the Union. It involves EU institutions rather than member states, and these institutions operate in the framework of the Union's institutional and substantive principles' (Hillion, 2018, p. 29). Withdrawal was an EU, not member state, competence designed to orchestrate an orderly exit and protect the constitutional integrity of the Union. The EU had to decide how to structure the negotiation process, who would negotiate on the Union's behalf and who would frame the guidelines. This involved designating responsibility within the institutions and establishing how the critical vertical and horizontal relationships would be organized and maintained. The institutional reflex was to insulate and isolate Brexit negotiations from the day-to-day routines of the EU policy-making. This contributed to building EU27 unity and to ensuring that the status of the UK evolved from that of partner to third country. Within two days of the referendum, the Council appointed Didier

Seeuws, Head of the Council's Brexit Special Task Force. The creation of the Task Force was initially regarded as pre-emptive strike by the Council to retain control over the negotiations. In fact, it contributed to the ease of engagement between the Council and the Commission and to the effectiveness of EU negotiations. The Council Task Force had responsibility for organizing and structuring the preparation of the 27 permanent representatives (Committee of Permanent Representatives) and of the General Affairs Council meetings on Brexit.

By 27 July 2016 President Juncker had appointed ex-Commissioner Michel Barnier as the Union's negotiator-in-chief, just one month after the British referendum. As a former vice-president of the Commission and a French government minister Michel Barnier was a political heavyweight. In welcoming his acceptance of the role, President Juncker was keen to emphasize Michel Barnier's credentials for the task ahead:

> I am very glad that my friend Michel Barnier accepted this important and challenging task. I wanted an experienced politician for this difficult job. Michel is a skilled negotiator with rich experience in major policy areas relevant to the negotiations … He has an extensive network of contacts in the capitals of all EU Member States and in the European Parliament, which I consider a valuable asset for this function. (Juncker, 2016b)

Michel Barnier had at his disposal newly created Commission Article 50 Task Force that began operations in October 2016. The Article 50 Task Force was staffed by some of the ablest and most experienced officials in the Commission and could call on the depth of expertise and knowledge in Commission DGs. A key EU27 decision was to agree to a single negotiating line, under Commission responsibility, which was achieved at a meeting of sherpas in the run up to the December 2016 European Council. The creation of the core institutional nodes was finalized with the establishment of a European Parliament Brexit Steering Group of six members under the chairmanship of Brexit coordinator Guy Verhofstadt, appointed on 8 September 2016. The European Parliament was a central player in the process as it would have to ratify the withdrawal agreement. The Brexit Steering Group offered a small, cohesive and manageable interlocutor for the Article 50 Task Force 50 in the European Parliament. It should be noted that Eurosceptic groups were excluded from the steering group.

The process of institutionalization and the establishment of roles and responsibilities meant that by the time Brexit negotiations opened in June 2017 the UK met a well-prepared and well-oiled EU machine (see Table 2 for an overview of negotiating methods found in EU documents). Over 60 per cent of all documents mentioned guidelines and procedures. Crucially, the EU27 stipulated in their 2017 April guidelines that '[s]o as not to undercut the position of the Union, there will be no separate negotiations between individual Member States and the United Kingdom' (European Council, 2017). This was a warning to the UK that it would be futile to bypass formal channels by going directly to capitals and was a commitment by the member states that they would not engage in bilateral negotiations. The HoSG were determined that they would not negotiate face to face with the UK prime minister at any stage, either collectively as European Council 27 or in smaller groupings.

Building confidence in the member states over the preparation and conduct of the negotiations was a priority. When Michel Barnier took office in autumn 2016 his first task was to travel Europe to meet key national actors. The chief negotiator was in both a

Table 2: EU27 Methods in Brexit Negotiations

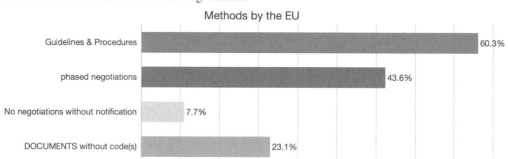

listening and a testing mode as he wanted to understand the core issues and concerns of member states and assess what topics had to be in the withdrawal agreement and how a transition period might be viewed. EU27 unity, so apparent in June 2016, had to be translated into a lasting unity of purpose. In Brussels the Council Task Force held 'confessionals' with every member state, attended by someone from the Commission Task Force. The Article Task Force had an open door policy and met repeatedly with governmental and stakeholder delegations from member states. Michel Barnier maintained constant contact with the member states throughout the negotiations, frequently travelling not just to capitals but to remote areas. As the negotiations proceeded the chief negotiator widened the range of contacts to include national parliaments, trade unions and employer's groups. Symbolically, he visited the Irish border and boarded a Danish fishing vessel that relied on access to North Sea fishing waters.

The decision to infuse the negotiations with maximum transparency was critical to the EU's capacity to build and maintain trust between Brussels and the member states as well as among the member states. At an early stage, Michel Barnier concluded that 'you could have transparency or leaks'.[4] It was, therefore, agreed that the member states would receive documents one day before they were published on the website. Beyond transparency, the EU was determined to hold press briefings so that its perspective reached the European public and to make sure that progress in the negotiations became part of the public record to be built on in the following round. The UK delegation did not want press briefings but as the EU was going to hold them anyway it had little choice. The EU devoted considerable time and deliberation to developing shared speaking lines so that when there was a significant Brexit development, such as a vote in the House of Commons, the EU reacted immediately. This contributed to the consistency of messaging across the institutions and the member states.

The use of time and the calendar technique, a well-developed aspect of the EU toolkit, proved significant in building the method. 'The clock is ticking' became a Barnier slogan during the negotiations and was the title of a documentary of the negotiations filmed by ARTE. Once the Union opted for no negotiations without notification, the EU deployed

[4]Interview with a member of Task Force 50, April 2019.

time as a formidable resource. Under Article 50 a departing state would automatically leave the union with or without a withdrawal agreement two years after formal notification unless the country in question revoked Article 50 or the EU agreed an extension. Within the two-year time frame the EU insisted that the negotiations would phased, starting with agreement on the terms of withdrawal and then talks on the future relationship. The phasing of negotiations was mentioned in 43.4 per cent of documents (see Table 2). The EU insisted on a bridge between the two phases; unless the European Council was satisfied that 'sufficient progress' had been made on the divorce issues it would not agree to opening discussions on the future relationship. The transition from phase one to two delivered concessions from the UK government across all three issues in time for the December 2017 European Council. Moreover, EU-27 agreed to extend the exit date to 31 October 2019 following a difficult discussion among the HoSG, although the UK may leave before then if it ratifies the withdrawal agreement. Time was also important in terms of cyclical pattern of negotiation process. When the formal negotiations began in summer 2017 the Union insisted on a 4-week negotiating cycle. This enabled the chief negotiator and his team to prepare the forthcoming negotiations with the member states, followed by a week of negotiations with the UK, a week to report back to the member states and a week to prepare the next cycle.

Planning for the actual negotiations involved meticulous homework that prepared the ground for every dimension of the UK's departure and was an exercise in collective fact finding and learning. The task forces used the time from autumn 2016 to the opening of negotiations in July 2017 to review the entire *acquis* and assess what Brexit meant for different policies and laws. This was an extremely demanding technical exercise for those concerned but they could call on the expertise of the Commission Directorates General to provide analysis and prepare papers. The legal services of the Commission and the Council were a vital resource. The challenge for the Union was not just to scan the *acquis* but to ensure that the member states were cognizant of the complexities involved and were confident that their interests were understood and taken into consideration. This hard and competent work was crucial in pursuing all three main objectives. It provided the EU with an advantage in understanding the available menu of options for the future EU-UK relationship, as it proved a compelling framing device for identifying the consequences of the UK's red lines. In addition, this display of capacity and command of the dossiers reinforced the member states' trust during the whole process. For instance, when the colour-coded draft withdrawal agreement was published in March 2018, Task Force 50 answered 700 questions from the member states within a short time-frame.

Protecting Interests

A feature of the Brexit negotiations was the marked difference in the projection of interests by both sides. When setting out the UK's approach to Brexit in her Article 50 notification letter, Prime Minister May claimed that the UK's objectives were 'not only in the interests of the United Kingdom but of the European Union and the wider world too'. This was followed by reference to 'the best interests of both the United Kingdom and the European Union' (UK, 2017). At no stage did the EU signal responsibility for the interests of the UK in the process. Brexit was a UK choice and the UK had to accept what that meant. The Union was clear that the 'overall objective in these negotiations will be to preserve its interests, those of its citizens, its businesses and its Member States' (European Council, 2017). When the EU published its guidelines on the Brexit talks in April 2017, three issues emerged as core interests: citizens, money and the Irish border (see Table 3 on the salience of these issues in official documents).

Securing the rights of EU citizens in the UK was 'the first priority for the negotiations' (European Council, 2017). This is borne out by the data in Table 3, showing that citizens were mentioned in 82.4 per cent of documents. From an EU perspective, 'Citizens who have built their lives on the basis of rights flowing from the British membership of the EU face the prospect of losing those rights' (European Council, 2017). The EU27 considered it essential that these rights be protected. When speaking on the issue at the European University Institute's State of the Union Conference in May 2017, Michel Barnier argued 'that protecting these rights will be both easy and complex at the same time. What do I mean by that? It should be easy to agree on general principles. But it will not be as easy to formulate all these principles neatly in a legally precise text' (Barnier, May 2017). There were challenging questions about who would be protected, for how long and what protections were included. In addition, the question of legal redress and the jurisdiction of the Court of the European Union were central.

Money was always a contentious issue in EU-UK relations. It formed part of the 1975 UK renegotiation and dominated Prime Minister Thatcher's European policy until it was addressed in 1984 at the Fontainebleau European Council with an agreement on a UK rebate. As the UK is a large net contributor to the EU budget, the EU wanted to ensure that UK commitments to the 2014–2020 financial framework and its other financial liabilities would be fully met (see Table 3). The UK's financial contribution is mentioned in 67.6 per cent of documents analysed. Because the EU budget was always politicized in UK discourse on membership, taking back control of money was both symbolic and material.

The elevation of the Irish border to a prominent place in the EU's negotiating objectives could not have been anticipated. The salience of the border is apparent in Table 3, which shows that it is mentioned in 77.9 per cent of documents. As the country most

Table 3: EU27 Interests in Brexit Negotiations

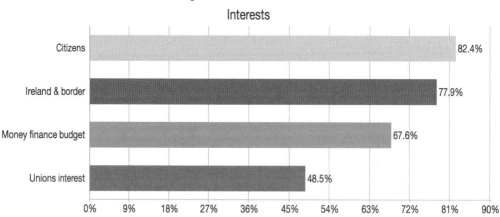

affected by Brexit, the Irish government and society were fully cognizant of the dangers of Brexit to Irish prosperity and peace. In autumn 2016, when it became increasingly clear that London was leaning towards a hard Brexit, Dublin launched an intensive process of bilateral discussions with its partners and EU institutions. Between June 2016 and March 2017, when UK Government triggered Article 50, Irish politicians and officials held 400 meetings with their counterparts in the other member states and with EU institutions. This was an enormous diplomatic effort by a small country but it succeeded when the Irish border was designated a phase one issue. Prime Minister May's Lancaster House speech in January 2017 confirmed to the Irish government that there had to be special arrangements for the Irish border, as the UK's stated preference to leave the single market and customs union were incompatible with the absence of a hard border on the island of Ireland.

The EU negotiating guidelines on the Irish border represented a strong commitment to solidarity with Ireland and to the Good Friday Agreement. The guidelines stated:

> The Union has consistently supported the goal of peace and reconciliation enshrined in the Good Friday Agreement in all its parts, and continuing to support and protect the achievements, benefits and commitments of the Peace Process will remain of paramount importance. In view of the unique circumstances on the island of Ireland, flexible and imaginative solutions will be required, including with the aim of avoiding a hard border, while respecting the integrity of the Union legal order. (European Council, 2017)

The Irish border has been the most challenging and contested issue during phase one of the negotiations. It almost derailed agreement on 'sufficient progress' in December 2017 and is one of the main reasons why Prime Minister May has failed to get the withdrawal agreement through the House of Commons. The UK election in May 2017 greatly complicated negotiations because the government in London became dependent for its survival on the votes of the Democratic Unionist Party of Northern Ireland, a unionist party that originally opposed the Good Friday Agreement. There are many reasons for the remarkable solidarity shown to Ireland during the Brexit negotiations. EU institutional actors and Ireland's partners were committed to the peace process and the EU's role in this. The objective of peace resonated with the foundations of the EU itself as a peace project.

Supporting Ireland served a wider strategic purpose for the Union. The Irish border was a wedge issue that illustrated the difficulties for the UK of exiting the Union. It allowed the EU to demonstrate that the integrity of the single market was central: the EU would be flexible and imaginative in relation to Northern Ireland but would not offer Great Britain the same flexibility. Solidarity with Ireland offered an opportunity to the EU as a collective to signal the benefits of membership to the 27 and to the UK. For the EU's small states, the majority of member states, the message was clear: you are stronger as a member state, and when you are faced with an existential issue the EU will support you. For the UK the message was compelling: a small member state has greater weight as a member state than the UK had as a third country in the making. When Ireland asked whether, if the Good Friday Agreement led to a united Ireland, Northern Ireland would automatically accede to the EU, the UK objected, but according to a Council official the response was, 'If this is what the Irish want, we're going to do it. They are around the table. You are not around the table' (Connelly, 2018, p. 20). In autumn 2017, when the UK needed to move the negotiations to phase two, there was a sense in London that solidarity with Ireland might wane. At a meeting with President Tusk on the 24 November 2017 Prime Minister May is alleged to have said: 'One country cannot hold up progress' and the UK was a 'much bigger and much more important country than Ireland' (Connelly, 2018). London had to learn that Ireland as an EU member state was on the stronger side of the table for the first time in their shared and turbulent history.

III. The EU as a Strategic Actor

The Brexit shock, which might have unleashed forces of disintegration and fragmentation in the Union, in fact enabled the EU to reassert dominance in its neighbourhood, to display capacity and to prove how and why membership mattered. Brexit revealed the Union's DNA as a political system, its public power and collective determination to protect the polity regardless of internal differences. The Brexit case reinforced the conclusion that 'political motives for being together prevail over purely economic interests' (van Middelaar 2019). Or to put it another way, the integrity of the single market by business interests was regarded as more important than economic exchange with the UK. Fears about the longer term material loss of the single market outweighed the disruption of Brexit. By maintaining unity, the EU played to its collective strength and reminded Europeans that the EU had capacity. The Union's three strategic goals were (1) to show that membership must matter, (2) to demonstrate the centrality of the EU to governing transnational relations in Europe and (3) to safeguard the EU as a rule-based system built on treaties, laws and institutions.

The first strategic goal was that membership must matter. Demonstrating the difference between being in the club and outside was essential. Put simply, there could be no privileged status for a former member state. This goal was systemic but reinforced by the apparent unwillingness of many in the UK to come to terms with what third country status might mean. The Union's commitment to ensuring that membership must matter also fed into the treatment of the Irish border in the negotiations. When London went into these negotiations, it would have expected to outgun Ireland comfortably in the negotiations, given the asymmetry of size. For the EU, however, a key goal was to show that it will protect its members and will not privilege the interests of a departing state over a member state.

The distinction between internal and external differentiated integration fed into the membership issue. By voting to leave the EU the UK exchanged differentiation within the Union for external differentiation. The Brexit negotiations have revealed the structural difference between these two forms of differentiation. As a member state a country participates fully in policy-making and if unanimity is required, a member state can block the progress of the others, which increases the incentive to consider opt-outs. External differentiation, on the other hand, is asymmetrical because the state on the outside has no veto capacity and faces a much more powerful partner at the table.

The second strategic goal was to affirm the Union's dominance in governing transnational relations in Europe. All European states must reach an accommodation with the EU if they are not part of the club and over time the Union has evolved a range of differentiated models of relationships with its neighbours. The depth and quality of the relationship represented by any one model is dependent on the balance between the rights and obligations that a third country is willing to accept and those that the EU is willing to grant. It is possible, albeit difficult, to untie the ties that bind EU member states, but the departing state must accept the trade-offs, costs and consequences involved. Membership delivers economic, political and diplomatic benefits to its members that are not available to a third country.

The third strategic goal was to protect the EU polity, its treaties, laws and institutions. The EU as a polity lacks the bonds of history, identity and institutional embeddedness that characterizes its member states as singular polities. As a voluntary association of states it relies on the glue provided by its treaties, laws and shared institutions to combine and bind its member states into a collective. The treaties provide the scaffolding for the Union, specifying what it may do and how it should do it. The Union becomes a living polity through collective policy-making and law-making overseen by the European Court of Justice, which has transformed the treaties into a European constitutional order. Laws and rules were the means of taming interstate relations in Europe and protecting member states from the arbitrary actions of their partners and EU institutions. Law is constitutive of the EU as a polity, a foundational source of its authority and a formidable resource, as captured in a pithy statement from a Council official: 'the EU is not strong on warfare but should not be taken on in lawfare'.[5] Moreover, protecting the polity involved protecting the integrity of the single market, which underpins the deep interdependence that characterizes the EU.

Conclusions

The date by which the UK was scheduled to leave the EU, March 29, 2019 has passed and it is still unclear how, when or even if the UK will finally leave. If the UK departs without an agreement the EU will have failed to achieve its negotiating objective of an 'orderly' departure of the UK. It did, however, conclude a withdrawal agreement with the UK on the terms of departure. The Brexit process has revealed a maturing of the EU polity and a will to survive. There are lessons for the EU from the Brexit process both in its internal and external governance. EU level institutions worked as a collective and the inclusive approach to consultation with the member states and sensitivity to their core concerns built trust. Brexit forced the Union to revisit its foundational principles and building blocks. In a Europe replete with fractured and fractious politics and deep differences among the member states, disintegrative tendencies are evident but not dominant. The EU polity, the collective, was on display in the Union's unity, capacity and power. Unity began as a pledge that was transformed into practice through framing, organization, consultation and communication. The Union's collective capacity was evident in the design of the Brexit negotiating track, the expertise and human resources that could be called upon, the use of process and procedure, the emphasis on transparency and the management of inter-institutional relations and relations between Task Force 50 and the member states. The collective power of the Union was deployed in the protection of the polity. Central to this was demonstrating that membership mattered and that a departing state was on the way to having a third country status with no special privileges. In the process, the EU polity was revealed as valued and valuable to its remaining member states.

[5]Interview with a member of President Tusk's Cabinet, January 2019.

References

Barnier, M. (2017) 'Speech at the 7th State of the Union Conference'. European University Institute, Florence, 5 May. Available online at: http://europa.eu/rapid/press-release_SPEECH-17-1236_en.htm. Last accessed: 3 July 2019.

Bettel, X. (2018) 'Remarks by Xavier Bettel, Prime Miinister of Luxemburg, 8 March'. Available online at: https://www.youtube.com/watch?v=JPXTkpGWD_g.

Connelly, T. (2018) *Brexit and Ireland: The Dangers, the Opportunities, and the Inside Story of the Irish Response* (London: Penguin).

European Council (2017) (Art. 50) Guidelines for Brexit Negotiations, 29 April. Available online at: https://www.consilium.europa.eu/en/press/press-releases/2017/04/29/euco-brexit-guidelines/. Last accessed: 3 July 2019.

European Parliament (2018) 'Resolution of 14 March 2018 on the Framework of the Future EU-UK Relationship'. Available online at: http://www.epgencms.europarl.europa.eu/cmsdata/upload/e9270809-8891-4d5d-bea4-1a764178e282/European_Parliament_resolution_on_the_framework_of_the_future_EU-UK_relationship_14_March.pdf. Last accessed: 3 July 2019.

EU (2016) 'Statement by the EU Leaders and the Netherlands Presidency on the Outcome of the UK Referendum, 24 June'. Available online at: https://www.consilium.europa.eu/en/press/press-releases/2016/06/24/joint-statement-uk-referendum/. Last accessed: 3 July 2019.

Heads of State and Government 27 (HoSG) (2016) 'Informal Meeting at 27 Statement, Brussels, 29th June'. Available online at: https://www.consilium.europa.eu/media/20462/sn00060-en16.pdf. Last accessed: 3 July 2019.

Hillion, C. (2018) 'Withdrawal under Article 50 TEU: An Integration-Friendly Process'. *Common Market Law Review*, Vol. 55, pp. 29–56.

Jensen, C.S. (2016) 'Neo-functionalism'. In Cini, M. and Borragán, N.P.-S. (eds) *European Union Politics* (Oxford: Oxford University Press), pp. 53–64.

Juncker, J.-C. (2016a) 'Remarks at Press Conference after European Council Meetings 28/29 June'. Available online at: https://www.consilium.europa.eu/en/press/press-releases/2016/06/29/tusk-remarks-informal-meeting-27/. Last accessed: 3 July 2019.

Juncker, J.-C. (2016b) P'ress Statement from President Juncker on the Appointment of Michel Barnier as Chief Negotiator, 27 July'. Available online at: http://europa.eu/rapid/press-release_IP-16-2652_en.htm. Last accessed: 3 July 2019.

Kingdon, J.W. (2011) *Agendas, Alternatives and Public Policies* (3rd edition) (Boston, MA: Longman).

Laffan, B. (2018) *Europe's Union in Crisis: Tested and Contested* (London: Routledge).

Moravcsik, A. (1998) *The Choice for Europe: Social Purpose and State Power from Messina to Maastricht* (London: UCL Press).

Snow, D.A. and Benford, R.D. (1992) 'Master Frames and Cycles of Protest'. In Morris, A.D. and Mueller, C.M. (eds) *Frontiers in Social Movement Theory* (New Haven, CT: Yale University Press), pp. 133–55.

Stone, D. (2002) *Policy Paradox: The Art of Political Decision Making* (3rd edition) (New York: Norton and Co).

Tusk, D. (2016a) 'Press Statement on the Outcome of the UK Referendum'. 24 June. Available online at: https://www.consilium.europa.eu/en/press/press-releases/2016/06/24/tusk-statement-uk-referendum/. Last accessed: 3 July 2019.

Tusk, D. (2016b) 'Speech at the European Policy Centre Conference, 13 October'. Available online at: https://www.consilium.europa.eu/en/press/press-releases/2016/10/13/tusk-speech-epc/. Last accessed: 3 July 2019.

Tusk, D. (2016c) 'Remarks at Press Conference after European Council Meetings 28/29 June'. Available online at: https://www.consilium.europa.eu/en/meetings/european-council/2016/06/28-29/. Last accessed 3 July 2019.

Tusk, D. (2018) 'Remarks by President Tusk after the Salzburg Informal Summit'. Available online at: https://www.consilium.europa.eu/en/press/press-releases/2018/09/20/remarks-by-president-donald-tusk-after-the-salzburg-informal-summit/. Last accessed 3 July 2019.

UK (2017) 'Letter of Notification to Leave the EU, 29 March'. Available online at:https://assets.publishing.service.gov.uk/government/uploads/system/uploads/attachment_data/file/604079/Prime_Ministers_letter_to_European_Council_President_Donald_Tusk.pdf. Last accessed 3 July 2019.

van Middelaar, L. (2019) *Alarums and Excursions: Improvising Politics on the European stage* (Newcastle-upon Tyne: Agenda).

JCMS 2019 Volume 57. Annual Review pp. 28–39   DOI: 10.1111/jcms.12919

House United, House Divided: Explaining the EU's Unity in the Brexit Negotiations

MADS DAGNIS JENSEN[1] and JESPER DAHL KELSTRUP[2]
[1]Department of International Economics, Government and Business, Copenhagen Business School, Frederiksberg [2]Department of Social Sciences and Business, Roskilde University, Roskilde

Introduction

The Brexit negotiations endured a turbulent year in 2018.[1] Nevertheless, member states and EU institutions were able to produce timely and coherent negotiating positions on Brexit. Just as importantly, they have appeared, by and large, united and have not broken rank in the negotiations despite some attempts by the UK to play a divide-and-conquer strategy (Kassim and Usherwood, 2018). This article sets out to explain the unexpected unity of the EU in the Article 50 negotiations.

The year commenced with the UK government submitting its European Union (Withdrawal) Bill to the House of Lords on 18 January after its approval in the House of Commons. The House of Lords began its readings, which led to several amendments, most of which were defeated in the Commons (Walker, 2019). On 26 June the bill received Royal Assent and thus became an Act of Parliament (Gov.UK, 2018a). *The European Union (Withdrawal) Act* sets out how to repeal the European Communities Act of 1972 and states that the UK Parliament must approve the negotiated withdrawal agreement between the government and the EU, as well as the way that EU laws are transposed into UK law (*European Union [Withdrawal] Act*, 2018).

After the terms of the divorce were defined, the next important event was the Chequers Plan, published on 12 July 2018, by Prime Minister Theresa May. The plan set out a detailed vision for the future relationship between the UK and the EU (Gov.UK 2018b). Special attention was paid to the economic relationship, where the aim was to maintain frictionless trade in goods after Brexit. Prior to launching the plan the Prime Minister gathered her ministers and asked for the collective support of her cabinet on 6 July 2018. Not all members of her cabinet could support the plan. The Secretary of State for Exiting the European Union David Davis (BBC News, 2018c), and Foreign Secretary Boris Johnson (BBC News, 2018a) both resigned in the wake of the meeting, before the plan was official. Both indicated that the government's vision of Brexit was too far from their respective visions.

The Chequers Plan got a lukewarm reception from the EU (Jensen and Kelstrup, 2018). On one hand, the EU wanted to recognize the new momentum after many months of limited progress in the negotiations. On the other hand, the EU could not support ideas in the plan that would allow UK companies free access to the single market without being legally bound to follow EU rules. At an informal meeting of the EU heads of state or government

---

[1]The outline of the events of 2018 was built primarily on Walker (2019).

in Salzburg on 20 September, President Donald Tusk stated that that the EU would not accept a deal where the UK could have free movement in goods without also accepting the other three freedoms (European Council and the Council of the European Union, 2018b).

As the negotiations approached the end, both parties stood far apart. The EU could not support any deal that would hamper the integrity of the single market, while the UK would not support a deal that would hamper the unity of England, Scotland, Wales and Northern Ireland. Despite their major differences, the UK government and EU negotiators managed to reach an agreement on 14 November 2018 (European Commission, 2018). The agreement determined the principles of how the UK would depart from the EU on 29 March 2019 and was accompanied by a political declaration on the future relationship between the two. The next day, the new Secretary of State for Exiting the European Union Dominic Raab and other ministers resigned from the Cabinet in opposition to the agreement (BBC News, 2018b). On 25 November 2018 the leaders of the remaining 27 member states gave their support for the withdrawal agreement and the political declaration (European Council and the Council of the European Union, 2018a). The House of Commons in the UK was supposed to do the same on 11 December but the Prime Minister decided to postpone the vote to January to gain more time to secure the necessary support (BBC News, 2018d).

Taken together, the EU remained surprisingly united while the UK became increasingly divided over the course of the negotiations in 2018 (Kassim and Usherwood, 2018). From both an empirical and theoretical point of view, previous crisis management and diverging interests in and between EU and member states provided reasons to expect that unity in the EU would be difficult to achieve and maintain. First, the EU has in recent years been faced with many crises, such as the economic crisis and the refugee crisis, in which it has been hard to find common ground (Seabrooke and Tsingou, 2019). Second, the EU is a fragmented political system with considerable division of powers among EU institutions, including the well-known rivalry between them (Jensen *et al*, 2014). Third, the member states of the EU are extremely heterogeneous in terms of their political systems, relationships with the UK and political and economic vulnerabilities to Brexit (Kassim and Usherwood, 2018).

In order to explain the unexpected unity of the EU27 and the EU's institutions, this article develops and operationalizes four different models; namely, the rational choice model, the identity model, the bureaucratic model and the framing model. Building on comprehensive empirical material, this article examines the explanatory value of the models. Third, it concludes by reflecting upon the utility of the theoretical framework.

I. Theorizing and Measuring the EU's Unity in the Negotiations

Inspired by Allison's classic study of decision-making (1969), this article utilizes four different theoretical models as lenses to illuminate the unity of the EU in the Brexit negotiations. Each model is discussed with regard to its theoretical foundation and causal mechanism and is operationalized in terms of a set of expectations, which are matched with empirical material in terms of policy documents, background interviews and academic sources.

Rational Choice Model

The rational choice model is based on economic theory and includes a number of prominent theories of European integration, such as classic intergovernmentalism (Hoffmann,

1966), liberal intergovernmentalism (Moravcsik, 1993) and principal-agent frameworks (Pollack, 2003). Although these theories differ in some important respects, they share some common basic assumptions about decision-making in the EU (Lewis, 2003). The member states are taken as the main unit of analysis and are assumed to act with instrumental rationality when faced with a strategic problem such as Brexit. That implies that the member states calculate the cost and benefits of different options with regard to European integration and work strategically for the one that is most likely to maximize their utility.

Identity Model

The identity model is derived from sociology and social psychology and is embedded in a neofunctional focus on changes in the loyalties of national actors (Haas, 1958), as well as other studies that focus on how national plenipotentiaries form and internalize common values and norms through socialization (Checkel, 1999; Lewis, 1998). A common assumption among these approaches is the idea that by interacting over time, actors in the EU develop a group identity with a set of shared norms and values. Common group identities are often associated with an in-group/out-group dynamic where the in-group tends to favour members coming from within it and to discriminate against members of the out-group (Tajfel and Turner, 1979). Based on this line of reasoning, the UK's decision to leave the EU has changed its status from being a part of the in-group to joining the out-group. This in turn has reinforced the common identity and unity of the remaining member states vis-à-vis the UK.

Bureaucratic Model

The bureaucratic model draws on organizational theory and is related to approaches that focus on the existence of a European administrative space in which national administrations and EU institutions are increasingly intertwined (Heidbreder, 2011; Olsen, 2003; Trondal and Peters, 2013). According to this model, the unity in the Brexit negotiations is a result of administrative action that has been successful in aligning the approach taken by national governments and EU institutions. Specifically, the bureaucratic model points to how the European administrative space has delivered a coordinated response among the multitude of national governments and EU institutions. This happened through the identification of common goals, which are associated with activities and actors through a system that manages interdependencies via resource allocation, sequencing and synchronizing (Malone and Crowston, 1994).

Framing Model

The framing model draws from agenda-setting, deliberative theories and political communication. Framing is an integral part of approaches in EU studies, emphasizing 'rhetorical action' (Schimmelfennig, 2001), 'communicative action' (Risse, 2000) and deliberative intergovernmentalism (Puetter, 2012). These approaches can be seen as argumentative ways to seek collective policy responses and as a type of non-hierarchical steering characterized by performative speech acts. Specifically, framing is the ability to construct a narrative of an issue so that it is likely to be interpreted in specific ways by the receiver.

If the model is valid, the unity of the EU can be ascribed to the ability of the actors which support unity in the EU27 to frame the Brexit negotiations as a situation where the united EU stands against a divided UK.

Summary of Theoretical Models

The four theoretical models are summarized in Table 1. Even though the models are sometimes seen as competing, this article follows Allison (1969) by applying them in a symbiotic way to answer why the EU has remained united in the face of heterogeneity.

II. Analysis

Brexit and the Rational Choice Model

Explanations based on rational choice reasoning are frequently used in media accounts covering the Brexit process as well as policy documents and academic analyses of it. This is hardly surprising as Brexit is a strategic problem in which strong national interests are at stake, and thus where it is reasonable to expect that the member states will act instrumentally to maximize their utility. In the media, the negotiations are covered using rational choice theoretical metaphors and concepts such as categorizing Brexit as 'lose-lose' (Gray, 2019), noting how the actors are deploying 'hardball tactics' (Macdonald and Baczynska, 2018) and how national interests – especially the German car industry – will prevail over EU unity at the end of the day (Posaner, 2017). In policy documents, the member states' preferences with regard to Brexit are frequently mapped, for example, the negotiating Brexit project led by Kassim and Usherwood (2017, 2018), the Institute for Government's mapping of 'the views of the EU27' (Durrant et al., 2018) and the House of Commons' 'The EU27: Internal Politics and Views on Brexit' (Fella et al., 2019). In academic studies the rational choice model has also been utilized to analyse the Brexit negotiations. In their study of the renegotiation of British membership, Kroll and Leuffen (2016, p. 1317) conclude that David Cameron failed to use domestic pressure to extract significant concessions from the EU because 'the cost-benefit structure of the other member states was not affected in such a way as to overcome the logic of the joint decision trap'. In another rational choice-guided analysis, Hix (2018) examines how the EU and UK ranked different Brexit options by factoring in both economic and political costs and identified the likely equilibrium outcome to be a basic free trade agreement.

The rational choice model holds some sway when analyzing the Brexit negotiations. Many member states have indeed made different estimations of the consequences of Brexit for them, which have fed into their domestic processes of preference formation (Kassim and Usherwood, 2017). Yet the standard rational choice model is challenged by the Brexit negotiations in two respects. First, the negotiations in 2018 and their likely outcome are characterized by observers as having a high degree of complexity and resting on incomplete information, which makes it difficult to search for an optimal solution. Though different outcomes can be placed on a continuum with a hard Brexit (that is, no deal) at one end and soft Brexit (that is, a European Economic Area) on the other, the degree of uncertainty is high. National preference formation, as described by people close to the process, is thus characterized more by bounded rationality and the search for satisfactory solutions in the face of the many unknowns (Cyert and March, 1992;

Mads Dagnis Jensen and Jesper Dahl Kelstrup

Table 1: Theoretical Models of EU Unity in Response to Brexit

	Rational choice	Identity	Bureaucratic	Framing
Expectations: EU unity is a function of	the interests of the member states	reinforced in-group identity	efficacious coordination	a shared interpretation
Logic	Utility maximizing	Collective identity	Administrative coordination	Common narrative
Questions	What are the costs and benefits of different options for the EU27 member states with regard to Brexit? Which option is most likely to maximize the utility of each member state?	How do the EU27 perceive themselves and each other? How do they perceive the UK before and after the EU referendum?	What organizational setups are there to handle Brexit? How is coordination between the various actors handled?	How is Brexit constructed rhetorically? To what extent do the EU27 agree on the master narrative of Brexit and how is it being reinforced?

Simon, 1957). Second, the cost-benefit calculations of each member state are often misconceived when applying the rational choice model. This leads to the erroneous conclusion that the EU ought to be more divided than it is because of the asymmetric impact of Brexit on the member states. To be more specific, policy reports have listed trade balances between each member state and the UK (Durrant *et al.*, 2018), whereas some academic studies have used more sophisticated gravity models to estimate the impact on member states' GDP under different Brexit scenarios (Chen *et al.*, 2018). However, when member states establish their preferences, they are not looking only at the net cost of the UK leaving versus the status quo. They are also calculating the net benefits they may receive from the single market without the UK and from the EU as a decision-making system for handling interdependence. More specifically, though some member states could in the short-run minimize the costs of Brexit by giving the UK a favourable deal that allows it access rights to the single market without being bound by many of its obligations, such a deal could be costly in the longer run, hampering the integrity of the single market. Such a deal would give the UK competitive advantages and perhaps undermine the EU's system. If this were to happen, the cost of Brexit would increase. Thus, to explain the EU's unity, one must operate with an advanced utility function of each member state, which also factors in the value they attach to the single market, to competitiveness and to the EU as a decision-making system. Moreover, collective action strengthens the EU27's chances of imposing preferences on the UK, thus giving the EU a collective advantage in the negotiations.

Brexit and the Identity Model

The departure of the UK from the EU implies the move from being part of a community to being in an out-group. The identity model captures different ramifications of this process and how it may have impacted upon, and in some respects strengthened, common identity and unity in the EU27 (see Laffan, 2019, in this issue). While the UK's EU referendum and the resulting decision to leave the EU have been widely understood to contrast with European values such as cosmopolitanism, tolerance, pragmatism and shared sovereignty (Adler-Nissen *et al.*, 2017), identity formation in response to the Brexit negotiations has several underpinnings.

The Brexit negotiations have contributed toward reinforcing a common EU identity based on the idea that the UK has always been an 'awkward partner' in the EU, tending to oppose European integration in many areas (George, 1994). Moreover, this level of awkwardness increased several years prior to the 2016 referendum as the UK moved away from its pragmatic approach to EU decision-making and took a more uncompromising stand (Jensen, 2017; Rasmussen, 2016). In the unfolding Brexit negotiations, it seems that the difficulties in managing Brexit have been much more obvious in London than in Brussels, where there has been almost consensual support for the EU's common principles adopted in 2016. EU identity was already visible in a joint response to the Brexit vote issue by the presidents of the European Council, the European Parliament and the European Commission the day after the referendum. The statement emphasized the survival of the EU27, their commitment to preserving EU unity in the negotiations and the importance of an orderly withdrawal, and it paved the way for treating the UK as a third party in the negotiations (Laffan, 2019, in this issue). In the unfolding negotiations the sense of unity has been reinforced by the idea that the single market signifies common European values in both economic and symbolic terms. In practice, the Article 50 negotiations also imply that the EU27 leaders now meet as a group and are 'visited' by the British prime minister, who eats by herself at lunches and dinners. As a result, the unfolding negotiations have consolidated a sense for the EU27 of remaining in an in-group with a joint purpose, if not a common identity. Small member states, in particular, enjoy the shared responsibility taken by the EU27 in the negotiations (Wishart, 2019).

However, the identity model faces several challenges. First, although the negotiations have been running for several years, they are by definition time-limited and it is, therefore, questionable whether they have similar long-term socializing effects to the regular European integration process. Second, as illustrated by the limited success in agreeing on new reform initiatives such as those suggested by French President Emmanuel Macron (Erlanger, 2018), it is questionable whether Brexit has triggered a new sense of common purpose in the EU. Rather, the EU's unity is about defending the status quo. Member states such as the Netherlands, Sweden and Denmark, which have tended to vote in similar ways to the UK in the Council (Hix, 2018) stand to lose a key ally after the UK leaves the EU. Such countries emphasize a shared free-market identity and are likely to pursue a close future relationship with the UK despite Brexit. The statements issued by the finance ministers from the eight countries in the so-called New Hanseatic League from March 2018 and onwards point in the same direction, although the future viability of the alliance remains uncertain (Korteweg, 2018).

Brexit and the Bureaucratic Model

The EU27 by and large have similar interests in relation to the UK, but was this a starting point or the result of a bureaucratic process? The bureaucratic model emphasizes the organizational setup around the negotiations, including the early and comprehensive use of the common principles that were adopted by the European Council on 26 June 2016. In this mode, the Article 50 Task Force under the Commission and the task forces that were established in many member states are important factors in explaining the unity of the EU27.

The common principles, that most notably maintain the integrity of the single market (popularized under the term "no cherry picking") and mandate that a task force would conduct the negotiations based on EU27 mandates and UK notifications, meant that important EU27 priorities as well as the negotiation procedures were evident from early on. The principles worked as a platform for establishing a common framework for managing the evolving negotiations, which were consolidated in an informal European Council meeting in December 2016 (Consilium Europa, 2016; Kassim, 2018). Both the priorities and the negotiation setup were results of EU-level actions and European Commission activities in coordination with the Article 50 Task Force, the European Council and the Article 50 Working Group in the Council as well as task forces in the member states. The close involvement of member states in the negotiations appears to have minimized concerns about EU-level negotiators becoming too distant from positions of EU member states. The horizontal and vertical coordination between these EU and member state actors dovetails with the idea of a common administrative space in the EU (Heidbreder, 2011). The setup for managing the negotiations remained in operation in 2018.

Importantly, responses have been coordinated around not only summits but also smaller issues relevant to Brexit. In coordination with the Council Secretariat and a variable geometry of Directorates-General (DGs), the Commission's Article 50 Task Force has made a difference by providing a horizontal framework that contrasts the sector-specific responses from the member states and EU institutions. A sector-specific approach would, if seen in isolation, tend to lead to a preference for the closest possible future relationship with the UK without considering common principles such as preserving the integrity of the single market and securing a broader balance between the UK's rights and obligations vis-à-vis the EU. Coordination in the EU's administrative space was applied to prepare for no-deal responses between affected member states in 2018.

Brexit and the Framing Model

While some of the other models have gained considerable traction in media coverage, policy documents and academic analysis, the framing model has received little attention. Framing studies have mainly focused on how the EU or Brexit is framed domestically in the media or by politicians rather than looking at the frames deployed in the negotiations (Koller *et al.*, 2019). However, the framing model has some explanatory power regarding EU unity in the Brexit negotiations. Before the result of the Brexit referendum was known on the evening of the EU Referendum in 2016, Tusk had cleared with the EU27 leaders the framing to be conveyed in case of a majority voting leave: 'The central message was that EU business would continue as usual, that everything was under control, and that there was "a pilot in the plane"' (Kassim, 2017). Subsequently, the EU27 heads of state or government came together at an informal European Council meeting on 27 June in Brussels, emphasizing in their statement:

> 'The outcome of the UK referendum creates a new situation for the European Union. We are determined to remain united and work in the framework of the EU to deal with the challenges of the 21st century and find solutions in the interest of our nations and peoples. We stand ready to tackle any difficulty that may arise from the current situation' (European Council, 2016).

The frame that the 'EU stands united in the face of Brexit and difficulties will be tackled' has been repeated regularly thereafter by different EU actors. Arguably, this frame serves the dual function of uniting the EU27 vis-à-vis the UK and reminding all remaining member states that EU membership is something that has to be fought for. Donald Tusk, Michel Barnier and Jean-Claude Juncker, among others, have underlined both that negotiations take place under time constraints with a fixed deadline and that it is important for the UK to provide clarity on what it wants.

At the outset of the negotiations, the EU and the member states were very conscious of emphasizing their unity vis-à-vis the UK. This was not in the least based on the fear that the EU would be divided as in previous crises (such as the Greek crisis and the refugee crisis). However, the need to frame the EU as a united bloc became less necessary as the negotiations progressed. The divisions in the UK government and Parliament and a united house in the EU overtook the framed versions. Thus, while this framing was initially intentionally created and synchronized, it soon became less necessary as events unfolded. In many cases EU actors, such as relevant ministers and EU officials, independently said that the EU was in agreement, while there was considerable internal disagreement within the UK. Yet the framing in terms of EU unity was not only rhetorical but has been implemented in the few instances when member states deviated from the EU's line. In those cases, the member state was informed of the importance of backing the EU's position and not creating fragmentation that the UK could use in a divide-and-conquer strategy.

Overall, the explanatory value of the framing model must be considered in conjunction with the other three models. First, the frame that the EU stands united was made feasible by a common material interest by all member states in defending the integrity of the single market and the EU's system in line with the rational choice model. Second, the common frame was also made possible by the shared norms and values among the actors on the EU's side, as claimed by the identity model. Third, the frame was supported by a system that first established a set of principles according to which the negotiations must be conducted and subsequently coordinated the activities among the various actors involved, following the bureaucratic model.

Conclusions

Given the fragmented nature of the EU, its unity in the Brexit negotiations is puzzling. Although the departure of a member state from the EU is exceptional, the unity of the EU has been maintained throughout the Article 50 negotiations. The rational choice, identity, bureaucratic and framing models have been deployed to explain the EU's unity in 2018. All models we found to be supported but were also challenged in some respects. A common economic interest in preserving the single market, a sense of common purpose among EU leaders, the early and comprehensive coordination of positions and the successful framing of the EU as a unitary actor in the negotiations all contribute to explaining the EU's unity in response to Brexit. However, the EU's unity is likely to be a function of the context-specific nature of the Brexit negotiations. The EU's unity in response to the Brexit divorce settlement is not likely to transpose to other third-party negotiations, and it may even be challenged when the future relationship between the EU and the UK is put on the table. Yet the four theoretical models used in this study to examine the Brexit divorce may also be utilized to identify factors causing disarray in other negotiations.

Acknowledgements

The authors of the article want to thank Theofanis Exadaktylos, Gorm Rye Olsen and Simon Usherwood for their valuable comments, which have helped improve this article.

References

Adler-Nissen, R., Galpin, C., & Rosamond, B. (2017) 'Performing Brexit: How a post-Brexit world is imagined outside the United Kingdom' *The British Journal of Politics and International Relations*, Vol. 19, No. 3, pp. 573–91.

Allison, G.T. (1969) 'Conceptual Models and the Cuban Missile Crisis'. *American Political Science Review*, Vol. 63, No. 3, pp. 689–718.

BBC News (2018a) 'Boris Johnson Resigns'. Available online at: https://www.bbc.com/news/av/uk-politics-44771278/boris-johnson-resigns-as-foreign-secretary. Last accessed: 2 May 2019.

BBC News (2018b) 'Brexit: Dominic Raab and Esther McVey among Ministers to Quit over EU Agreement'. Available online at: https://www.bbc.com/news/uk-politics-46219495. Last accessed: 2 May 2019.

BBC News (2018c) 'Brexit Secretary David Davis Resigns'. Available online at: https://www.bbc.com/news/uk-politics-44761056. Last accessed: 2 May 2019.

BBC News (2018d) 'Theresa May Sets January Date for MPs' Brexit Vote'. Available online at: https://www.bbc.com/news/uk-politics-46586673. Last accessed: 2 May 2019.

Checkel, J.T. (1999) 'Norms, Institutions, and National Identity in Contemporary Europe'. *International Studies Quarterly*, Vol. 43, No. 1, pp. 84–114.

Chen, W., Los, B., McCann, P., Ortega-Argilés, R., Thissen, M. and van Oort, F. (2018) 'The Continental Divide? Economic Exposure to Brexit in Regions and Countries on Both Sides of the Channel'. *Papers in Regional Science*, Vol. 97, No. 1, pp. 25–54.

Consilium Europa (2016) 'Informal meeting at 27 Brussels, 29 June 2016 Statement'. Available online at: https://www.consilium.europa.eu/media/20462/sn00060-en16.pdf. Last accessed: 30 April 2019.

Cyert, R.M. and March, J.G. (1992) *A Behavioral Theory of the Firm* (2nd edition) (Malden, MA: Blackwell).

Durrant, T., Stojanovic, A. and Lloyd, L. (2018) *Negotiating Brexit: the Views of the EU27: Our Brexit Work*. Available online at: https://www.instituteforgovernment.org.uk/sites/default/files/publications/IfG_views-eu-27-v5_WEB.pdf. Last accessed: 26 June 2019.

European Commission (2018) *Draft Agreement on the Withdrawal of the United Kingdom of Great Britain and Northern Ireland from the European Union and the European Atomic Energy Community*. Available online at: https://ec.europa.eu/commission/sites/beta-political/files/draft_withdrawal_agreement_0.pdf. Last accessed 27 June 2019.

European Council and the Council of the European Union (2018a) 'Special Meeting of the European Council (Art. 50) Conclusions, 25 November 2018'. Available online at https://www.consilium.europa.eu/en/press/press-releases/2018/11/25/european-council-art-50-con-clusions-25-november-2018/. Last accessed 27 June 2019.

Erlanger, S. (2018) 'Macron Had a Big Plan for Europe. It's Now Falling Apart'. New York Times. Available online at: https://www.nytimes.com/2018/04/19/world/europe/emmanuel-macron-eu-reform.html. Last accessed: 26 April 2019.

European Council and the Council of the European Union (2018b) 'Remarks by President Donald Tusk after the Salzburg Informal Summit'. Available online at: https://www.consilium.europa.eu/en/press/press-releases/2018/09/20/remarks-by-president-donald-tusk-after-the-salzburg-in-formal-summit/. Last accessed: 2 May 2019.

European Union (Withdrawal) Act (2018). Available online at: http://www.legislation.gov.uk/ukpga/2018/16/pdfs/ukpga_20180016_en.pdf. Last accessed: 2 May 2019.

Fella, S., Miller, V., and Walker, N., (2019) 'The EU27: Internal Politics and Views on Brexit'. Briefing Paper, House of Commons, Number 8362, 18 January 2019. Available online at: https://researchbriefings.parliament.uk/ResearchBriefing/Summary/CBP-8362#fullreport. Last accessed: 26 April 2019.

George, S. (2004) *An Awkward Partner: Britain in the European Community* (2nd edition) (Oxford: Oxford University Press).

Gov.UK (2018a) 'The EU (Withdrawal) Bill receives Royal Assent'. Available online at: https://www.gov.uk/government/news/the-eu-withdrawal-bill-receives-royal-assent. Last accessed: 2 May 2019.

Gov.UK (2018b) *The Future Relationship between the United Kingdom and the European Union.* Available online at: https://www.gov.uk/government/publications/the-future-relationship-between-the-united-kingdom-and-the-european-union/the-future-relationship-between-the-united-kingdom-and-the-european-union-html-version. Last accessed: 2 May 2019.

Gray, S. (2019) 'Luxembourg Fears A Lose-Lose Brexit Despite Financial Sector Gains'. *Financial Times*. Available online at: https://www.ft.com/content/14a32bb0-1e63-11e9-a46f-08f9738d6b2b. Last accessed: 26 April 2019.

Haas, E.B. (1958) *The Uniting of Europe: Political, Social and Economic forces,* 1950–7. (Stanford: Stanford University Press).

Heidbreder, E.G. (2011) 'Structuring the European Administrative Space: Policy Instruments of Multi-level Administration'. *Journal of European Public Policy*, Vol. 18, No. 5, pp. 709–27.

Hix, S. (2016) Does the UK have influence in the EU legislative process?. *The Political Quarterly*, Vol. 87, No. 2, pp. 200–8.

Hix, S. (2018) 'Brexit: Where is the EU–UK Relationship Heading?''. *Journal of Common Market Studies*, Vol. 56, No. S1, pp. 11–27.

Hoffmann, S. (1966) 'Obstinate or Obsolete? The Fate of the Nation-state and the Case of Western Europe'. *Daedalus*, Vol. 95, No. 3, pp. 862–915.

Jensen, M.D. (2017) 'Exploring Central Governments' Coordination of European Union Affairs''. *Public Administration*, Vol. 95, No. 1, pp. 249–68.

Jensen, M.D. and Kelstrup, J.D. (2018) 'Denmark'. In Kassim, H. and Usherwood, S. (eds) *Negotiating Brexit: Where Now?* (Norwich: University of East Anglia) pp. 11–13.

Jensen, M.D., Koop, C. and Tatham, M. (2014) 'Coping with Power Dispersion? Autonomy, Co-ordination and Control in Multilevel Systems'. *Journal of European Public Policy*, Vol. 21, No. 9, pp. 1237–54.

Kassim, H. (2017) 'The European Council, the Council of the European Union, and the European Commission'. In Kassim, H. and Usherwood, S. (eds) *Negotiating Brexit: What Do the UK's Negotiating Partners Want?* (Norwich: University of East Anglia) pp. 7–10.

Kassim, H. (2018) 'The View from "Brussels". The European Institutions and the EU27'. In Kassim, H. and Usherwood, S. (eds) *Negotiating Brexit: Where Now?* (Norwich: University of East Anglia), pp. 44–8.

Kassim, H. and Usherwood, S. (eds) (2017) *Negotiating Brexit: What do the UK's Negotiating Partners Want?* (Norwich: University of East Anglia).

Kassim, H. and Usherwood, S. (eds) (2018) *Negotiating Brexit: Where Now?* (Norwich: University of East Anglia). Available online at: https://ukandeu.ac.uk/wp-content/uploads/2018/11/Negotiating-Brexit-Where-Now.pdf. Last accessed: 23 April 2019.

Koller, V., Kopf, S. and Miglbauer, M. (2019) *Discourses of Brexit* (Abingdon-on-Thames: Routledge).

Korteweg, R. (2018) 'Why a New Hanseatic League Will Not Be Enough'. *Clingendael Spectator*. Available online at https://spectator.clingendael.org/en/publication/why-new-hanseatic-league-will-not-be-enough. Last accessed 24 May 2019.

Kroll, D.A. and Leuffen, D. (2016) 'Ties that Bind, Can Also Strangle: The Brexit Threat and the Hardships of Reforming the EU'. *Journal of European Public Policy*, Vol. 23, No. 9, pp. 1311–20.

Lewis, J. (1998) 'Is the "Hard Bargaining" Image of the Council Misleading? The Committee of Permanent Representatives and the Local Elections Directive'. *Journal of Common Market Studies*, Vol. 36, No. 4, pp. 479–504.

Lewis, J. (2003) 'Institutional Environments and Everyday EU Decision Making'. *Comparative Political Studies*, Vol. 36, No. 1–2, pp. 97–124.

Macdonald, A. and Baczynska, G. (2018) 'EU Leaders Prepare Hardball Brexit Summit for May'. Available online at: https://www.reuters.com/article/uk-britain-eu-hardball/eu-leaders-prepare-hardball-brexit-summit-for-may-idUSKCN1MQ2DE. Last accessed: 26 April 2019.

Malone, T.W. and Crowston, K. (1994) 'The Interdisciplinary Study of Coordination'. *ACM Computing Surveys*, Vol. 26, No. 1, pp. 87–119.

Moravcsik, A. (1993) 'Preferences and Power in the European Community: A Liberal Intergovernmentalist Approach'. *Journal of Common Market Studies*, Vol. 31, No. 4, pp. 473–524.

Olsen, J. (2003) 'Towards A European Administrative Space?' *Journal of European Public Policy*, Vol. 10, No. 4, pp. 506–31.

Pollack, M.A. (2003) *The Engines of European Integration: Delegation, Agency, and Agenda Setting in the EU* (Oxford: Oxford University Press).

Posaner, J. (2017) 'German Industry to UK: We Won't Undermine Single Market over Brexit'. *POLITICO*. Available online at: https://www.politico.eu/article/german-industry-to-uk-we-wont-undermine-single-market-over-brexit/. Last accessed: 30 April 2019.

Puetter, U. (2012) 'Europe's Deliberative Intergovernmentalism: The Role of the Council and European Council in EU Economic Governance'. *Journal of European Public Policy*, Vol. 19, No. 2, pp. 161–78.

Rasmussen, M.K. (2016) '"Heavy Fog in the Channel. Continent Cut Off"? British Diplomatic Relations in Brussels after 2010'. *JCMS*, Vol. 54, No. 3, pp. 709–24.

Risse, T. (2000) '"L" "Let's Argue!": Communicative Action in World Politics'. *International Organization*, Vol. 54, No. 1, pp. 1–39.

Schimmelfennig, F. (2001) 'The Community Trap: Liberal Norms, Rhetorical Action, and the Eastern Enlargement of the European Union'. *International Organization*, Vol. 55, No. 1, pp. 47–80.

Seabrooke, L. and Tsingou, E. (2019) 'Europe's Fast- and Slow-burning Crises'. *Journal of European Public Policy*, Vol. 26, No. 3, pp. 468–81.

Simon, H.A. (1957) *Models of Man: Social and Rational: Mathematical Essays on Rational Human Behavior in a Social Setting* (New York: John Wiley & Sons).

Tajfel, H. & Turner, J. (1979) An integrative theory of intergroup conflict. In W. Austin, & S. Worchel (Eds.) *The social psychology of intergroup relations* Monterey, CA: Brooks/Cole pp. 33–47.

Trondal, J. and Peters, B.G. (2013) 'The Rise of European Administrative Space: Lessons Learned'. *Journal of European Public Policy*, Vol. 20, No. 2, pp. 295–307.

Walker, N. (2019) 'Brexit Timeline: Events Leading to the UK's Exit from the European Union'. Commons Briefing Papers CBP-7960. Available online at: https://researchbriefings.parliament.uk/ResearchBriefing/Summary/CBP-7960#fullreport. Last accessed: 23 April 2019.

Wishart, I. (2019) 'Stick Up for the Little Guy, Ireland's Varadkar Tells EU'. Bloomberg. Available online at: https://www.bloomberg.com/news/articles/2019-02-06/stick-up-for-the-little-guy-ireland-s-varadkar-tells-eu. Last accessed: 19 May 2019.

JCMS 2019 Volume 57. Annual Review pp. 40–48   DOI: 10.1111/jcms.12918

Making the Eurozone Sustainable by Financial Engineering or Political Union?

PAUL DE GRAUWE[1] and YUEMEI JI[2]
[1]London School of Economics, London [2]University College London, London

Introduction

2018 was the year when policymakers and official institutions in the Eurozone embraced the intellectual idea that financial markets can be used to impose budgetary discipline and that suitably constructed financial assets can promote financial stability in the Eurozone. This idea has become popular among Eurozone policy-makers because of a realisation that achieving discipline and stability by political means, such as political integration, has hit a wall preventing any further progress.

During 2018, a group of French and German economists proposed various schemes such as sovereign bankruptcy procedures and triggers that would force governments to issue different tranches of debt in the hope of garnering the disciplining powers of the markets (Benassy-Quéré *et al.*, 2018; Lane and Langfeld, 2018).[1] The European Systemic Risk Board (ESRB) published a report containing a proposal to create a "safe asset" for the Eurozone that is based on a repackaging of the risks of sovereign bonds (2018). The European Commission followed up on this and came forward supporting the idea of creating a safe asset (European Commission, 2018). The hope is that this financial engineering will stabilise an otherwise unstable system of sovereign bond markets in the Eurozone. Thus, during 2018, official policy has become very much based on using market forces to discipline and to stabilise the Eurozone.

In a way all this is quite surprising. One thing we have learned from the financial crisis is that financial markets cannot be trusted as a disciplining device. During the booming years prior to the crisis, euphoria dominated in financial markets leading consumers, banks, firms, and investors to be blind for risk. As a result, encouraged by equally euphoric rating agencies, they took up massive amounts of debt disregarding the risks they took on their balance sheets. This was the time financial markets considered Greek sovereign bonds to exhibit the same risk as German sovereign bonds. Financial markets were an engine of indiscipline.

When the crash came, financial markets panicked. Suddenly they detected risks everywhere forcing consumers, firms and governments into excessive austerity thereby deepening the recession (e.g. Eurozone sovereign debt crisis, see De Grauwe and Ji, 2013). Financial markets became engines of excessive discipline.

All this is not new. Economic historians (Kindleberger, 1978; Minsky, 1986) have taught us for some time that financial markets almost never apply the right amount of

---

[1]For a more general criticism of the French-German reform proposals, see Messori and Micossi (2018).

discipline. During booms markets apply too little discipline thereby amplifying the boom and during recessions they impose too much discipline thereby making the downturn worse.

In this article, we discuss the recent proposals that aim at garnering financial markets to discipline and stabilise the Eurozone, and we analyse whether the financial engineering that is implicit in these proposals will help to stabilise the Eurozone. We argue that financial engineering cannot stabilise a financial system that is fundamentally unstable. Our conclusion is that further steps towards political integration are key in making the Eurozone sustainable in the long run.

I. Government Bond Markets in the Eurozone Are Unstable

Let us first describe the nature of the instability of the government bond markets in a monetary union (see De Grauwe, 2011; De Grauwe and Ji, 2013). We then analyse whether these proposals will succeed in stabilising government bond markets in the Eurozone in sections II and III.

The instability of the sovereign bond markets in the Eurozone can be described as follows. National governments in a monetary union issue debt in a currency that is not their own, but is equivalent to a foreign currency. As a result of this lack of control over the currency in which the bonds are issued, these governments cannot guarantee that the bondholders will always be paid out at maturity. This contrasts with governments of countries issuing their own currency. These governments can give a full guarantee to the bondholders because they know that the central bank stands ready to provide liquidity in times of crisis. In turn, this leads to a situation in which government bond markets in a monetary union can be hit by self-fulfilling crises: investors distrusting the capacity (or willingness) of a government to continue to service its debt, sell the bonds thereby raising the yields and making it more difficult for that government to rollover its debt. A liquidity crisis erupts which results from a fear that the government will be hit by a liquidity crisis. This usually happens during recessions when budget deficits and government debts increase automatically. Investors will then single out those governments perceived to be most at risk, sell their bonds, and acquire bonds issued by governments perceived to be less risky. As a result, massive capital flows across the borders of the monetary union are set in motion destabilising the whole system. This is exactly what happened during the sovereign debt crisis of 2010–2012.

The instability of the government bond markets in a monetary union is aggravated by a possible doom loop between the banks and the sovereign. When banks are in trouble, the sovereign who is obliged to save the banks will also be hit by a liquidity and possibly a solvency crisis. This was the problem of Ireland. The reverse can also happen: a sovereign debt crisis leads domestic banks, holding large amounts of domestic sovereign bonds, into illiquidity and insolvency. This was the case of Greece. The doom loop amplifies a sovereign debt crisis. That does not mean though that sovereign debt crises and the ensuing destabilising capital flows cannot erupt in the absence of a banking crisis.

Let us now turn to the proposals mentioned earlier.

II. Introducing Market Discipline

In this section we concentrate on two proposals that aim at enforcing market discipline by financial engineering. The first one proposes to change the existing structural budget balance rule by an expenditure rule that, if exceeded, would force governments to issue junior debt. The second proposal wants to enforce sovereign debt default procedures on governments that have become insolvent. Let us discuss these consecutively.

Tranching Government Debt

The idea behind the proposal to force governments to issue junior debt if their expenditures exceed some threshold value is that this will subject governments to more market discipline. The reasoning is the following. When governments spend too much they are forced to finance the extra spending by issuing junior bonds. As a result, the buyers of these bonds will face more risk and demand a risk premium. Thus, these governments will pay a higher interest rate which will enforce more discipline. The market will do its job of reining in the tendency of governments to spend too much.

All this sounds plausible. The evidence of past financial cycles of booms and busts, however, is that this disciplining mechanism typically fails. During booms, euphoria prevails and few investors perceive risks. As mentioned earlier, during the Eurozone boom years, investor saw no difference in risks between Greek and German sovereign bonds. It is likely that when euphoria prevails they will see no significant difference in risks between the different tranches of outstanding government bonds.

During the downturn, exactly the opposite will happen. In fact, the existence of junior bonds will work as wake-up call and set in motion panic reactions of flight. As a result, governments, which have issued junior bonds, are more likely to be hit by a self-fulfilling liquidity crisis forcing them into excessive discipline and austerity.

The reality is that financial markets are not well-equipped to enforce discipline on sovereigns. The introduction of some new financial instrument will not change that reality.

Sovereign Default Procedures

The second proposal aiming at using market forces to discipline governments uses a formal sovereign debt restructuring procedure. Governments that are insolvent should be forced to restructure their debt. In other words, the holders of these governments' bonds should be forced to accept losses. As a result, investors would realise that, without a possible bailout of the sovereign, their investments would be risky. This would lead them to ask for a risk premium, thereby introducing market discipline on the behavior of the sovereign.

Again, at first sight this sounds reasonable. The same criticism, however, applies here to the one we leveled against the forced issue of junior bonds. There is very little evidence that investors ask for risk premia during boom phases. That's when euphoria blinds them in not seeing risks properly. And during the bust phase the opposite occurs. That's when the knowledge of the existence of debt restructuring procedures will act as triggers that create fear and panic. As a result, the existence of a sovereign restructuring procedure may actually trigger crises more easily during the bust.

There is an additional problem with this proposal. This has to do with identifying when governments are insolvent. It is easy to say that an insolvent sovereign should be forced to restructure his debt. It is much more difficult, during crises moments, to distinguish between solvency and liquidity problems of sovereigns. This difficulty arose during the sovereign debt crisis of 2010–2012. In the case of Greece, it was relatively easy to conclude that the Greek government was insolvent. But what about countries like Ireland, Spain, and Portugal? These countries were gripped by massive sales of their sovereign bonds leading to a liquidity crunch that made it impossible to rollover their debt at normal market conditions. Quite a lot of economists concluded that these countries were insolvent and should restructure their debt. It turned out that this advice was wrong and that these countries were solvent but had become illiquid. Had they been forced to restructure their debt economic recovery would have been much more difficult (see also Tabellini, 2017).

III. The Safe Asset Proposal

The proposal to create a safe asset in the Eurozone, which was made by the European Systemic Risk Board (ESRB), explicitly aims at eliminating the destabilising capital flows across the borders of the monetary union and to stabilise the system. Will this proposal actually achieve this goal? This is the question we now turn to.

In contrast with earlier proposals to create Eurobonds (see De Grauwe and Moesen, 2009; Delpla and von Weizsäcker, 2010) which assumed that participating governments are jointly liable for the service of the national debts, the "safe asset" proposal makes no assumption of joint liability. Instead, in this proposal national governments are individually liable for their own debt. As a result, there is no pooling of risks.

The "safe asset" is created when financial institutions (private or public) buy a portfolio of national government bonds (in the primary or in the secondary markets) and use this portfolio as a backing for their own issue of bonds, called "sovereign bond backed securities" (SBBS). The latter have the following characteristics. One tranche, i.e. the junior tranche, is risky. When losses are posted on the underlying portfolio of government bonds the junior tranche takes the hit.[2] The second tranche, i.e. the senior tranche, is safe. The proponents of these SBBS take the view that a 30% junior tranche is large enough as a buffer to take potential losses on the underlying sovereign bonds so as to make the senior tranche (70%) risk free. Based on simulations of underlying risk patterns, the authors claim that their proposal will allow to more than double the size of safe assets in the Eurozone. In addition, they claim that the existence of SBBS will replace the destabilising capital flows across national borders in the Eurozone by a movement from the risky asset (the junior tranche) into the safe asset (the senior tranche)—thereby eliminating the instability in the Eurozone.

How likely is it that these SBBS will help to stabilise the Eurozone? It is worth noting that in the way we formulate the question we do not dispute that in normal times the creation of a safe asset may not increase the efficiency of the financial system in the Eurozone. It will probably do so by supplying a new type of asset that can provide for a better diversification of normal risks. The issue is whether the safe asset will be an

---

[2]In the ESRB (2018) proposal this tranche is split further into two tranches, a junior tranche proper with the highest risk (10%) and a mezzanine tranche (20%) which takes the losses after the junior tranche has been depleted.

instrument for dealing with systemic risks in times of crisis? Our answer is negative for the following reasons.

First, the creation of a safe asset does not eliminate the national government bond markets. This is recognised by the proponents of a safe asset (see Brunnermeier *et al.*, 2016; ESRB, 2018). In fact, these proponents have made the continuing existence of national sovereign bond markets a key component of their proposal. According to the ESRB "the SBBS issuance requires price formation in sovereign bond markets to continue to be efficient" (2018: 33). The markets for sovereign bonds must remain large enough so as to maintain their liquidity. That is also why the ESRB proposes to limit the total SBBS issuance to at most 33% of the total outstanding stock of sovereign bonds.

This constraint on the issue of SBBS implies that national sovereign bond markets will be "alive and kicking". As a result, the major problem that we identified earlier, i.e. the potential for destabilising capital flows across the borders of the monetary union will still be present. However, since the markets of sovereign bonds will have shrunk the yields are likely to be more volatile during crisis periods.

Second, we observe that during crises, the correlation pattern of yields changes dramatically. During normal times all yields are highly positively correlated (see Tables 1 and 3 for the pre- and post-crisis periods). During crisis times, as investors are looking for safe havens, the yields in the safe assets tend to decline sharply and become negatively correlated with the high-risk yields. This pattern was very pronounced during the sovereign debt crisis of 2010–2012. In their simulations of the risks involved in SBBS, Brunnermeier *et al.* (2016) indeed consider the fact that risks can be correlated. However, this correlation pattern is fixed, while during periods of crisis correlation patterns change dramatically. We show this feature in Table 2. We find that during the sovereign debt crisis of 2010–2012, the government bond yields of the periphery countries under stress were highly positively correlated. At the same time, these yields were negatively correlated with the yields of the core (safe) countries like Germany, Finland, Austria, France, and the Netherlands.

The implication is that during crises it is very unlikely that the senior tranche in the SBBS can maintain its status of safe asset. It will consist of bonds investors dump and "safe-haven" bonds. The senior tranche will continue to depend on the cash flow generated by bonds that panicking investors deem to be extremely risky. The perception that

Table 1: Correlation of yields before crisis (2000 M1-2009 M12)

	Germany	Finland	Netherlands	Austria	France	Belgium	Italy	Spain	Ireland	Portugal	Greece
Germany	1.00										
Finland	0.97	1.00									
Netherlands	0.97	1.00	1.00								
Austria	0.94	0.99	0.99	1.00							
France	0.98	1.00	1.00	0.99	1.00						
Belgium	0.95	1.00	0.99	1.00	0.99	1.00					
Italy	0.89	0.97	0.96	0.99	0.96	0.98	1.00				
Spain	0.94	0.99	0.99	1.00	0.98	1.00	0.99	1.00			
Ireland	0.61	0.78	0.76	0.83	0.74	0.81	0.88	0.83	1.00		
Portugal	0.90	0.98	0.97	0.99	0.96	0.99	0.99	0.99	0.87	1.00	
Greece	0.68	0.83	0.82	0.87	0.80	0.86	0.92	0.88	0.96	0.91	1.00

Source: European Central Bank and authors' own calculation Note: The yields are yields on 10-year government bonds

Table 2: Correlation of yields during crisis (2010 M1-2012 M09)

	Germany	Finland	Netherlands	Austria	France	Belgium	Italy	Spain	Ireland	Portugal	Greece
Germany	1.00										
Finland	0.98	1.00									
Netherlands	0.99	0.99	1.00								
Austria	0.89	0.93	0.91	1.00							
France	0.83	0.89	0.87	0.98	1.00						
Belgium	0.45	0.58	0.54	0.74	0.80	1.00					
Italy	−0.66	−0.57	−0.58	−0.34	−0.21	0.28	1.00				
Spain	−0.62	−0.60	−0.55	−0.48	−0.34	0.02	0.81	1.00			
Ireland	0.16	0.24	0.24	0.28	0.38	0.68	0.38	0.44	1.00		
Portugal	−0.62	−0.52	−0.54	−0.32	−0.19	0.29	0.88	0.73	0.54	1.00	
Greece	−0.82	−0.79	−0.78	−0.62	−0.50	−0.13	0.81	0.81	0.23	0.85	1.00

Source: European Central Bank and authors' own calculation Note: The yields are yields on 10-year government bonds

Table 3: Correlation of yields after crisis (2012 M10-2017 M12)

	Germany	Finland	Netherlands	Austria	France	Belgium	Italy	Spain	Ireland	Portugal	Greece
Germany	1.00										
Finland	1.00	1.00									
Netherlands	1.00	1.00	1.00								
Austria	1.00	0.99	1.00	1.00							
France	0.99	0.99	0.99	0.99	1.00						
Belgium	0.99	0.99	0.99	0.99	0.99	1.00					
Italy	0.92	0.91	0.92	0.93	0.95	0.95	1.00				
Spain	0,90	0.90	0.90	0.92	0.92	0.94	0.97	1.00			
Ireland	0.93	0.93	0.93	0.95	0.95	0.96	0.97	0.99	1.00		
Portugal	0.78	0.78	0.79	0.82	0.83	0.85	0.93	0.93	0.92	1.00	
Greece	0.31	0.31	0.31	0.35	0.34	0.38	0.45	0.58	0.55	0.57	1.00

Source: European Central Bank and authors' own calculation Note: The yields are yields on 10-year government bonds

this senior tranche is equally safe as the safe-haven sovereign bonds (e.g. German bonds) is very unlikely when markets are in panic mode. As a result, it is also likely that investors will flee the senior tranches of the SBBS to invest in the "real thing", i.e. super safe sovereign national bonds.

A third problem is related to the previous one. During normal times, the safe asset will have been used in the pricing of derivatives and other financial instruments and it will be an important part of the repo market providing liquidity in that market. As a result, a large part of the financial markets in the Eurozone will depend on the perceived safety and liquidity of the SBBS construction. During crisis periods, when the safety of that construction is put into doubt (as we argued in the previous section), liquidity will tend to disappear and the whole financial sector of the Eurozone will be at risk. In the end, we may have more rather than less financial stability in the Eurozone.

There is an historical analogy here. During the boom years, collateralised debt obligations (CDOs) were created backed by different types of securities, e.g. mortgages. At the time, many people were enthusiastic about this and believed that CDOs would make financial markets more efficient by spreading the risks better. It was believed that ultimately, this would lead to more financial stability. The SBBS proposed by the ESRB has the same CDO structure as the previous ones. It would be surprising that financial engineering would manage to stabilise financial markets, having failed dismally to do so in the past.

Conclusion: The Inevitability of Political Union

We have argued that various proposals made during 2018 aimed at stabilising the Eurozone by financial engineering do not eliminate the inherent instability of the sovereign bond markets in a monetary union. During crises this instability becomes systemic and no amount of financial engineering can stabilise an otherwise unstable system.

The proposals made by the French and German economists (Benassy-Quéré *et al.,* 2018) have clearly been inspired by concerns about moral hazard. These concerns are very intense among German economists and have left their mark on the reform proposals of the French-German group of economists. Moral hazard means that agents consciously take too much risk because they expect others to bail them out. It is very unlikely, however, that the sovereign debt crisis had much to do with moral hazard. It stretches the imagination to believe that the Greek, Irish, Portuguese or Spanish governments decided to allow their debt levels to increase in the expectation that they would be bailed out by the governments of Northern Eurozone countries. Our hypothesis that the sovereign debt crisis erupted as a result of a boom that led private and public agents to disregard risk makes more sense. But even if moral hazard was a cause of the crisis, those who took on too much risk will have learned that the punishment for being bailed out by Northern Eurozone governments is severe. It should by now be clear that no government would wish to be bailed out by these governments.

Stabilisation by financial engineering will not work. Real stabilisation of the Eurozone goes through two mechanisms. The first one is the willingness of the European Central Bank (ECB) to provide liquidity in the sovereign bond markets of the Eurozone during times of crisis. The ECB has set up its outright monetary transactions (OMT) programme to do this. However, the OMT programme is loaded with austerity conditions, which will be counterproductive when used during recessions (which is when crises generally occur). That is why a second mechanism is necessary. This consists of creating Eurobonds that are based on joint liability of the participating national governments. Without such joint liability it will not be possible to create a common sovereign bond market. The creation of such a common bond market makes it possible to eliminate the inherent instability of a monetary union that has centralised money but kept the national government bond markets alive. It is therefore also a *conditio sine qua non* for long-term stability in the Eurozone.

Issuing common Eurobonds presupposes a very intrusive process of political unification with further substantial transfers of sovereignty. The issuer of such common bonds has to be *de facto* a European government with the power to tax and to spend. Such a power must be embedded in a democratic decision-making process involving the European Parliament. The political willingness to go in this direction, however, is non-existent today. There is no willingness to provide a common insurance mechanism that would put taxpayers in one country at risk of having to transfer money to other countries. Under those conditions the sovereign bond markets in the Eurozone will continue to be prone to instability.

Although the willingness to create a political union today that is necessary to sustain the euro does not exist, it is important to keep a political momentum alive that this remains necessary for the long-term survival of the Eurozone. Such a momentum can be created by a *strategy of small steps* (Enderlein *et al.*, 2012), such as the creation of a limited fiscal space at the level of the Eurozone. Other proposals such as a common unemployment insurance mechanism come to mind as part of a strategy of small steps (Van Rompuy *et al.*, 2012; Alcidi and Thirion, 2015).

With the election of Emmanuel Macron as French President in 2017 there was some hope that such a strategy of small steps could be set in motion. Macron's proposal to create an embryonic government budget for the Eurozone seemed to open the door for such a strategy. The political events of 2018, however, seem to have closed that door for the time being. Macron's proposal was effectively buried during the December 2018 summit meeting of the European Heads of State, when it was decided to make it part of the European Union (EU) budget. This ensured that this budget would remain infinitesimally small for the time being.

The danger of financial engineering proposals is that they create a fiction allowing policymakers to believe that they can achieve the objective of stability by some technical wizardry without having to pay the price of a further transfer of sovereignty. This fiction could become an impediment to taking the necessary steps to further political unification that alone can ensure the sustainability of the Eurozone in the long run.

References

Alcidi, C., and Thirion, G., (2015), Feasibility and Added Value of a European Unemployment Benefit Scheme, Interim Report, CEPS, Brussels

Benassy-Quéré, A. *et al.* (2018) 'Reconciling risk sharing with market discipline: A constructivae approach to euro area reform'. *CEPR Policy Insight*, Vol. , No. 91, 1–24. https://cepr.org/sites/default/files/policy_insights/PolicyInsight91.pdf.

Brunnermeier, M. Langfield, S., Pagano, M., Reis, R., Van Nieuwerburgh, S., Vayanos, D., (2016), ESBies: Safety in the tranches, ESRB Working Paper Series, no. 21.

De Grauwe, P., (2011) The Governance of a Fragile Eurozone, CEPS Working Documents, Economic Policy, May 2011 http://www.ceps.eu/book/governance-fragile-eurozone

De Grauwe, P. and Ji, Y. (2013) 'Self-fulfilling Crises in the Eurozone: An Empirical Test'. *Journal of International Money and Finance*, Vol. 34, pp. 15–36.

De Grauwe, P., and Moesen, W. (2009) 'Gains for All: A Proposal for a Common Eurobond', Intereconomics, May/June.

Delpla, J., and von Weizsäcker, J., (2010), the Blue Bond Proposal, Bruegel Policy Brief, May.

Enderlein, H., *et al.*, (2012), Completing the Euro. A road map towards fiscal union in Europe, Report of the "Tomaso Padoa-Schioppa Group", Notre Europe, June.

European Commission (2018), http://europa.eu/rapid/press-release_MEMO-18-3726_en.htm

European Systemic Risk Board (ESRB), (2018), Sovereign bond-backed securities: a feasibility study; January.

Kindleberger, C.P. (1978) *Manias, Panics and Crashes: A History of Financial Crises* (Wiley, New York).

Lane, Ph., and Langfeld, S., (2018), The feasibility of sovereing bond backed secutities in the euro area, https://voxeu.org/article/feasibility-sovereign-bond-backed-securities-euro-area

Messori, M and Micossi, S., (2018), *Counterproductive Proposals on Euro Area Reforms by French and German Economists, Centre for European Policy Studies*, https://www.ceps.eu/system/files/PI2018_04_MMandSM_PI91.pdf

Minsky, H. (1986) *Stabilizing an Unstable Economy* (New Haven: Yale University Press).

Tabellini, G. (2017), "Reforming the eurozone: Structuring vs Restructuring Sovereign Debts", Voxeu.org, 23 November.

Van Rompuy, H. in close collaboration with Barroso, J.M., Juncker, J.C., Draghi, M. (2012)., "Towards a Genuine Economic and Monetary Union", European Council, 5 December, Final Report.

JCMS 2019 Volume 57. Number . pp. 49–61   DOI: 10.1111/jcms.12941

The Juncker Presidency: The 'Political Commission' in Practice

HUSSEIN KASSIM[1] and BRIGID LAFFAN[2]
[1]University of East Anglia, Norwich [2]European University Institute, Florence

Introduction

Appearing before the European Parliament (EP) in July 2014 as candidate for the European Commission Presidency, Jean-Claude Juncker declared that his would be a 'political Commission' (2014a). With this formulation, which he would repeat continually over the coming months (2014b, 2015) and indeed throughout his mandate, Juncker served notice that, after his appointment he had no intention simply of picking up where the outgoing Commission signed off. His administration would be different: it would take political responsibility for its actions, respond to the interests of citizens, and be prepared to defend the European Union (EU) and itself.

Even if the Commission has always been a hybrid of the political and the technocratic (Coombes, 1970), combining competing organizational logics to carry out its mission (Christiansen, 1997), few Commission presidents have chosen to highlight the political dimension. Most have rested their claims to legitimacy on the Commission's technical expertise rather than their mode of election or electoral mandate. A few went as far as to speak of the Commission's 'technical charisma'. Juncker, the first Commission president to be selected via the *Spitzenkandidaten* process, provoked anxieties by his insistence on framing his Commission as political. Some feared that it signalled an end to the institution's neutrality and independent action based on expertise, and that herald both a new importance to political parties and a further step in a process of parliamentarianisation that would threaten its non-majoritarian status (Majone, 2002).

This article critically reflects on the Juncker Commission. It considers the political and organizational strategy that lay behind Juncker's conception of the Commission, how that vision informed institutional changes introduced at the beginning of its term, and shaped relations with other EU institutions. It situates the Commission with its treaty-accorded roles in the complex system of EU institutions, considers its political, legal and regulatory responsibilities, and examines how the operationalisation of the 'political Commission' affected the institution's internal organisation.

The discussion starts with the origins of the political Commission in the *Spitzenkandidaten* process. It considers the implications of this innovation in EU governance for the theory and practice of the Commission's role in the EU system. It then explores the impact of the experiment on relations with the European Council and the EP before assessing how it affected the performance of the functions entrusted to the Commission under the treaty. The fourth section examines the views of Commission staff.

I. The Origins of the 'Political Commission'

The *Spitzenkandidaten* process represents a further stage in the EU's politicization following the ratification of the Maastricht Treaty. It altered the political context of EU institutions and brought electoral and party politics to the fore. It also marked the origins of the 'political Commission'. 'This time it's different' was the bold slogan, emblazoned on billboards adopted by the EP for the 2014 European elections and later on an awning on the Commission's Berlaymont headquarters. The slogan was an act of institutional positioning, a claim by the EP to greater influence in the EU's political system through linking the appointment of the president of the Commission directly to the results of the European elections.

This innovation in EU governance was made possible by an amendment introduced by the Lisbon Treaty. Article 17.7 of the revised Treaty on European Union stated that

> *[t]aking into account the elections to the European Parliament* and after having held the appropriate consultations, the European Council, acting by a qualified majority, shall propose to the European Parliament a candidate for President of the Commission. *This candidate shall be elected by the European Parliament* by a majority of its component members [italics added].

The highlighted phrases were seized upon by the EP to expand its power. An EP resolution dated 22 November 2012, which built upon an earlier initiative taken by the European People's Party (EPP) at the Estoril Congress, urged the parliament's political groups to appoint lead candidates for the EP elections (Westlake, 2014).

In the lead-up to the 2014 elections, five of the EP's main party families – the Party of European Socialists (PES), the EPP, the Alliance of Liberals and Democrats in Europe (ALDE), the Party of the European Left, and the European Green Party – each nominated a candidate. The Alliance of European Conservatives and Reformers, and the Movement for a Europe of Liberties and Democracies – both on the eurosceptic right – opted not to. The EU electorate was thereby given a choice of lead candidates on the left–right spectrum, although not on the EU as a project. The candidates, especially Martin Schulz (PES) and Jean-Claude Juncker (EPP) who represented the two largest political families, put considerable effort into a transnational campaign, which included a series of televised debates conducted between 9 April and 20 May 2014.

Scholarly assessments of the process distinguish between the impact on interinstitutional relations and on input legitimacy (Christiansen, 2016; Hobolt, 2015). As an exercise designed to Europeanize the EP elections, the *Spitzenkandidaten* process reportedly had a minor impact. However, it did disrupt the institutional balance between the European Council, which brings together the political leaders of member states, elected via national processes and accountable to national parliaments, and the EP, which is directly elected by citizens of EU member states every five years.

Although European political parties were quick to put their weight behind the winning candidate after the May 2014 elections, the European Council was reluctant to accept a direct link between the elections and the appointment of the Commission president that would deprive its members of a power that they believed rightly belonged to them. Eventually Chancellor Merkel, whose position in the aftermath of the elections was pivotal, conceded to domestic pressure and gave her backing to Jean-Claude Juncker as the lead candidate of the party that had headed the poll. Most of the European Council followed suit. The EP thereby emerged as the dominant player in the 2014 selection of the Commission president.

II. Juncker's Vision of the 'Political Commission'

Juncker used the formulation 'political Commission', first as candidate president, then incoming president, to highlight the democratic credentials that issued from the *Spitzenkandidaten* process and to differentiate his administration from previous commissions. He also used it as a device to emphasize his own substantial political experience, including eighteen years as prime minister of Luxembourg. He repeated the same formulation, including the sources of his mandate, in the mission letters sent to members selected for the College (see, for example, Commission, 2014a) as well as a document circulated at their first formal meeting (Commission, 2014b):

> The new European Commission, its composition, its political orientation and its ambition, are the result of the European Parliament elections on 22–25 May 2014; and of the joint will of the Heads of State and Government of all 28 EU Member States to implement a 'Strategic Agenda for the Union in Times of Change', agreed by the European Council on 27 June 2014. We took up this mission in the Political Guidelines of 15 July 2014, which underline the commitment of the new European Commission to a new start for Europe, and to an Agenda for Jobs, Growth, Fairness and Democratic Change with ten priorities. I was elected President on the basis of this Agenda; as a College, after parliamentary hearings, we got the consent of the European Parliament for this new Agenda; and the European Council appointed the new European Commission on this basis.

In speeches and statements between June and October 2014, Juncker communicated his vision of the 'political Commission'. The first was that his election marked a new start for Europe. As the EPP's *Spitzenkandidat*, Juncker had campaigned on a platform of five priorities. Before appearing before the EP in June 2014, he fleshed out these political guidelines. Drawing on exchanges with leaders of political groups in the EP and the European Council's Strategic Agenda (2014), he presented his ten-point policy programme, 'Agenda for Jobs, Growth, Fairness and Democratic Change', which aimed to turn the page on austerity, focused on a 'positive agenda' for Europe, and addressed the challenges that had been neglected while the EU had been absorbed by the financial and economic crisis.[1]

Secondly, the 'political Commission' would take a programmatic – targeted and selective – approach to policy. It would prioritize action in fields where the EU could make a difference. As Juncker declared: 'I want a European Union that is bigger and more ambitious on big things, and smaller and more modest on small things' (2014a). Other policy areas would be left to the member states in accordance with principles of subsidiarity and proportionality.

---

[1]The ten priorities were: a new boost for jobs, growth and investment; a connected digital single market; a resilient energy union with a forward-looking climate change policy; a deeper and fairer internal market with a strengthened industrial base; a deeper and fairer economic and monetary union; a reasonable and balanced free trade agreement with the USA; an area of justice and fundamental rights based on mutual trust; towards a new policy on migration; Europe as a stronger global actor; and a union of democratic change.

Thirdly, Juncker emphasized the 'special working relationship' between the Commission and the EP that he expected to emerge: 'For the first time', he noted, 'a direct link has […] been established between the outcome of the European Parliament elections and the proposal of the President of the European Commission. […] It has the potential to insert a very necessary additional dose of democratic legitimacy into the European decision-making process, in line with the rules and practices of parliamentary democracy'.

At the same time, Juncker's fourth message was that the Commission and the EP would be European community players. The 'political Commission' would not be 'working against the European Council or against the Council of Ministers. We are not building Europe in opposition to countries or nations', he declared. Indeed, Juncker stressed repeatedly that he was not an advocate of a European federation and emphasised that the EU needed to be built upon and fully respect European states. He was also careful to underline the input of the Strategic Agenda adopted by the European Council in June 2014 on his programme.

Juncker's final message was that, while the Commission would work closely with other institutions, it would not be subservient to them. Although the European Council 'proposes the President of the Commission', he noted, 'that does not mean he is its secretariat. The Commission is not a technical committee made up of civil servants who implement the instructions of another institution. The Commission is political'. Similarly, even though he had been elected by the EP, Juncker warned that he was not going to be its 'lackey'.

Juncker's description of the 'political Commission' prior to taking office was both fuller and more nuanced than it was or has been reported subsequently. Although keen to emphasise the uniqueness of his mandate due to the *Spitzenkandidaten* process, he also observed that, in virtue of the definition of its role under the treaties, the Commission is inevitably political. He emphasized that not all the actions of the Commission could, would or should be political. He was also careful not to emphasise political parties or suggest that partisanship would be important in the Commission's work.

There were some obvious tensions between some of these messages. Could a close relationship with the EP be reconciled with good cooperation with the Council? Also, although the stability and growth pact was an area identified by Juncker as an example of where the rules allowed flexibility, it was exactly in the performance of its implementation and enforcement functions that the idea of the 'political Commission' threw doubt on whether it could continue its traditional role of neutral arbiter.

III. Operationalizing the 'Political Commission'

A 'political Commission' would require experienced politicians of the first rank if it was to play the leadership role that Juncker envisaged. Drawing on his long years in European circles, Juncker defied convention by making personal approaches to candidates he favoured for particular portfolios and appealed to his electoral mandate when prime ministers, suggested individuals that he did not like, or challenged his authority to select who he wanted as members of the College. The new team announced on 10 September 2014 included: '5 former Prime Ministers, 4 Deputy Prime Ministers, 19 former Ministers, 7 returning Commissioners and 8 former Members of the European Parliament' (Commission, 2014c).[2]

Juncker and his transition team worked with the secretariat general on how best to operationalize the 'political Commission'. They considered how the leadership capacity of the Commission could be strengthened in order to ensure the effective delivery of the President's programme, and how to organise the work of the College to suit the incoming President's management style. The creation of project teams around a vice president was the main innovation. Each of the seven vice presidents was assigned responsibility for one or more elements of the President's programme. There was also an effort to balance the party ticket in each project team (see de Marcilly, 2014). Most vice presidents had prime ministerial experience, which, it was thought, made them ideally qualified to play a coordinating role within the College.

The responsibilities of the vice presidents were described in the mission letters sent to the commissioners and spelled out in a communication of 11 November, which detail the 'new ways of working'. As well as steering and coordinating work in their respective areas of responsibility, the vice presidents would be gatekeepers in the policy process: 'As a rule, the President will not include a new initiative in the Commission Work Programme or place it on the agenda of the College unless [...] recommended by one of the Vice-Presidents, on the basis of sound arguments and a clear narrative that is coherent with the priority projects of the Political Guidelines'. Vice presidents would take the lead in 'the follow-up, implementation, and communication of the Commission's priority policies across the Union and internationally', as well as deciding who should represent the Commission in the EP and the Council. In their work, vice presidents without responsibility for a directorate general would be supported by the secretariat general and were expected to work closely with the president's cabinet.

As first vice president, Frans Timmermans, a former Dutch foreign minister affiliated to the PES, occupied a key position. He was responsible for several portfolios, including interinstitutional relations, the rule of law and the Charter of Fundamental Rights, and the Better Regulation portfolio. In the president's own words, Timmermans would be his 'right-hand man'. His status was symbolized by the first vice president's power to decide whether initiatives would be discussed by the College or included in the Commission's annual work programme.

Several changes to the presidential services were included in a wider reorganization of Commission departments. The secretariat general received 80 extra staff to enable it to manage its expanded workload. The Directorate General for Communications became a presidential service, and the Spokesperson Service, of which it was part, was centralized so that commissioners no longer had their own spokesperson. The Bureau of European Political Affairs, the Commission's in-house think tank, was replaced by the European Political Strategy Centre, and a new leadership was appointed.

Overall, these changes were intended to ensure that the Commission would have the necessary capacity to steer through the president's programme. The aim was to strengthen political leadership within the institution, give greater coherence to the work of the College and unify political messages within the 'house', and streamline, expedite and

---

[2]In addition, '[o]ne third of the members of the new Commission (9 out of 28 eight), including the President-elect, campaigned in the 2019 European elections reaching out to citizens and seeking their support'.

improve decision-making by bringing the political coordination of policy to the beginning of the process rather than leaving it until the end. The sections below examine how the 'political Commission' played out in three areas.

IV. The 'Political Commission' and Interinstitutional Relations

The impact of the 'political Commission' on relations with other institutions varied between institutions and changed over time. The relationship between the Juncker Commission and the European Council was mixed. Early indications were not promising. The European Council had been divided on the *Spitzenkandidaten* process, and few heads of government were persuaded that the EU's democratic credentials had been enhanced. There were concerns that the 'political Commission' would erroneously apply a parliamentary model to the EU, ignoring not only the European Council's status, authority and claims to legitimacy but its importance as the EU's supreme institution in crisis management. Suspicions that the Commission was trying to usurp its leadership role lay behind the European Council's decision to adopt a Strategic Agenda in June 2014 – prior to the formal appointment of the new College and some months before it would take office. Moreover, smaller states were worried that a 'political Commission' would no longer protect them.

Despite these misgivings, the fact that Juncker had been a member of the European Council for close to two decades, and chair of the Eurogroup, eased the relationship in practice, at least initially. Although Juncker's had pledged to be more assertive than his predecessor in European Council meetings, relations between the Commission president and President of the European Council, Donald Tusk, started on cordial terms. In a reversal of the division of labour that had developed between their predecessors Tusk took the lead in international affairs and Juncker in economic policy. The two presidents met weekly, and Juncker's involvement in the 'Five Presidents' report' on Eurozone reform indicated a preparedness to recognise the Commission President's expertise and experience.

Within a year, however, differences over how the EU should respond to the handling of the migration crisis, however, and specifically the Juncker Commission's dogged pursuit of a solidarity mechanism that included compulsory quotas for the resettlement of refugees between member states, led to a souring of relations between the two presidents within a year. Although it did not ultimately prevent the Commission and the European Council from cooperating closely on related issues, such as the west Balkan route and negotiations with Turkey, and in other areas, including the Ukraine, the Greek crisis and Brexit, migration remained an enduring source of tension.

The 'political Commission' reinforced and to some extent extended the institution's privileged relationship with the EP established under the Barroso Commission. The annual delivery of the State of the Union speech and the 2010 framework agreement were two key legacies. Under the Juncker presidency, the Commission has been more frequently represented by commissioners rather than officials in the Parliament and in legislative negotiations with the Parliament and the Council (trilogues). Its relationship with the EP was closer under the first presidency (2014–17) of the eighth parliament than the second (2017–19). Not only had the EP been the main advocate of the *Spitzenkandidaten* process, but the leaders of the EPP, Progressive Alliance of Socialists and Democrats (S&D), and ALDE had struck a quid pro quo with the candidate

Commission president: they pledged their support for Juncker's nomination provided that his political guidelines responded to their key demands.

Moreover, after his defeat as the *Spitzenkandidat* of the S&D Group, Martin Schulz – an old friend of the Commission President – became president of the EP, and the EPP and S&D signed up to a power-sharing agreement. They formed a grand coalition, commanding a working majority of Members of the European Parliament (MEP), that was largely supportive of the Commission's legislative programme. Regular meetings involving Juncker, Timmermans, Schulz, Manfred Weber, chairman of the EPP and S&D group president, Gianni Pitella – the so-called 'G5' (Palmeri, 2015) – helped to maintain good working relations between the two institutions.

Following Schulz's departure from the EP, EPP MEP Antonio Tajani became EP president, and a return to adversarial politics appeared to be a possibility. Although the relationship between the Commission and the Parliament became more complex, provisional analysis of parliamentary roll calls suggest that the voting patterns of the 'grand coalition' survived in practice (Maurice *et al.*, 2019). Indeed, although the EP became more assertive in its relations with the Commission, few proposals were blocked or rejected (see below).

In its relations with the Council of the European Union, the Juncker Commission adopted a more aggressive strategy than its predecessors. Rather than seeking the consensus that member states and the Council preferred, the Commission was satisfied when it was able to muster a qualified majority – an approach that did not endear it to national capitals. Nonetheless, at the end of its term, the Commission (2019) was able to report that no less than 90 per cent of the legislative proposals adopted by the Council had been reached by consensus.

V. The 'Political Commission and the Commission's Responsibilities under the Treaties

The Commission has achieved some notable successes in its function as the EU trade negotiator – notably, in agreements with Japan and Canada, the joint EU–US statement, and for being nominated as EU negotiator with the UK, which was not a given – and thereby demonstrated the level of responsiveness to which the President aspired. The effects of the 'political Commission' have also been felt in its responsibilities for the initiation, implementation and enforcement of policy. Although the Barroso Commission nursed the same ambition to control the Commission's output, the Juncker Commission has gone considerably further, introducing instruments of a different order. A programmatic approach to policy initiation, enforced by the system of vice presidents, together with the introduction of a Regulatory Scrutiny Board and the work of the Task Force on subsidiarity, proportionality and doing less more efficiently, have been especially effective. Only in exceptional cases – the prohibition of single-use plastic is an example – have new legislative proposals that did not originate from among the president's ten priorities been able to make it to the College. The prohibition of single-use plastics is an example.

Symbolizing the new approach and the new start, the Juncker Commission immediately withdrew 80 measures that had been tabled by its predecessor. Its decision was controversial,[3] not least because some of the measures that were withdrawn related to environmental

---

[3]In a case brought by the Council, the Court of Justice of the European Union outlined the conditions under which Commission could withdraw proposals (Crisp, 2015).

policy, provoking fears about its green credentials. On entering office the Commission moved quickly to introduce the Juncker investment plan – a flagship initiative intended to signal the turning of the page on austerity – and to advocating the use of the flexibility written into the rules of the stability and growth pact to aid recovery. The administration's measured approach was evident at both its beginning and its end: the Juncker Commission's first annual work programme listed a mere 23 new initiatives and by the summer of 2018 it had tabled all the proposals it had promised, allowing it to focus its attention on the inter-institutional diplomacy necessary to maximise the chances of their adoption.

As its term of office drew to a close, the Commission was able to report that of 515 proposals tabled – 471 by the Juncker Commission, 44 carried over from previous commissions, and 75 per cent fewer each year than its predecessor – 348 had been agreed by the Parliament and the Council (Commission, 2019).[4] EP figures are similar (Bassot & Hiller, 2019). By the EP's reckoning, the Commission delivered 512 of the 547 proposals it had programmed. Of these, 361 (66 per cent) were adopted. Of the 151 remaining, 115 (21 per cent) were progressing as normal. Only 36 (7 per cent) had made slow progress or been blocked.

Space does not permit a detailed overview of the fate of the legislative proposals made by the Commission,[5] but its top achievements included the creation of the Juncker Fund, measures to strengthen the eurozone, keeping Greece in the euro, the creation of the European Border and Coast Guard Agency, the regulation for general data protection, the end of roaming charges, reforms of the posting of workers directive, the gas directive, and the European Citizen's Initiative, a European Pillar of Social Rights, the creation of the European Labour Authority, and a ban on single-use plastic. By contrast, all seven proposals on reform of the common asylum system remained on the table. Its more ambitious initiatives to strengthen the economic and monetary union and the banking union were also unsuccessful, while proposals on e-privacy, e-evidence and the prevention of disseminating terrorist content online, and social security coordination were also left in limbo.

Perhaps, the greatest anxieties about how the 'political Commission' would approach the institution's traditional responsibilities concerned implementation and enforcement. The stability and growth pact was a case in point, which Juncker had cited as an area where the Commission could exercise discretion and on which subject it issued an interpretative Communication. A furore greeted the Commission's decision in May 2016 to allow France more time to redress its fiscal deficit, especially when – jokingly – the Commission president appeared to justify the decision on the grounds that 'France is France'. However, despite the anxieties expressed, there appeared to be a vindication of this view, since all the Commission's decisions were supported in the Council.

Finally, there was little evidence of a tendency on the part of the 'political Commission' either to favour large member states or to pull its punches in enforcement. In competition policy, the Commission fined the Swedish truck manufacturer Scania for participating in a price cartel, and fined Google three times for breaching anti-trust rules. It also required the recovery of illegal tax benefits from Apple and blocked a proposed merger between Siemens and Alstom in the railway sector. This merger was the subject

---

[4]As a senior official in Council observed in an interview with one of the authors, 'If everything it proposed is adopted, the Commission has not been ambitious enough'.
[5]See Commission (2019), Bassot and Hiller (2019) and Blockmans (2019).

of intense lobbying by the French and German governments and the Commission was strongly criticized for impeding EU industrial policy.

One important change, however, saw the Juncker Commission take a new approach to infringements. Rather than prosecute all suspected infringements, the Commission decided both to prioritise and to attempt to resolve cases with member states without going to Court. By June 2019 it could claim to have closed more than 500 cases each year following such negotiations with national authorities. The Commission president also decided that, as a matter of political principle, the College as a political body rather than permanent officials in the services should be responsible for delegated decisions and, in the same spirit, proposed a reform to comitology that would compel member states to own the decisions taken.

VI. Intrainstitutional Views on the 'Political Commission'

Insights into how staff view the 'political Commission' are provided by an online survey ($n = 6400$) administered to all staff and interviews conducted across the organization ($n = 204$) as part of an independent research project, 'The European Commission: Where now? Where next?'.[6] Asked, 'Which of the following developments have been positive and should be retained?', 72 per cent of respondents to the survey agreed or strongly agreed with the proposition 'the identification of political priorities by the President prior to election'. Altogether 69 per cent approved of 'the use of the annual State of the Union to set Commission priorities' and 68 per cent approved of 'a desire to be present in political debates in the member states'.

Views were more mixed on the 'new ways of working'. A plurality of staff agreed or strongly agreed with the following four propositions: that the new working methods had improved the ability of the Commission to speak with a single voice (38 versus 21 per cent who disagreed or strongly disagreed); that Commission policy was now owned by the College as a whole (31 versus 21 per cent who disagreed or strongly disagreed); that policy proposals were now carefully thought through by the relevant services (30 versus 24 per cent who disagreed or strongly disagreed); and that cooperation was better between services (30 versus 25 per cent who disagreed or strongly disagreed). While the level of disagreement ranged between 16 and 25 per cent, between 18 and 24 per cent held a neutral view and a further 18 to 26 per cent did not know. The analysis of the survey responses revealed considerable variation between and within directorates general. Perhaps unsurprisingly members of cabinet, staff in the European Political strategy centre, and the secretariat general were the most positive about the 'new ways of working'. Logistical support services, by contrast, and the Commission's legal service, were among the least enthusiastic, while line directorates general took positions in between (see Bauer *et al.*, 2019).

[6]The research team, which included Brigid Laffan, Michael W. Bauer, Pierre Bocquillon, Renaud Dehousse and Andrew Thompson, was led by Hussein Kassim and Sara Connolly. For further information, see the project website at https://www.uea.ac.uk/political-social-international-studies/research/the-juncker-commission. We should like to express our gratitude to all members of staff who completed the survey or agreed to be interviewed for 'The European Commission: Where now? Where next?', as well as the officials on both sides of the Rue de la Loi who, on a strictly non-attributable basis, offered their thoughts on the topics covered in this article.

Interviews among commissioners, cabinet members and senior managers offer a detailed account of the inner workings of the 'political Commission'. According to these accounts, the new ways of working had affirmed the primacy of the President's cabinet vis-à-vis other cabinets. They had increased demands on cabinets due notably to the coordinating role of the vice presidents' cabinets and the higher levels of interaction necessary at the cabinet level, especially in the early stages of the policy process. There was wide agreement that the new system had strengthened the secretariat general. Interestingly, interviewees did not think that the 'political Commission' had promoted party politics or partisanship within the institution.

Asked how they evaluated the changes, interviewees thought that the 'political Commission' had been a positive development, which had made clear where responsibility lay within the organization. The adoption of a policy programme established priorities, enabled the effective monitoring of planning and programming of policy initiation, and allowed greater predictability in interinstitutional relationships. It enabled the Commission to react to emerging issues, double up on the Commission's presence, often covering both sides of the political spectrum, which was particularly useful on key topics when the Commission needed to reach out, and to ensure that all commissioners remained engaged. Interviewees welcomed the new ways of working, because the new procedures enforced early political coordination between commissioners and cabinets, strengthened the College and improved quality control. Few of them thought that the 'political Commission' had made political parties or party affiliation more important in the Commission.

The interviewees also reported downsides. There were fears that the political Commission could undermine the Commission's independence in the exercise of its implementation and enforcement responsibilities, its neutrality between member states, and its equidistance between the European Council and the EP. Dangers included over-centralization, an undervaluing of technical expertise and adverse effects on morale in areas not designated as a priority. On the new ways of working, interviewees expressed concerns about the creation of extra layers of hierarchy, the exclusion of directors general from political coordination, and a disconnection between interdisciplinarity at the political level and the persistence of administrative silos. The encroachment by the secretariat general into the substance of policy making was an additional problem for some.

Several suggestions for making the model more effective were raised in the interviews. Many focused on the system of vice presidents. Interviewees proposed better delineation of the responsibilities of vice presidents and portfolio commissioners, stronger administrative support for vice presidents and a more effective choreographing of project team meetings. Others wondered about the size, focus and composition of project teams, and whether they should be reviewed and revised during the mandate. A few reflected on the conditions that had made the system work and wondered whether they were reproducible. According to one senior manager: 'The model works if you assume all the politicians get on and want to work together. Either they compromise or they apportion roles enabling them to work harmoniously. It also depends on the strength at the top. So, Martin [Selmayr – the head of the president's cabinet and then secretary general plays a necessarily role] as an enforcer. Without a strong centre it doesn't work. This model with Prodi would have been a complete disaster'.

Finally, whatever their reservations about the new ways of working, respondents to the survey were extremely positive about the performance of the Juncker Commission. Asked to offer their assessment along four dimensions: effectively managing the house, setting a policy agenda, delivering on policy priorities and defending the Commission in the EU system, staff rated the 'political Commission' more highly than its immediate predecessor: 44 versus 18 per cent, 70 versus 19 per cent, 52 versus 18 per cent, and 50 versus 16 per cent, respectively.

Conclusion

The above discussion has presented three arguments. The first is that Jean-Claude Juncker used the phrase 'political Commission' as a frame to legitimize a new model of Commission leadership. The formulation was intended both to capture the distinctiveness of the mandate he claimed as a result of his selection through the *Spitzenkandidaten* process and to signal that his Commission would be very different from its predecessors. Secondly, the 'political Commission' was operationalized in a form that distinguished it sharply from previous commissions, including its immediate predecessor (see Kassim *et al.*, 2019). Restructuring the work around several vice presidents was a key innovation. More fundamental, however, was a reading of the mandate derived from the *Spitzenkandidaten* process to reshape the Commission in a form that would ensure the delivery of the programme on which the Commission had been elected.

The third argument is that the 'political Commission' had important effects in the three areas discussed above. Inter-institutionally, it created friction with the European Council, which had opposed the *Spitzenkandidaten* process and saw the 'political Commission' as an attempt to contest its leadership role. By contrast, it reinforced the strengthening of relations with the EP that had begun under the Barroso Commission. In terms of the Commission's responsibilities under the treaties, the 'political Commission' largely delivered the policy initiatives it had promised, even if a number of important proposals remained under negotiation or were not adopted, while its record of implementation and enforcement did not justify the fears about its neutrality and independence that were initially raised. Within the institution, views on the 'political Commission' were positive. Although the assessment of the new ways of working were more varied, overall staff rated the Juncker Commission highly.

A number of questions remain unanswered, however. The first is whether the 'political Commission' would be possible without the mandate delivered as result of the *Spitzenkandidaten* process. A second question that arises is whether a politician with less experience of the EU than Jean-Claude Juncker would be able to fulfil the presidential role in the same way. A related issue concerns the conditions, including appointments and particular personalities, that made the success of the 'political Commission' possible. As one director general commented: 'The model works if you assume all the politicians get on and want to work together. […] It also depends on the strength at the top. Without a strong centre it doesn't work. This model with Prodi would have been a complete disaster'. For these reasons, in the EU system where institutionalization has not proceeded as far as in national states, it remains unclear whether the 'political Commission' is a one-off, a staging post, or an endpoint.

References

Bassot, E. and Hiller, W (2019) 'The Juncker Commission's Ten Priorities. An End-of-term assessment'. European Parliamentary Research Service, PE 637.943.

Bauer, M.W., Connolly, S.,Kassim, H. Laffan, B. and Thompson, A. (2019) 'Bureaucrats and administrative reform. The responses of EU civil servants to President Juncker's "political Commission"', paper prepared for presentation at the 2019 EUSA International Biennial Conference, Denver May 9-11, 2019.

Blockmans, S. (ed.) (2019) *What Comes after the Last Chance Commission? Policy Priorities for 2019–2024* (Brussel: Centre for European Policy Studies).

Christiansen, C. (2016) 'After the *Spitzenkandidaten*: Fundamental Change in the EU's Political System?' *West European Politics*, Vol. 39, No. 5, pp. 992–1010.

Christiansen, T. (1997) 'Tensions of European Governance: Politicized Bureaucracy and Multiple Accountability in the European Commission'. *Journal of European Public Policy*, Vol. 4, No. 1, pp. 73–90.

Commission (2014a) 'President Juncker's Mission Letter Addressed to First Vice-President Frans Timmermans'.

Commission (2014b) 'The Working Methods of the European Commission 2014–2019'. Communication from the President, 11 November.

Commission (2014c) 'Questions and Answers: The Juncker Commission'. Memo, 10 September 2014.

Commission (2019) 'Europe in May 2019. Preparing for a More United, Stronger and More Democratic Union in an Increasingly Uncertain World'. The European Commission's contribution to the informal EU27 leaders' meeting in Sibiu (Romania) on 9 May 2019.

Coombes, D. (1970) *Politics and Bureaucracy in the European Community* (Sydney: Allen & Unwin).

Crisp, J. (2015) 'Judges Limit Commission's Power to Retract EU laws', *Euractiv*, 28 April. Available online at: https://www.euractiv.com/section/science-policymaking/news/judges-limit-commission-s-power-to-retract-eu-laws/ Last accessed 27 July 2019.

de Marcilly, C. (2014) 'The Juncker Commission, the Return of Politics?' Fondation Robert Schuman, European Issue no. 330.

European Council (2014) 'Strategic Agenda for the Union in Times of Change'. European Council Conclusions 26/27 June 2014.

Hobolt, S.B. (2015) 'A Vote for the President? The role of *Spitzenkandidaten* in the 2014 European Parliament Elections'. *Journal of European Public Policy*, Vol. 21, No. 10, pp. 1528–40.

Juncker, J.-C. (2014a) 'A New Start for Europe: My Agenda for Jobs, Growth, Fairness and Democratic Change Political Guidelines for the next European Commission'. Opening Statement in the European Parliament Plenary Session' Strasbourg, 15 July 2014.

Juncker, J.-C. (2014b) 'Setting Europe in Motion: President-elect Juncker's Main Messages from his Speech before the European Parliament'. Statement in the European Parliament plenary session ahead of the vote on the College, Strasbourg, 22 October 2014.

Juncker, J.-C. (2015)' State of the Union Address 2015: Time for Honesty, Unity and Solidarity'. Strasbourg, 9 September 2015.

Kassim, H., Connolly, S., Laffan, B. and Bocquillon, P. (2019) 'The Juncker Commission: A New Model of Presidentalism?' Paper prepared for presentation at the 2019 EUSA International Biennial Conference, Denver 9–11 May, 2019.

Majone, G. (2002) 'The European Commission: The Limits of Centralization and the Perils of Parliamentarization'. *Governance*, Vol. 15, No. 3, pp. 375–92.

Maurice, E., Hellot, C., Bougassas-Gaullier, D. and Menneteau, M. (2019) 'Review of the 8th Legislature of the European Parliament'. Fondation Robert Schuman, European issues, no 512, 23 April 2019.

Palmeri, T. (2015) 'The Most Exclusive Dining Club in Brussels'. Politico online, 18 June 2015. Available online at: https://www.politico.eu/article/g5-brussels-most-exclusive-dining-club/. Last accessed 14 June 2019.

Westlake, M. (2014) 'Chronicle of an Election Foretold: The Longer-term Trends leading to the '*Spitzenkandidaten*' Procedure and the Election of Jean-Claude Juncker as European Commission President'. LSE 'Europe in Question' Discussion Paper Series, Paper No. 102/2016. http://www.lse.ac.uk/european-institute/Assets/Documents/LEQS-Discussion-Papers/LEQSPaper102.pdf Last accessed 8 August 2019.

JCMS 2019 Volume 57. Number . pp. 62–76   DOI: 10.1111/jcms.12949

European Integration and Disintegration: Feminist Perspectives on Inequalities and Social Justice

EMANUELA LOMBARDO[1] and JOHANNA KANTOLA[2]
[1]Departamento de Ciencia Política y Administración; Instituto de Investigaciones Feministas, Universidad Complutense de Madrid, Madrid [2]Tampere University, Tampere

Introduction

The year 2018 marked the tenth anniversary of unprecedented challenges to the European integration processes. Beginning in 2008, the global financial crisis, which later turned into a eurocrisis, started a chain of events that shook the process of European integration. From Brexit to the rise of European populist parties and to attacks to democracy in member states such as Hungary and Poland, each ensuing development suggests there was a move towards European *disintegration*. At the same time the EU sought to reply to these challenges by strengthening *integration* in some areas. The EU established new mechanisms of economic governance, moving decision-making power away from member states and the European Parliament. Moreover, a stronger social dimension was debated, as evidenced by the European Pillar of Social Rights. In many ways 2018 was the year when European disintegration as a process entered mainstream discourse and thinking. The juxtaposition of deeper integration in some areas, coupled with less democratic forms of governance, can be understood as part of balancing integration and disintegration that is at the very core of the year under examination here.

Scholarly debates about the European crisis are marked by contestation about whether we can speak of disintegration and how to identify it (see Rittberger and Blauberger, 2018). In this contribution, we examine what insights *feminist political analysis* can bring to these contradictory processes of integration and disintegration and how we may theorize these competing processes. We argue that feminist political analysis shows that mainstreaming gender as a core analytical category of European integration theory is a litmus test for the whole integration process. It is an indicator of the democratic health of the EU. Scrutinizing real-world challenges to European integration from an intersectional gender perspective shows that when gender equality is dismantled, attacked or marginalized in the EU, it is not just one tiny slice of social and political reality that is affected; the democratic character of whole integration process is at stake.

We apply a fivefold analytical framework of gender (Kantola and Lombardo, 2017a, 2017b) to selected key challenges to European integration to illuminate these questions and pull out the significance of different gender perspectives for understanding European integration. Of five feminist approaches: women, gender, deconstruction, intersectionality and post-deconstruction, the first two – women and gender – have been most extensively applied in gender and politics research. In this contribution we highlight the importance of the last three. Our key argument is that European integration theory can improve its analytical capacity vis-à-vis current disintegration challenges in theory and the real world by including analytical and methodological insights from feminist deconstruction, intersectional and post-deconstruction approaches. These methods are particularly suitable for linking theory and praxis, for addressing power dynamics between different embodied people and for identifying discursive and intersectional oppositions and counterforces, as well as the affective contexts in which current processes of disintegration and integration develop.

I. Theorizing European Disintegration

Our argument draws upon two recent sets of scholarly debates: firstly, the EU literature on European disintegration and, secondly, the gender and EU literature on European integration. From the former, we adopted the idea that, in contrast to the approach of much of current literature, it is imperative to focus on real-world challenges to integration and its discursive and affective framings. From the latter we discerned the centrality of gendered power relations to analysing both integration and disintegration.

European integration theory faces a number of challenges in making sense of the new political context of potential disintegration. Classic definitions of European integration conceive it as a process in which political actors give rise to a 'new political community' because they 'are persuaded to shift their loyalties, expectations and political activities towards a new centre, whose institutions possess or demand jurisdiction over pre-existing national states' (Haas, 1958, p. 16). More recently, Webber (2017, p. 336) identified three dimensions of political (dis)integration; a *horizontal* dimension that concerns the increase or reduction in the number of countries that join the EU; a *vertical* dimension that includes the increase or reduction of competence and power of EU supranational institutions such as the European Commission, the European Parliament and Court of Justice and a *sectoral* dimension that implies a growth or decrease in the number of issue areas in which the EU adopts common policies in the member states.

'Differentiated integration', in turn, is the process by which member states go towards a similar goal of involvement in the EU but at different speeds. Yet, in the face of member states' increasing differentiation in the post-crisis context, scholars now treat differentiated integration as a '"normal" feature of regional integration' (Leruth and Lord, 2015, p. 760). Furthermore, the profound transformations of the EU political context exemplified by the rise of Brexit, populist and eurosceptic parties, have recently moved researchers to argue that understanding processes of integration requires studying both differentiated integration but also *differentiated disintegration* (Leruth and Lord, 2015; Rittberger and Blauberger, 2018).

The topic of disintegration had been notably absent from European integration theories until recently. However, to respond to the EU crisis political setting, concepts and theories are being refined to improve our understanding not only of why and how states integrate but also why and how they disintegrate (Rittberger and Blauberger, 2018). Drawing on these debates, while the existence of disintegration is contested, some elements allowed us to define the phenomenon. These included: the exit of states (Brexit) (Rosamond, 2016; Schimmelfennig, 2017), or the *horizontal* dimension of disintegration; the reduction of competence of EU supranational institutions, or the *vertical* disintegration; a decrease in the issue areas in which the EU adopts common policies, or the *sectoral* disintegration (Webber, 2017); and democratic decline in countries such as Hungary and Poland and in some of the political responses to the economic crisis (Kreuder-Sonnen, 2018).

We also took from scholarly debates on European disintegration the message that it was important to address both integration and disintegration as part of the same process (Rosamond, 2016). European integration is not a linear process. Looking at integration and disintegration as part of the same process ensures a greater analytical balance, thus enabling a more comprehensive and sophisticated understanding of this complex political process. Addressing disintegration and integration together on the political phenomena that characterized EU politics in 2018 could reveal the contradictory nature of the EU's socio-political reality and the dynamics of enabling and repressive powers that are at work.

As Tanja Börzel (2018, p. 480) puts it: 'If we do not find compelling evidence for disintegration, maybe our search has been tainted by theories that have missed out on important dimensions' of analysis 'beyond economic transactions, regional institution-building, and European identity' and comprehensive analyses that account for

> 'variation across time and, possibly, issues. If discourses become more nationalist and practices more non-compliant, we need theories that tell us how and when these tendencies of disintegration will undermine economic transactions, regional institution-building, and the dependable expectations of peaceful change among Europeans'.

She therefore recommends that European integration scholars should be concerned about '*discursive* and *behavioural practices* that could turn into disintegration' rather than interdependence, institutions and identities (Börzel, 2018, p. 480, emphasis ours).

While European integration theory has clearly identified the problems the EU is currently facing and has advanced in conceptualizing them, it has not addressed such problems in depth and it has missed important analytical and methodological dimensions. In other words, to grasp disintegration, we need to give more weight to the study of exclusionary nationalist discourses and practices, as well as the dynamics of gender and other inequalities that have intensified in the context of the EU economic crisis and Brexit. Understanding EU disintegration requires new lenses that can be offered by using non hegemonic approaches in the European integration discipline. This is why we argue that gendering European integration through feminist approaches is especially able to analyse the current EU (dis)integration challenges that have come to define EU politics in 2018.

II. Gendering European Integration Theories

Gender scholars who have explicitly engaged with European integration theories denounce their gender blindness and masculine bias (Abels and MacRae, 2016; Hoskyns, 2004; 1996; Kronsell, 2012, 2016). These theories are based on depictions of abstracted processes, structures and actors, whose gendered underpinnings are not of interest. Mainstream scholarship has paid little attention to the fact that most key actors in the EU are men (as heads of states, commissioners, bankers or top civil servants). Furthermore, the structures of economic and political integration may signify different things to the women, men and minorities living in the EU or working within its institutions (for example, feminine characteristics and life situations may be devalued as opposed to masculine ones); and integration processes themselves may be gendered, prioritizing masculine structures and failing to advance gender equality and diversity (Haastrup and Kenny, 2016). The same lack of understanding of the way in which gender shapes the world is evident in the concepts and methods used to study European integration (Kronsell, 2012). The omission of gender analyses in dominant European integration approaches reduces scholars' analytical potential for understanding the EU as it 'produce[s] ignorance of the asymmetrical impact of critical junctures (e.g., Brexit) and governance structures (e.g., negotiations) on different socioeconomic groups' (Guerrina *et al.,* 2018, p. 254).

At the same time – and perhaps as a result – gender and EU studies have not made sustained efforts to theorize 'integration as such' (Abels and MacRae, 2016, p. 22), with a couple of notable exceptions (Abels and MacRae, 2016; Kronsell, 2005, 2012, 2016). According to Abels and MacRae (2016) a gender approach to integration theory boils down to three issues. The first is a 'new epistemology and ontological approach' that studies 'power relations, agency, and dynamics of formal and informal institutional interactions' (2016, p. 27). The second is the fact that there is not one feminist approach but rather many. Thirdly, 'as integration scholarship has generally reached the end of the grand debates and there has been a blurring of formerly strict boundaries, the opportunity opens up for an increased gendered theorizing' (Abels and MacRae, 2016, p. 22).

We make two observations and wish to make two contributions to these debates. The first observation is that despite their sensitivity to different perspectives, Abels and MacRae (2016) deal with only two gender approaches to political analysis: namely, what we would term 'women', and 'gender' approaches (Kantola and Lombardo, 2017a, 2017b). The second observation is that our assessment of 2018 calls for the need to draw on three other feminist approaches to political analysis: deconstruction, intersectionality and post-deconstruction.

We have discussed the framework of the five approaches at length elsewhere (Kantola and Lombardo, 2017a, 2017b) but we here link them to integration theory in a novel way. To analyse European integration using the perspective of *women and integration* entails asking where women are in European integration processes and theory and adding the topic of women to existing European integration theories. Hence, the perspective of women and integration illustrates the marginal position of women and the dominant position of men in the key places, processes and institutions of European integration. The category of gender is reduced to the category of women, which in turn is seen as a unified and stable category with common interests (Haastrup and Kenny, 2016, p. 204).

In the *gender and integration* approach gender is the analytical category. This shifts scholarly attention to the gendered structures of European integration: how gender shapes socially constructed roles assigned to women and men in integration processes, placing the former in a position of disadvantage with respect to the latter; how gender power reflects unequal gender relations; and how different values attached to masculinities and femininities underpin European integration processes and structures. Haastrup and Kenny explain that the historical exclusion of women from EU political institutions has meant that sets of masculine practices have become the dominant norms and logics of these institutions (2016, p. 202). This expansive notion of gender requires, as Hoskyns suggests (2004, p. 33), rethinking the very concepts of European integration. One example is the notion of power, which is narrowly defined in mainstream integration theory (Bieling and Diez, 2016, p. 282). It omits broader notions of power, which, according to feminist theory, is a relation between diverse embodied people rather than just between institutions

or polities (Kronsell, 2012), which not only constrains women's opportunities by domi-
nating them but also empowers gendered subjects through their resistance to domination.

We discerned three additional feminist approaches to integration theory. The concepts
of d*econstruction and integration* expose the dominant gendered discourses and norms
that underpin ideas about integration, and have powerful effects on people. Three issues
are central to gender in relation to social constructionism and European integration theory:
the notion that European integration is a social construction, the ways in which structures
and agency are mutually constituted and the role of norms and discourses (Lombardo,
2016, p. 124). Feminist analyses of EU gender policy have been inspired by this deconstructionist approach and have illustrated how the problem of gender inequality in the
EU and its solutions can be represented in different ways, and that a fixed particular conceptualization or solution to the problem at the same time silences other representations of
the problem and its solutions, with gender and intersectional effects on the people (for example, Cavaghan, 2017; Kantola and Lombardo, 2017b Rolandsen Agustín, 2013; Verloo,
2007). An approach to integration based on the Foucauldian idea of governmentality addresses 'how gendered norms and rationalities of government are discursively constructed
through policies and politics and how these in turn are influenced by mostly essentialist
gender norms and assumptions' (Wöhl, 2016, p. 239). Governmentality approaches stress
the ambivalent effects of EU's political and economic power, which can be both repressive
and enabling or empowering (Wöhl, 2016, p. 239; Eräranta and Kantola, 2016).

In the *intersectionality and integration* approach analyses how gender intersects with
other inequality categories such as race, ethnicity, class, disability or sexuality, and the
power hierarchies, privileges and exclusions that are produced between embodied people.
Power, in this approach, is related to the interacting dynamics of sexism-racism-homo-
phobia-classism and other privileging or marginalizing inequalities that people experience
and politics produces. Structures of inequality shape the lives of different women and men
in the EU and beyond (structural intersectionality) and inform the policies put forward by
the EU (political intersectionality) (see Crenshaw, 1991; Rolandsen Agustín, 2013).
European integration theory most often fails to account for these acute inequalities and
power imbalances that lie at the heart of the EU (Lombardo, 2016, p. 131). This is all
the more shocking, considering the colonial history of the Europe and the way this past
lives on in the postcolonial present, together with the institutionalized racism and inequalities that underpin its processes and policies (Bassel and Emejulu, 2017).

Post-deconstruction and integration is a novel approach that is widely debated in feminist theory and cultural studies but is still not employed in gender and EU studies or in
political analysis. Post-deconstruction approaches 'are interested in understanding what
affects, emotions and bodily material do in gender and politics' (Kantola and Lombardo,
2017, p. 43). According to these perspectives, significant social change cannot be
achieved solely by deconstructing discourses: we need to understand and alter the
material conditions, affect and interests that these discourses serve (Coole and Frost,
2010, p. 25). Affect and emotions are perceived as shaping individual and collective bod-
ies, cementing sexed and raced relations of domination, and being collectively organized
around particular figures (for example, the 'asylum seeker'), by attaching emotions of disgust or empathy to people who are constructed as 'the other' (Ahmed, 2004; Pedwell,
2014). Post-deconstruction approaches have been marginal in research in both European
integration and gender and politics. However, these approaches are relevant for

understanding how emotions and affect currently challenge European integration. Populism is a good example of the need to employ a post-deconstruction perspective to understand how gendered and raced emotions are mobilized in a EU in which prime ministers attack academic institutions and gender studies (for example, Orbán's Hungarian government) and scientific data (for example, Salvini's Italian government by attacking data on the role of migrant women and men in the pension system).

III. Feminist Approaches to European Disintegration: Economic Crisis, Populism and Brexit

In this section, using the three feminist approaches discussed above we analyse three key challenges to European integration that became manifest in 2018. Our cases are illustrative and our key aim is to make visible what feminist approaches can add to our understanding of integration and disintegration in the current European politics. To do this we discuss, firstly, the economic crisis though intersectionality; secondly, populism through deconstruction; and thirdly, Brexit through post-deconstruction.

Economic Crisis and Intersectionality

The economic crisis has challenged European integration by reviving long-standing tensions, such as the uneasy relationship between economic productivity and the EU social model, inequalities between member states and the democratic deficit (Kantola and Lombardo, 2017; Walby, 2015). Analyses of the economic crisis through *intersectional* lenses reveal dimensions of disintegration, such as the marginalization of minoritized women and men in the integration project, sectoral disintegration in different policy fields, and de-democratization. At the same time, they also show the pressures towards further integration that the crisis has triggered, which reveal that processes of inclusion, gender equality policy advances and re-democratization are on course.

EU austerity politics has created socioeconomic and other inequalities between European citizens (for example, by impoverishing Greek citizens), and the exclusion and marginalization of third-country nationals. Intersectional theory moves us to ask; 'integration or disintegration for whom?' The exclusion and marginalization of EU women citizens produced by the crisis could be taken as an indicator of the declining capacity of EU to include them, through targeted policies, and thus be interpreted as a sign of sectorial disintegration. Gender analyses show that austerity cuts to the public sector services, benefits and jobs, unemployment, and poverty have increased in the EU, especially for racialized minority women (Karamessini, 2014).

Above all, when intersectional lenses are adopted, integration failures, so prevalent in the analysis of 2018, appear as long-standing issues rather than exceptional problems brought about by the crisis. While prevailing narratives of the crisis picture the negative effects of austerity politics on women in EU member states in terms of their increasing inequality and precarity in the labour market, this representation, argue Bassel and Emejulu (2017), reflects only the experience of majority women who enjoyed more economically privileged situations before the crisis. Minority women, in contrast, have to face 'routinized crises' in their everyday work and life due to attracting economic and social inequalities based on their race, ethnicity, class, sexuality, legal status or religion.

Work precarity, everyday inequalities and lack of full integration in the EU political community predated the 2008 crisis for minority women. The decline in sectoral integration as a result of the economic crisis exists only when seen it is from the perspective of some, not all women, as the demands of minority women are still met by the EU (Bassel and Emejulu, 2017).

As the EU economic governance in times of crisis has promoted gendered and racialized hierarchies (Klatzer and Schlager, 2014), similarly, the EU official narrative of a positive economic recovery in 2017 is problematized by Cavaghan and O'Dwyer (2018), who ask: 'A Recovery for Whom?'. Whose interests are considered when EU institutions claim we have recovered normality in a 'post-crisis' context in which women's unpaid reproductive work has increased as a consequence of austerity politics and backsliding gender equality policies? Whose demands are included when ethnic minority women are still unequally treated in the EU labour market and society? When intersectional lenses are applied to the analysis of the economic crisis, the European integration process presents new and old disintegrative dynamics.

At the same time, intersectional approaches allow researchers to identify the integrative processes that the economic crisis had triggered. Anti-austerity feminist struggles enacted in civil society as a response to the economic crisis have contributed to promoting a project of European integration based on equality, solidarity, inclusion and democracy. Feminist activists in Spain have woven intersecting alliances with Indignados social movements struggling for real democracy and defending public health, housing and education policies from the neoliberal attacks that intensified during the economic crisis, at the same time as they advanced the feminist project of gender equality (Lombardo, 2017). Ethnic minority women in the UK and France have made intersecting alliances to promote social justice and counteract the invisibilization of their long-standing demands now that the privileged white middle classes face the precarious economic and societal conditions that constitute the norm for minority women (Bassel and Emejulu, 2017). New autonomous feminist movements and trade unions in Finland joined in struggles against the neoliberalism, racism and conservatism of the right-wing government's austerity politics (Elomäki and Kantola, 2017, 2018). Such feminist struggles, which often make intersecting alliances with other social movements, have promoted a project of European integration based on equality and social inclusion. Moreover, they have promoted the dynamics of re-democratization of the European public sphere in response to austerity politics (Roggeband and Krizsán, 2018; Verloo and Patternotte, 2018), which we consider to be a key element of European integration.

To account for such integrative dynamics, European integration theory needs to include the study of empowering intersectional coalitions of equality projects. An analysis of EU policymaking from intersectional perspectives also contributes to European integration theory by showing the extent to which EU policies are inclusive of different people and therefore capable of promoting further integration among the people of Europe's increasingly diverse societies (Lombardo and Rolandsen, 2016).

Populism and Deconstruction

For decades the EU has been used strategically and discursively by national actors for a variety of purposes. It has become an easy target for populist politicians who blame it for a multiplicity of national, European and global problems. Populist right-wing parties challenge the EU's legitimacy to represent the people and reject European integration, presenting themselves as the 'only defenders of national sovereignty and culture', both of which, they claim, are under threat by the process of European integration and globalization (Gómez-Reino, 2018, p. 63). The EU's bureaucracy is represented as excessive, its legislation and laws as irrelevant or harmful to national interests, and the EU as lacking in democratic legitimacy (Pirro and van Kessel, 2017, p. 407). While this increasing questioning of EU supranational competence by populist eurosceptic parties has not led to the actual renationalization of EU policies, it is a sign of a shift towards 'vertical' disintegration, or the decreasing power of supranational institutions, at least in discourse (Webber, 2017, p. 336).

Anti-gender discourses are an important part of populist anti-EU integration rhetoric because the EU tends to be associated with gender equality. *Deconstruction approaches* show that, if gender equality is marginalized in the narrative of the economic crisis, populist discourses seem to be in direct opposition to gender equality. Mieke Verloo (2018, p. 6) defines such opposition as any activity in which a perspective opposing feminist politics and gender+ equality policy is articulated in a way that can be expected to influence or is actually influencing politics or policymaking at any stage. This discourse opposes EU Treaty articles on equality and antidiscrimination and has detrimental effects on democracy. Deconstructionist perspectives show how the discourse of radical right populist groups in Europe is anti-feminist and anti-lesbian, gay, bisexual, transgender, and intersex, conservative, nationalist, racist, xenophobic and islamophobic (Köttig *et al.,* 2017; Norocel, 2013; Spierings and Zaslove, 2015) and expose the ways in which gender equality discourse is used against migrant people (Keskinen *et al.,* 2016; Meret, 2015; Siim *et al.,* 2016). Discourses against gender ideology, which misrepresent gender equality policies and gender studies, presenting them as dangerous, reveal that gender is a scapegoat for right populists both at national level (Kuhar and Paternotte, 2017) and in misogynist speeches by members of the European Parliament (Kantola and Rolandsen Agustin, 2016, 2019). Anti-gender discourses foster disintegration because, as Kuhar and Paternotte (2017) explain, they construct the EU as the gender equality project of the elites, as opposed to the people and the people, thus delegitimizing the EU and fuelling more euroscepticism. Radical right-wing groups in the European Parliament believe that the EU should not intervene in gender equality; they emphasize subsidiarity and treat this matter as a national issue.

Sectoral disintegration through backsliding and the dismantling of gender equality policies has occurred in member states such as Poland and Hungary in the last ten years (Roggeband and Krizsán, 2018). This has gone together with the discursive de-legitimation of gender equality policies in 'morality' areas, such as abortion, sexual and reproductive rights, sexual education, family policies and violence against women. If gender were taken more seriously in European integration theory, the analysis of discursive attacks on gender equality and backsliding in gender policies in some member states could have attracted earlier mainstream scholarly attention to rising euroscepticism in these countries. This is because gender equality is perceived as a specifically EU value that the EU supports. Interestingly, in central European countries 'Anti-discrimination policies, economic issues such as women in the labour market or in leadership, equal pay, and sexual harassment, which are all mainly regulated in alignment with EU norms, have been left remarkably untouched by the wave of policy dismantling' (Roggeband and Krizsán, 2018, p. 379). This is a profound finding, which could show that European integration still holds, because discursive attacks and policy backsliding have affected only those areas that the EU does not regulate. Once again, feminist political analysis can provide European integration theory with insights to understand current (dis)integration processes better.

Gender research also connects the opposition to gender equality expressed by populist parties and other forces with de-democratization (Verloo, 2018; Verloo and Paternotte, 2018). Discursive attacks on gender equality are considered in gender research as attacks on democracy because gender equality is not just one slice of democracy; it is an integral part of it. As a result, when gender equality is attacked democracy is attacked, and vice versa. Feminist scholarship brings empirical evidence to the 'clear democratic decline in Europe' and its detrimental effects on equality and inclusion (Verloo, 2018, p. 238) and suggests that theories about opposition and de-democratization and their interaction need to be included in European integration studies. The curtailing of space for the expression of views in civil society and of free speech in Europe has detrimental effects on feminist struggles.This is turn has further de-democratization consequences, considering the contribution of feminist struggles to the democratization of the political space through their challenge to processes of domination and exclusion (Verloo and Paternotte, 2018). If European integration theory does not address opposition to gender equality and lesbian, gay, bisexual, and transgender rights it will miss the important indicators of disintegration and de-democratization that became highly salient in 2018.

Feminist approaches point to a variety of integrationist dynamics and offer helpful insights for European integration. The role of civil society, in particular, the discursive and material struggles of feminist movements in reaction to right-wing populism, is an important issue that gender approaches bring to light and should be included in European integration analyses, as it indicates that there are dynamics towards democratization that are of interest to integration. In Finland, for example, right-wing populism has activated women into politics through a new feminist movement that is much more mobilized than before and articulates discourses that contrast with the radical right-wing agenda of the populist Finns Party (Elomäki and Kantola, 2018).

Deconstruction approaches provide elements for capturing the genderedness of contexts that counteract disintegration practices and mobilize people towards European integration grounded on solidarity and human rights. One example is the intersectional activism and solidarity movements that European citizens have formed to counteract the exclusionary processes of right-wing populism and neo-nationalism, and to support equality and inclusive human rights in Europe (Siim *et al.,* 2018). To grasp integrative dynamics, European integration theory needs to include the study of citizens' solidarity movements (for example, with migrants, refugees and asylum-seekers). Another example of integrative practices is that offered by politicians who speak in a different, more reconciliatory and eurofriendly language than the oppositional stance of right-wing populist leaders (for example, compare Macron and Sánchez with Orbán and Salvini) or that have revitalised practices of dialogue with European citizens about the future of the EU (for example, Macron and Timmermans).

Deconstructionist approaches help us to understand why right-wing populists oppose gender in their discourses, how gender is used in populist discourses to attack the democracy of the European polity and how central gender is in integrative dynamics when people react against the racism, sexism, xenophobia and homophobia of right-wing populist parties to defend equality, inclusion and democracy. While right-wing populism explicitly opposes gender equality (and expresses eurosceptic positions), gender analyses of European left-wing populism show that, at a discursive level, left-wing populist parties such as Podemos in Spain are better allies of feminist politics than right-wing ones (Kantola and Lombardo, 2019).

In conclusion, deconstructionist approaches contribute to showing the disintegration dynamics of populism and to enrich European integration theory by introducing the concept of *opposition to gender equality* and through analyses of discursive attacks against gender in member states and EU institutions, and attending to gender backsliding and gendered de-democratization as indicators of disintegration. Gender approaches also reveal the integrationist dynamics of feminist re-democratization struggles, solidarity in civil society and differences within populist discourses, with the left developing more progressive than previously equality discourses. Feminist research shows that the gender component is not marginal but is in fact central to populist discourse and that the EU is associated with the support of gender equality as a value. It is therefore important to adopt gender lenses to make sense of (dis)integration dynamics.

Brexit and Post-deconstruction

Brexit dominated European politics in 2018, with its key dates, negotiations, parliamentary debates and votes in the UK House of Commons. Brexit is the clearest example of disintegration in light of Webber's (2017, p. 336) dimension of 'horizontal disintegration' or a simple reduction in the numbers of EU member states (Rosamond, 2016; Schimmelfennig, 2017). As Brexit is shaped by, based on and brings to the fore strong emotions for and against it, we suggest that what we have called post-deconstruction is a useful analytical lens in this context.

Post-deconstruction foregrounds the role of emotions and affect in politics, not as an individual but rather as a social phenomenon. Negative emotions about the European integration project are prominent in Brexit. The populist right-wing parties that promoted Brexit mobilized people's disgust, fear or anger against migrants and the EU. In doing this, they expressed their own gendered ethos and masculinist attitudes. Arguments for Brexit mobilized nostalgic feelings for an imaginary past, as shown by the slogan 'Take back control' of the Vote Leave campaign. While positive emotions about the integration project are far harder to articulate in the analysis of Brexit, events such as the London 'Put it to the people' march of 23 March 2019 show integrationist dynamics in the positive feelings and affective attachments to the European project that thousands of people manifested (Adams, 2019).

Feminist analytical perspectives to Brexit capture the 'highly emotive nature of the debate' and suggest this was 'deeply gendered' prior to the 2016 referendum (Guerrina *et al.,* 2018, p. 388). The debate reproduced political binaries of high versus low politics and policy, marginalizing social and gender equality and women's concerns (Guerrina *et al.,* 2018). At the same time, during the campaign the media gave minimum coverage

(17.5 per cent of media coverage) to women, according to Guerrina *et al.* (2018, p. 391). The potentially negative effects for UK gender equality policies in exiting the EU were also silenced (Guerrina and Masselot, 2018). As Guerrina *et al.* (2018) argue, the symbolic context of the referendum reproduced a gendered public–private dichotomy of political participation in which men were represented the 'strong publics', engaged with high political issues of the referendum, and women were represented as the 'weak publics', undecided about their vote, less confident about their knowledge about the EU and displaying less political engagement with the referendum's issues (Guerrina *et al.,* 2018: 392). The referendum campaign took place in a context of political violence (as exemplified by the murder of Jo Cox), and in social media aggression and personal threats to women experts arguing for the remain option.

Brexit negotiations also revealed emotional political contexts full of toxic masculinity (Guerrina, 2019). The political debates have been highly confrontational, focused on the theme of winners versus losers, with politics conceived as a winner-takes-it-all game in which individual performance and power, rather than collective social consequences, were considered important. Guerrina (2019) argues that attitudes of 'compromise and cooperation' often associated with 'women's skills' in politics, were presented as 'weakness' to be avoided during negotiations. In her words, 'Acknowledging the interests of under-represented groups requires empathy, something that has been sadly lacking throughout the Brexit process' (Guerrina, 2019). By failing to address this matter the debate disregards the impact of Brexit on underprivileged and underrepresented socioeconomic groups, let alone caring for their interests, as the Fawcett Society and the Women's Budget Group have demonstrated. It has also prevented negotiators from exploring all possible options in the search for a way forward in the Brexit challenge.

Overall, when analysed from a gender post-deconstructionist approach, Brexit is not only the clearest example of horizontal disintegration (Webber, 2017), but also a good example of the effects that the marginalization of women's voices and gender perspectives in a context of toxic masculinity can have on gender equality and the goals and shaping of European integration. The political consequences of marginalizing gender issues and positive emotions of empathy towards most unprivileged groups in the Brexit process, and of representing compromises during the negotiations as a form of weakness, include the strengthening of gender and other intersecting inequalities in the political process (Guerrina and Masselot, 2018; Guerrina, 2019). For this reason, Guerrina *et al.* (2018, p. 253) urge scholars of European integration to take gender seriously, because otherwise this lack 'puts the discipline in danger of reproducing structures of power that keep traditionally marginal groups, including women, ethnic minorities and migrants, on the periphery of the EU project'. They argue that the construction of knowledge and feelings about the European integration political procestedess, and the gender biases in this construction, contribute to shape existing social inequalities in the EU by promoting or counteracting them.

Conclusion

In this contribution we have explored the impact of the confluence of key events in 2018 on the way we think about European integration and disintegration. Specifically, we argued for a detailed engagement with feminist political analyses in the development of integration and disintegration theories. It has been our contention that feminist political analyses have key contributions to make; and not just any feminist political analyses but the three approaches that have had the hardest time in making an impact on political science and EU studies. These include deconstruction, intersectionality and post-deconstruction. The first focuses on deconstructing dominant discourses and gender norms and showing their impact on political processes; the second foregrounds the ways in which gender is always cut through with other inequalities such as race and ethnicity, class, ability and sexuality, which together with gender shape political realities; the last illustrates how emotions and affect drive politics, including European integration and disintegration. In this way, our contribution represents a plea not just to include a gender perspective in European integration and disintegration debates but to engage with the insights of these often marginalized perspectives.

Our key contention has been that without an understanding of intersectional gender dynamics and feminist analysis European integration theories will only ever be partial and will continue to be unable to explain disintegration. Gender equality is at the heart of integration and disintegration and subtle and overt attacks on it, including scaling down gender equality policies, commitments and priorities, are key signals of the difficulties the European integration project faces.

We have illustrated our argument by focusing on three defining cases of 2018: the economic crisis, populism and Brexit. We analysed what an intersectionality approach would reveal of the economic crisis and showed that it demonstrates, even better than a gender approach, the unevenness of integration and disintegration moments. We approached populism through a deconstruction perspective to show the key role that discursive constructions – as prominent and powerful ideas – of European integration play in populist politics. They are underpinned by constructed norms about gender and European gender equality project - both constructed as particularly elitist or as signs of dangerous "gender ideology" and therefore to be attacked. Finally, Brexit illustrates the usefulness of feminist post-deconstruction to analyse the role that emotions and affect play in politics and in perceptions about European integration and disintegration.

One of our key conclusions is that integration and disintegration are present in all these cases. For instance, intersectional gender analyses expose the challenge that the economic crisis posed to European integration, identifying both disintegration and integration dynamics. While the dismantling of EU gender equality policies, the marginalization of minoritized women and de-democratization indicate disintegration, intersectional approaches expose the existence of integrative dynamics activated by the crisis, such as inclusive processes, re-democratization struggles and some advances in the EU social agenda.

Acknowledgements

We would like to thank the Editors of the JCMS Annual Review Roberta Guerrina and Theofanis Exadaktylos for their constructive feedback on a former draft of this article.

Correspondence:
Emanuela Lombardo Departamento de Ciencia Política y Administración Facultad de Ciencias Políticas y Sociología Universidad Complutense de Madrid Campus de Somosaguas, 28223 Pozuelo de Alarcón (Madrid), Spain.
email: elombardo@cps.ucm.es.

References

Abels, G. and MacRae, H. (2016) 'Why and How to Gender European Integration Theory? Introduction'. In Abels, G. and MacRae, H. (eds) *Gendering European Integration Theory. Engaging New Dialogues* (Berlin: Barbara Budrich), pp. 9–37.

Adams, T. (2019) 'Put it to the People March: A Formidable Sea of Humanity and Powerful Strength of Feeling'. The Guardian, 23 March. Available online at https://www.theguardian.com/politics/2019/mar/23/put-it-to-the-people-march-against-brexit-london-revoke-remain-re-form. Last accessed 29 July 2019.

Ahmed, S. (2004) *The Cultural Politics of Emotions* (Edinburgh: Edinburgh University Press).

Bassel, L. and Emejulu, A. (2017) *Minority Women and Austerity: Survival and Resistance in France and Britain* (Bristol: Policy Press).

Bieling, H.-J. and Diez, T. (2016) 'Linking Gender Perspectives to Integration Theory'. In Abels, G. and MacRae, H. (eds) *Gendering European Integration Theory. Engaging New Dialogues* (Berlin: Barbara Budrich), pp. 279–92.

Börzel, T.A. (2018) 'Researching the EU (Studies) into Demise?' *Journal of European Public Policy*, Vol. 25, No. 3, pp. 475–85.

Cavaghan, R. (2017) 'The Gender Politics of EU Economic Policy: Policy Shifts and Contestations before and after the Crisis'. In Kantola, J. and Lombardo, E. (eds) *Gender and the Economic Crisis in Europe. Politics, Institutions, and Intersectionality* (Basingstoke: Palgrave Macmillan), pp. 49–72.

Cavaghan, R. and O'Dwyer, M. (2018) 'European Economic Governance in 2017: A Recovery for Whom?' *JCMS*, Vol. 56, No. S1, pp. 96–108.

Coole, D. and Frost, S. (2010) 'Introducing the New Materialisms'. In Coole, D. and Frost, S. (eds) *New Materialisms: Ontology, Agency and Politics* (Durham, NC: Duke University Press), pp. 1–46.

Crenshaw, K.W. (1991) 'Demarginalizing the Intersection of Race and Sex: A Black Feminist Critique of Antidiscrimination Doctrine, Feminist Theory and Antiracist Politics'. In Bartlett, K. and Kennedy, R. (eds) *Feminist Legal Theory: Readings in Law and Gender* (San Francisco, CA: Westview Press), pp. 57–80.

Elomäki, A. and Kantola, J. (2017) 'Austerity and Feminist Resistance in Finland: Between Established Women's Organisations and New Movements'. In Kantola, J. and Lombardo, E. (eds) *Gender and the Economic Crisis in Europe* (Basingstoke: Palgrave Macmillan), pp. 231–55.

Elomäki, A. and Kantola, J. (2018) 'Theorizing Feminist Struggles in the Triangle of Neoliberalism, Conservatism, and Nationalism'. *Social Politics*, Vol. 25, No. 3, pp. 337–60.

Eräranta, K. and Kantola, J. (2016) 'The Europeanization of Nordic Gender Equality: A Foucauldian Analysis of Reconciling Work and Family', *Gender, Work & Organization* 23 (4), 414–30

Gómez-Reino, M. (2018) 'The Populist Nationalist Party Family and the European Cleavage'. In Gómez-Reino, M. (ed.) *Nationalisms in the European Arena: Nationalisms in the European Arena* (Basingstoke: Palgrave Macmillan), pp. 63–85.

Guerrina, R. (2019) 'Hyper-masculinity in Brexit is Stopping Us from Finding Another Way Forward'. 28 March. Available online at: https://inews.co.uk/opinion/comment/brexit-hyper-masculinity-limited-opportunities-alternative-ways-forward/. Last accessed 29 July 2019.

Guerrina, R. and Masselot, A. (2018) 'Walking into the Footprint of EU Law: Unpacking the Gendered Consequences of Brexit'. *Social Policy & Society*, Vol. 17, No. 2, pp. 319–30.

Guerrina, R., Haastrup, T., Wright, K.A.M., Masselot, A., MacRae, H. and Cavaghan, R. (2018) 'Does European Union Studies have a Gender Problem? Experiences from researching Brexit'. *International Feminist Journal of Politics*, Vol. 20, No. 2, pp. 252–7.

Haas, E.B. (1958) *The Uniting of Europe: Political, Social, and Economical Forces, 1950–1957* (Stanford, CA: Stanford University Press).

Haastrup, T. and Kenny, M. (2016) 'Gendering Institutionalism: A Feminist Institutionalist Approach to EU Integration Theory'. In Abels, G. and MacRae, H. (eds) *Gendering European Integration Theory* (Berlin: Barbara Budrich), pp. 197–216.

Hoskyns, C. (2004) 'Gender Perspectives'. In Wiener, A. and Diez, T. (eds) *European Integration Theory* (Oxford: Oxford University Press), pp. 217–36.

Kantola, J. and Lombardo, E. (2017) 'EU Gender Equality Policies'. In Heinelt, H. and Münch, S. (eds) *Handbook of European Policies: Interpretive Approaches to the EU* (Cheltenham: Edward Elgar), pp. 331–52.

Kantola, J. and Lombardo, E. (eds) (2017a) *Gender and the Economic Crisis in Europe. Politics, Institutions, and Intersectionality* (Basingstoke: Palgrave Macmillan).

Kantola, J. and Lombardo, E. (2017b) *Gender and Political Analysis* (Basingstoke: Palgrave Macmillan).

Kantola, J. and Lombardo, E. (2019) 'Populism and Feminist Politics: The Cases of Finland and Spain'. *European Journal of Political Research*. https://doi.org/10.1111/1475-6765.12333.

Kantola, J. and Rolandsen Agustin, L. (2016) 'Gendering Transnational Party Politics: The Case of European Union'. *Party Politics*, Vol. 22, No. 5, pp. 641–51.

Kantola, J. and Rolandsen Agustin, L. (2019) 'Gendering the Representative Work of the European Parliament: A Political Analysis of Women MEP's Perceptions of Gender Equality in Party Groups'. *JCMS*.

Karamessini, M. (2014) 'Introduction – Women's Vulnerability to Recession and Austerity. A Different Context, a Different Crisis'. In Karamessini, M. and Rubery, J. (eds) *Women and Austerity: The Economic Crisis and the Future for Gender Equality* (London: Routledge), pp. 3–16.

Keskinen, S., Norocel, C. and Jørgensen, M. (2016) 'The Politics and Policies of Welfare Chauvinism under the Economic Crisis'. *Critical Social Policy*, Vol. 36, No. 3, pp. 321–9.

Klatzer, E. and Schlager, C. (2014) 'Feminist Perspectives on Macroeconomics: Reconfiguration of Power Structures and Erosion of Gender Equality through the New Economic Governance Regime in the European Union'. In Evans, M., Hemmings, C., Henry, M., Madhok, S. and Waring, S. (eds) *Feminist Theory Handbook* (London: Sage), pp. 483–500.

Köttig, M., Bitzan, R. and Pető, M. (eds) (2017) *Gender and Far Right Politics in Europe* (Basingstoke: Palgrave Macmillan).

Kreuder-Sonnen, C. (2018) 'An Authoritarian Turn in Europe and European Studies?' *Journal of European Public Policy*, Vol. 25, No. 3, pp. 452–64.

Kronsell, A. (2005) 'Gender, Power and European Integration Theory'. *Journal of European Public Policy*, Vol. 16, No. 2, pp. 1022–40.

Kronsell, A. (2012) 'Gendering Theories of European Integration'. In Abels, G. and Mushaben, J. (eds) *Gendering the European Union. New Approaches to Old Democratic Deficits* (Basingstoke: Palgrave Macmillan), pp. 23–40.

Kronsell, A. (2016) 'The Power of EU Masculinities: A Feminist Contribution to European Integration Theory'. *JCMS*, Vol. 54, No. 1, pp. 104–20.

Kuhar, R. and Paternotte, D. (2017) *Anti-gender Campaigns in Europe: Mobilizing against Equality* (Lanham, MD: Rowman & Littlefield).

Leruth, B. and Lord, C. (2015) 'Differentiated Integration in the European Union: A Concept, a Process, a System or a Theory?' *Journal of European Public Policy*, Vol. 22, No. 6, pp. 754–63.

Lombardo, E. (2016) 'Social Constructivism in European Integration Theories: Gender and Intersectionality Perspectives'. In Abels, G. and MacRae, H. (eds) *Gendering European Integration Theory: Engaging New Dialogues* (Berlin: Barbara Budrich), pp. 123–46.

Lombardo, E. (2017) 'The Spanish Gender Regime in the EU Context: Changes and Struggles in the Wake of Austerity Policies'. *Gender, Work & Organization*, Vol. 24, No. 1, pp. 20–33.

Lombardo, E. and Rolandsen, L. (2016) 'Intersectionality in European Union Policymaking: The Case of Gender-based Violence'. *Politics*, Vol. 36, No. 4, pp. 364–73.

Meret, S. (2015) 'Charismatic Female Leadership and Gender: Pia Kjærsgaard and the Danish People's Party'. *Patterns of Prejudice*, Vol. 49, No. 1–2, pp. 81–102.

Norocel, C. (2013) ''Give Us Back Sweden!' A Feminist Reading of the (Re)interpretations of the Folkhem Conceptual Metaphor in Swedish Radical Right Populist Discourse'. *Nordic Journal of Feminist and Gender Research*, Vol. 21, No. 1, pp. 4–20.

Pedwell, C. (2014) *Affective Relations: The Transnational Politics of Empathy* (Basingstoke: Palgrave Macmillan).

Pirro, A.L.P. and van Kessel, S. (2017) 'United in Opposition? The Populist Radical Right's EU-pessimism in Times of Crisis'. *Journal of European Integration*, Vol. 39, No. 4, pp. 405–20.

Rittberger, B. and Blauberger, M. (2018) 'Introducing the Debate Section: The EU in Crisis: EU Studies in Crisis?' *Journal of European Public Policy*, Vol. 25, No. 3, pp. 436–9.

Roggeband, C. and Krizsán, A. (2018) 'Reversing Gender Policy Progress: Patterns of Backsliding in Central and Eastern European New Democracies'. *European Journal of Politics and Gender*, Vol. 1, No. 3, pp. 367–85.

Rolandsen Agustín, L. (2013) *Gender Equality, Intersectionality and Diversity in Europe* (Basingstoke: Palgrave Macmillan).

Rosamond, B. (2016) 'Brexit and the Problem of European Disintegration'. *Journal of Contemporary European Research*, Vol. 12, No. 4, pp. 864–71.

Schimmelfennig, F. (2017) 'Theorising Crisis in European Integration'. In Dinan, D., Nugent, N. and Paterson, W.E. (eds) *The European Union in Crisis* (Basingstoke: Palgrave Macmillan), pp. 316–35.

Siim, B., Krizsán, A., Gruziel, D. and Nissen, A. (2016) D9.7 'Report of Case Studies on Gender Equality as a Focus Point of National and Nativist Discourses'., 16 June. Available online at: https://www.uu.nl/en/research/beucitizen-european-citizenship-research/publications.   Last accessed 29 July 2019.

Siim, B., Krasteva, A. and Saarinen, A. (eds) (2018) *Citizens' Activism and Solidarity Movements: Contending with Populism* (Basingstoke: Palgrave Macmillan).

Spierings, N. and Zaslove, A. (2015) 'Gendering the Vote for Populist Radical-right Parties'. *Patterns of Prejudice*, Vol. 49, No. 1–2, pp. 135–62.

Verloo, M. (ed.) (2007) *Multiple Meanings of Gender Equality: A Critical Frame Analysis of Gender Policies in Europe* (Budapest: Central European University Press).

Verloo, M. (ed.) (2018) *Varieties of Opposition to Gender Equality in Europe* (London: Routledge).

Verloo, M. and Paternotte, D. (2018) 'The Feminist Project under Threat in Europe'. *Politics and Governance*, Vol. 6, No. 3, pp. 1–5.

Walby, S. (2015) *Crisis* (Cambridge: Polity Press).

Webber, D. (2017) 'Can the EU survive?'. In Dinan, D., Nugent, N. and Paterson, W.E. (eds) *The European Union in Crisis* (Basingstoke: Palgrave Macmillan), pp. 336–359.

Wöhl, S. 2016. Gendering Governmentality and European Integration Theory in G. Abels and H. MacRae (eds.) *Gendering European Integration Theory* (Opladen: Budrich Press), 237–55.

JCMS 2019 Volume 57. Annual Review pp. 77–89   DOI: 10.1111/jcms.12930

Euroscepticism behind the Victory of Eurosceptic Parties in the 2018 Italian General Election? Not Exactly

NICOLA MAGGINI and ALESSANDRO CHIARAMONTE
University of Florence, Florence

I. The 2018 Italian General Election: Context and Question

On 4 March 2018 Italy went to the polls amidst an intense wave of anti-establishment sentiment. The parties that contributed most to, and capitalized from, this political climate were the Movimento 5 Stelle (M5S, Five Star Movement) and the Lega Nord (Lega, Northern League), that is, the challenger, populist parties. In spite of the outcome of a hung Parliament, they turned out to be the true political winners, having significantly increased their share of votes compared with the previous general election of 2013 and together received more than 50 per cent of the support of the electorate. On the contrary, mainstream parties such as the incumbent Partito Democratico (PD, Democratic Party) and Forza Italia (FI, Go Italy) suffered heavy vote losses.

Given the eurosceptical nature of the M5S and even more of the Lega (Emanuele *et al.*, 2016), the election result has been regarded by many as a blow to Europe. Indeed, Italian voters have shifted from pro-European to eurosceptic positions over the past 25 years, particularly after the 2009 great recession and the following austerity measures implemented in 2011 by the technocratic government led by Mario Monti. As shown by the autumn of 2017 Eurobarometer survey, conducted only few months before the March 2018 election, about 40 per cent of Italians 'totally agreed' or 'tended to agree' that 'the country could better face the future outside the EU'. Although anti-EU and anti-euro sentiments do not account for the majority of views in Italy, these data signal a growing discontent with the European integration process, fuelled by the migration and economic crises (Bellucci and Serricchio, 2016; Conti and Memoli, 2015; Lucarelli, 2015).

However, while the victory of eurosceptic parties in the 2018 election is a matter of fact, whether euroscepticism was one of the main explanations for it remains to be determined. Thus, the goal of this contribution was to assess exactly the role played by euroscepticism in the outcome of the 2018 Italian general election. For this purpose, we tried to see how and to what extent EU-related issues were able to shape parties' strategies and voters' preferences. More specifically, we examined, on the one hand, the emphasis given to them by the parties both in their manifestos and in their official Twitter feeds during the electoral campaign, and, on the other hand, the voters' preferences and priorities on those issues and, in comparison, on other issues.

II. Parties, Coalitions and Electoral Manifestos

In October 2017, just 4 months before the end of the legislature, the Italian Parliament passed a new electoral law with the support of all the main parties except the M5S (Massetti and Farinelli, 2019). The new electoral systems for the Chamber of Deputies and the Senate are mixed in nature, combining proportional representation for the nationwide distribution of two-thirds of the total seats with a first-past-the-post system in single-member districts for the remaining one-third (Chiaramonte and D'Alimonte, 2018).

Although allocating most seats through a proportional representation system, the new electoral systems provided a strategic incentive to parties to form pre-electoral coalitions supporting joint candidates in the single-member districts. The parties reacted differently to this. The M5S maintained its traditional decision to maximize brand recognition, running on its own, as it had already done in 2013. The centre-right parties adopted the opposite strategy. They formed a unified coalition including Berlusconi's FI, the Lega – that since 2013 had been transformed by the new leader Matteo Salvini from a northern regionalist party into a populist radical right-wing party with nationwide appeal (not by chance, the word 'Northern' was cancelled from the party's electoral symbol), the post-fascist Fratelli d'Italia (FDI, Brothers of Italy), and the minor party alliance Noi con l'Italia–Unione di Centro (NCI-UDC, Us with Italy–Union of the Centre). Unlike the centre right, and in spite of numerous attempts to overcome the divisions, the centre-left parties were not able to form a unified front. Liberi e Uguali (LEU, Free and Equal), the joint list of parties to the left of the PD, ran for election separately from the PD. The latter created a coalition with three allies: the centrist Lista Civica Popolare (CP, Popular Civic List); +Europa (+EUR, More Europe) led by Emma Bonino, former EU Commissioner; and Insieme (Together), a joint list of Greens, Socialists and other leftist groups.

Turning to the analysis of the electoral manifestos of the main Italian parties, we find that the EU is one of the issues dealt with, although with different degree of relevance. On the centre left the PD dedicated an entire section to the EU issue, supporting pro-EU stances directed to strengthen democratic mechanisms and institutions at the EU level, to reform EU economic governance towards a new common fiscal policy, a social union and a common immigration policy towards asylum seekers and refugees. Their ultimate goal is the creation of a United States of Europe. Very similar goals are supported by +EUR, whose electoral manifesto and party label itself put the EU issue at the centre of the party platform. More Europe, indeed, is the key message of the electoral list led by Emma Bonino, who is a strong supporter of EU federalism. Compared with PD, EU issues are more relevant in the +EUR platform and in terms of content +EUR supports free-market measures and fiscal stability in the context of greater integration of fiscal, energy, banking, transport and services.

On the left, no specific section of LEU electoral manifesto is devoted to EU issues. Nevertheless, in the preamble of its manifesto LEU states that their choice is clearly pro-European, but it is in contrast to the technocratic drift that Europe has taken. They advocate a fairer, more democratic Europe, supporting a greater role of the European Parliament in electing a real government of European citizens, and also overcoming the intergovernmental dimension that dictates duties and does not guarantee rights because of austerity policies.

As regards parties of the centre right, the Lega, FI and FDI developed a common electoral platform in 10 summary points, one of which is labelled 'fewer constraints from Europe'. The European issue is not dealt with in depth, but centre-right parties simply list a series of measures to eliminate the flaws of the EU or the powers they consider excessive: opposition to austerity policies and to excessive EU regulations that hinder economic development; calls for a review of European treaties; call for less bureaucracy in Europe; for the reduction of the surplus of Italian annual payments to the EU budget; demand that the Italian Constitution should prevail over community law, following the German model (that is, for the recovery of sovereignty); and call for the protection of Italian interests, starting with ensuring the security of savings and the protection of the 'Made in Italy' brand. Nevertheless, the Lega created its own manifesto, in which eurosceptic stances emerge more clearly. Indeed, the party led by Salvini dedicated a section of its manifesto to Europe, stating that the Lega wants to stay within the EU only upon the condition that the Italian government will review all the treaties that place constraints on the exercise of full and legitimate Italian sovereignty, and returns to the European Economic Community before the Maastricht Treaty. The euro is considered to be the main cause of Italian economic decline and therefore the Lega advocates embarking on a shared path of agreed exit from the eurozone. Furthermore, the party aims to recover national sovereignty on several issues, advocating exclusive competence on commercial policy, the restoration of the full control of each state within its own borders, (that is, repealing Schengen and the Dublin regulation); supremacy of member states' law over that of the Union, EU Court of Justice case law and the EU legal personality (that is, the power to conclude international agreements on behalf of the member states); the restoration of subsidiarity by returning most of the areas of shared competence and all areas of supporting action under the exclusive competence of each member state and by strengthening the power of national parliaments and regions to monitor the application of the principle of subsidiarity. Finally, none of the 20 points of the electoral manifesto produced by M5S is specifically dedicated to the EU.

To conclude, the main Italian parties deal explicitly with EU issues in their manifestos, with the significant exception of the M5S. The salience of EU issues varies, with some parties (such as +EUR) putting the EU at the centre of their manifesto and others (such as the LEU) mentioning it only in the preamble. Moreover, we noticed a clear contrast between pro-EU positions on the centre left (with some nuances) and anti-EU stances on the right (especially the Lega). However, electoral manifesto data do not tell us about the actual behaviour of the parties during the electoral campaign. In this regard, we can expect parties to adopt strategic choices on social networks much more than on their electoral platforms. Hence, the next section analyses the feeds on Twitter of the main parties and their leaders, which represent the most widely accessible form of party communication.

III. Twitter Campaign Analysis

To comprehend the interaction between party strategies and electoral incentives we relied on two different data sources, which allowed us to capture and measure the parties' strategies in terms of both their emphasis on issues and the issue opportunities for parties. The first goal was reached by coding all the messages posted on Twitter by the main Italian parties and their leaders during the electoral campaign. The second goal was reached by a pre-campaign survey on a representative sample of the Italian voting-age population.[1] In particular, comparing party strategies during the electoral campaign and issue opportunities among voters before election allows us to understand (1) whether the parties politicized issues related to the EU by emphasizing them through their Twitter feeds, and (2) whether the party strategies actually exploited EU-related issue opportunities available among voters.[2]

We start with the Twitter campaign analysis. Although it can be claimed that the Twitter audience in most countries is scarcely representative of the entire population, we consider that the use of Twitter feeds for measuring issue emphasis should allow us to detect the parties' strategic priorities in a campaign. Indeed, in line with De Sio *et al.* (2018), we believe that political parties use Twitter mostly to provide official statements and positions to the media and the public (as a press release tool), even in countries with low or elite-only Twitter penetration, as shown by empirical research (Kreiss, 2016; Parmelee and Bichard, 2011). All tweets in the Twitter accounts of the main parties and party leaders competing in the election were collected in the 2 months preceding the election day (7 January to 4 March). We scrutinized the official Twitter accounts for seven parties – PD, M5S, FI, Lega, FDI, LEU, +EUR – and their leaders – Matteo Renzi, Luigi Di Maio, Silvio Berlusconi, Matteo Salvini, Giorgia Meloni, Pietro Grasso and Emma Bonino. After removing retweets and replies, 17,667 tweets remained for scrutiny. During the coding procedure human coders manually assigned each of the 1,292 policy tweets to one of the 34 issues included in the survey,[3] while tweets not related to policy issues were deleted (92.8 per cent). The issue selection process was designed to address all topics debated during the campaign and to cover different policy domains, namely the economy, Europe, immigration and social issues. We identified both positional and valence issues (Stokes, 1963). To summarize, positional issues are those on which two rival goals are preferred by only portions of the electorate (such as progressive tax versus a flat tax), while valence issues concern goals shared by the whole electorate (such as the fight against unemployment).

Table 1 reports, for each of the selected Italian parties, their top five issue goals in terms of their issue emphasis, along with their specific share of tweets. It is worth noticing that EU issues were not at the centre of party campaign strategies, with the (expected) exception of +EUR. Indeed, EU issues are not included among the top five issue goals in terms of issue emphasis (that is, share of tweets) by the Italian parties. As anticipated, the only exception is +EUR, which dedicated 39 per cent of their tweets to the goal 'stay in the EU', by far the issue most emphasized by the party led by Emma Bonino. In addition, a valence issue related to the EU ('make Italy count more in Europe') appears among the most emphasized issues by the party (5 per cent of tweets). Overall, 44 per cent of +EUR tweets focused on the EU. This is consistent with the party's electoral manifesto

---

[1]These investigations were carried out in the Issue Competition Comparative Project conducted by Italian Centre for Electoral Studies (see http://cise.luiss.it/iccp/).
[2]For a more comprehensive analysis of the interaction between issue opportunity structure and strategic choices of Italian parties, see Emanuele *et al.* (2019, forthcoming).
[3]Specifically, two coders coded all tweets independently, deciding to which of the 34 issues measured in the electoral survey it belonged. The validity of our ex ante issue selection was confirmed by the very low number of tweets dedicated to issues not included in the original 34-item list (19 of a total of 17,667 tweets), leading us to exclude these 19 tweets from the analysis. The intercoder reliability was very high, as measured by the Cohen's kappa statistic (0.90): according to Fleiss *et al.* (2013), values over 0.75 can be considered excellent. Consequently, we decided to keep only the classification of the coder assigning the highest number of tweets to issue content.

Table 1: Top Five Goals by Issue on Twitter for Italian Parties (EU Issues in Bold)

Party	Issue goal	Issue emphasis
PD	Support economic growth	0.14
	Fight unemployment	0.13
	Keep progressive tax on income	0.12
	Make citizens safer from crime	0.07
	Increase economic bonuses to families with children	0.07
M5S	Fight pollution and disruption of territory	0.32
	Improve Italian education	0.26
	Ensure the good functioning of the health-care system	0.13
	Lower the pensionable age	0.06
	Renew Italian politics	0.06
Lega	Limit the number of refugees	0.27
	Lower the pensionable age	0.15
	Introduce a flat tax	0.09
	Make citizens safer from crime	0.06
	Decriminalize excessive self-defence	0.05
FI	Introduce a flat tax	0.39
	Limit the number of refugees	0.14
	Fight unemployment	0.14
	Reduce poverty in Italy	0.10
	Support economic growth	0.07
FDI	Limit the number of refugees	0.22
	Making citizens safer from crime	0.22
	Decriminalize excessive self-defence	0.09
	Fight pollution and disruption of territory	0.08
	Increase economic bonuses to families with children	0.06
LEU	Fight pollution and disruption of territory	0.21
	Ensure the good functioning of the health-care system	0.14
	Keep progressive tax on income	0.12
	Improve Italian education	0.09
	Scrap the cost of university tuition fees	0.06
+EUR	**Stay in the EU**	0.39
	Continue to accept refugees as now	0.16
	Support economic growth	0.10
	Make Italy count more in Europe	0.05
	Renew Italian politics	0.05

+EUR, More Europe; FDI; Fratelli d'Italia; FI, Forza Italia; LEU; Liberi e Uguali; M5S, Movimento 5 Stelle; PD, Partito Democratico.

and is not surprising, as +EUR can be considered a niche party founded precisely around the EU issue, with a strong pro-EU and federalist stance (Table 1).

Therefore, as far as EU issues are concerned, the actual party communication strategies in general do not reflect their electoral manifestos. This is particularly evident for PD and the Lega, whose pro and anti-EU positions did not emerge during their electoral campaign on Twitter. Conversely, the lack of emphasis on EU issues by M5S is consistent with its electoral manifesto.

By looking at the specific strategies of four major parties (M5S, PD, Lega, and FI), we notice that the M5S chose a non-ideological campaign, given that it emphasized only one positional goal – lowering the pensionable age, while it focused its message on non-divisive, valence issues (Stokes, 1963) such as reducing pollution, improving the education and health-care system, and renewing Italian politics. Conversely, the PD emphasized mostly economically progressive goals (progressive tax and bonuses for children), while FI campaigned on both cultural and economic conservative goals (fewer refugees and flat tax). Finally, the Lega mostly campaigned on right-wing cultural policies, but also on two economic goals of a different ideological weight: the flat tax – a clearly right-wing economic measure – and reducing the pensionable age – a traditional social-democratic economic goal.

Election results: to what extent did the EU shape voters' preferences and behaviour?

The outcome of the election turned out to be a hung parliament, with none of the main competitors capable of winning the majority of seats in the Chamber and in the Senate (Table 2).

The centre-right coalition came first with 37 per cent of the votes and 42.1 per cent of seats in the Chamber, and 37.7 per cent of the votes and 43.5 per cent of seats in the Senate. It increased its 2013 vote share by roughly 8 percentage points, with the Lega growing by 14 points, and FI losing over 7 points. As a consequence, the Lega became, for the first time, the most-voted party of the coalition, achieving its best electoral result ever.

Table 2: Results of the 2018 Italian General Election in the Chamber of Deputies and in the Senate

Party lists and coalitions	*Chamber*				*Senate*			
	Votes		*Seats*		*Votes*		*Seats*	
	No.	*%*	*No.*	*%*	*No.*	*%*	*No.*	*%*
Lega	5,705,925	17.3	125	19.8	5,334,049	17.6	58	18.4
FI	4,586,672	13.9	103	16.3	4,358,101	14.4	57	18.1
Fratelli d'Italia	1,440,107	4.4	32	5.1	1,286,887	4.3	18	5.7
NCI-UDC	431,042	1.3	5	0.8	362,131	1.2	4	1.3
FI, FDI, MNVA	5,533	0.0	0	0.0	5,223	0.0	0	0.0
Total right	*12,169,279*	*37.0*	*265*	*42.1*	*11,346,391*	*37.5*	*137*	*43.5*
M5S	10,748,372	32.7	227	36.0	9,747,701	32.2	112	35.6
PD	6,153,081	18.7	112	17.8	5,788,103	19.1	53	16.8
Più Europa (+EUR)	845,406	2.6	3	0.5	716,136	2.4	1	0.3
Insieme	191,489	0.6	1	0.2	163,903	0.5	1	0.3
Civica Popolare	180,539	0.5	2	0.3	152,505	0.5	1	0.3
SVP, PATT	134,613	0.4	4	0.6	128,336	0.4	3	1.0
PD, UV, UVP, EPAV	14,429	0.0	0	0.0	15,958	0.1	1	0.3
Total centre left	*7,519,557*	*22.9*	*122*	*19.4*	*6,964,941*	*23.0*	*60*	*19.0*
LEU	1,114,298	3.4	14	2.2	990,715	3.3	4	1.3
Others	1,354,919	4.1	2	0.3	1,226,064	4.0	2	0.6
Total	*32,906,425*	*100*	*630*	*100*	*30,275,812*	*100*	*315*	*100*

+EUR, More Europe; EPAV, Edelweiss Popolare Autonomista Valdostano; FDI, Fratelli d'Italia; FI, Forza Italia; LEU, Liberi e Uguali; M5S, Movimento 5 Stelle; MNVA, Movimento Nuova Valle d'Aosta; NCI-UDC, Noi con l'Italia-Unione di Centro; PATT, Partito Autonomista Trentino Tirolese; PD, Partito Democratico; SVP, Südtiroler Volkspartei; UV, Union Valdôtaine; UVP, Union Valdôtaine Progressiste. Source: authors' elaboration of data from the Italian Ministry of the Interior.

The M5S followed with 32.7 per cent of the votes and 36 per cent of the seats in the Chamber, and 32.2 per cent and 35.6 per cent of the votes and the seats in the Senate, respectively. It increased its 2013 vote share by 7 percentage points. In 2013 the M5S had achieved a record high for a new party at its first electoral outing in the whole of western Europe since the Second World War. Five years later, at the subsequent national election, not only did the M5S manage not to lose support, but it was able to build on what was already a record performance.

Finally, the centre-left coalition led by the incumbent PD trailed third, with only 22.9 per cent of the votes and 19.4 per cent of seats in the Chamber, and with 23 per cent and 19 per cent of votes and seats in the Senate, respectively. Its 2013 vote share fell by about 7 percentage points and it was the clear loser of this election. While the lack of a clear winner was a largely expected outcome, the overall performance of individual parties came as a surprise. The success of the challenger parties, the M5S and the Lega, was greater than was predicted by most polls – as was the defeat of the mainstream parties, the PD and FI. While a comprehensive explanation of the election outcome goes beyond the remit of this contribution, we address the question whether EU issues have played a major role in shaping priorities and preferences of Italian voters.

In order to comprehend how party strategies – as outlined in the previous section – were consistent with the issue opportunities available among their voters, we need to look at public opinion data. In this regard, a computer-assisted web interviewing survey was carried out before the 4 March election (6–12 February) among a quota sample of 1,000 Italian citizens over the age of 18 years. The sample was representative of the voting-age population in Italy based on gender, age group, geographical area, and education. The response rate was 49 per cent.[4] Respondents were asked about their policy preferences and priorities (namely, the same items that we detected in the Twitter campaign analysis).

Before discussing the details of each party constituency, it is worth briefly looking at the issue preferences and priorities of the overall Italian electorate. Table 3 presents the systemic salience of both valence and positional issues[5] for our whole sample and, for positional issues only, the favourite and most salient rival goal – with its level of support and percentage points of predominance in terms of salience compared with the rival goal. The first point to be stressed is that on the European dimension, Italians are in favour of the country both staying in the EU (66 per cent) and the eurozone (61 per cent), with a good level of salience of both issues (74 per cent and 72 per cent, respectively). In comparison with other issues, EU issues fall in an intermediate position in terms of salience. All eight most-salient issues are valence, with unemployment, corruption and the health-care system at the top of voters' agenda. The only positional issues showing levels of salience comparable with valence issues are pensions, refugees and tax evasion. We thus note a mixture of conservative cultural goals on immigration and social-democratic goals on the economy, which are considered more salient. Roughly three-quarters of Italians are in favour of progressive taxation, increasing benefits for families with children, reducing income differences, introducing a minimum hourly wage, reducing economic austerity

---

[4]The response rate of 49 per cent is definitely good because it is usually around 33 per cent in non-random computer-assisted web interviewing surveys and even less in telephone surveys.

[5]The systemic salience of an issue is calculated as the percentage of all respondents that considers the issue as a high priority, with respondents reporting medium priority being counted as half.

Table 3: Italian Public Opinion Configuration before the Election (Valence Issues in Italics, EU Issues in Bold)

Issue	Systemic salience (% of respondents)	Most supported and salient goal	Goal support (% of respondents)	Salience differentials between rival goals (in percentage points)
Fight unemployment	93			
Improve healthcare	92			
Fight corruption	92			
Reduce costs of politics	90			
Fight poverty	90			
Increase safety from crime	89			
Support economic growth	89			
Protect from terrorism	84			
Tax evasion	83	Increase tax evasion fight	85	+67
Number of refugees	82	Limit the number of refugees	80	+56
Renew politics	82			
Protect environment	81			
Pensionable age	81	Lower the pensionable age	80	+59
Improve education	80			
Make Italy count more in Europe	78			
Tax progressivity	77	Keep tax progressivity	74	+39
Vaccines	76	Keep vaccines compulsory	78	+48
The EU	**74**	**Stay in the EU**	**66**	**+26**
The eurozone	**72**	**Stay in the eurozone**	**61**	**+18**
Economic benefits for families with children	71	Increase benefits for children	85	+55
Income differences	71	Reduce income differences	79	+49
Minimum hourly wage	71	Introduce minimum hourly wage	80	+53
Make political economy of the EU more flexible or not	71	More EU economic flexibility	76	+44
Basic income	69	Introduce basic income	73	+41
Self-defence	69	Decriminalize excessive self-defence	69	+31
Freedom of enterprise	64	Reduce freedom of enterprise	60	+17
Welfare chauvinism	63	Restrict welfare for immigrants	60	+22
Citizenship for immigrants' children	60	No easier citizenship	56	+11
Living will	59	Keep living will legislation	76	+33
Globalization	58	Limit globalization	55	+8
Soft drugs	53	Don't legalize soft drugs	52	+11
Prostitution	51	Legalize prostitution	70	+26
University tuition	51	Abolish university tuition fees	62	+20
Same-sex unions	43	Keep same-sex unions	67	+15

Figure 1: EU, economic and cultural issues: preferences and salience of major Italian party constituencies.+EUR, More Europe; FDI; Fratelli d'Italia; FI, Forza Italia; LEU, Liberi e Uguali; M5S, Movimento 5 Stelle; PD, Partito Democratico. [Colour figure can be viewed at wileyonlinelibrary.com]

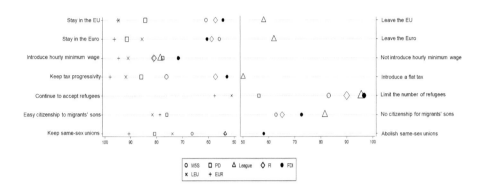

and introducing a basic income for people in poverty. The first item is particularly interesting, as its rival goal (introducing a flat tax) has been the signature campaign proposal on the economy of the most-voted coalition – the centre right. The only economic issue splitting the electorate into two portions with about the same weight is regulating the job market. Nevertheless, 60 per cent of Italians chose the left-wing goal – reducing the freedom of entrepreneurs to fire and hire.

In parallel to their observed preference for social-democratic economic goals, Italians favour demarcationist cultural goals (Kriesi *et al.,* 2006). In addition to 80 per cent of Italians who want a reduction in the number of refugees, most also prefer not easing elegibility for citizenship for immigrants' children born in Italy and reducing welfare services for legal immigrants. On these issue dimensions, then, the centre right appears to be much more in line with the preferences of the electorate.

The issue dimension that is least salient for Italians is social issues. End-of-life regulations, legalizing prostitution or soft drugs, and gay-couples' rights are all at the bottom of the Italian agenda, with the last-named being the only issue whose level of salience is below 50 per cent. This is something worth underlying: despite the fact that the pro-choice goal is usually preferred on these issues, their low salience makes it harder to move them to the centre stage during the campaign.

In order to investigate the configuration of issue opportunities for Italian parties which stays behind the general patterns shown by Table 3, now it is worth looking at the preferences and priorities of party constituencies on positional issues. The latter, as stated, consist of two rival goals, which can vary in terms of salience and within-party agreement. Any goal on which its voters agree most and perceive as salient can provide a political party with a higher electoral opportunity than can a divisive and less salient goal.[6] Figure 1 shows, for the selected parties, where their electorates stand on the EU positional

---

[6]In this regard, we are in line with the theoretical insights of issue yield theory (De Sio and Weber, 2014; De Sio *et al.,* 2018), which considers that contemporary party competition is best understood in terms of issue competition (Carmines and Stimson, 1980; Green-Pedersen, 2007).

issues, along with their relative salience (represented by the size of the indicator). Apart from EU-related issues, Figure 1 also includes a selection of economic and cultural positional issues, which can be clearly interpreted according to the progressive-conservative antithesis (Middendorp, 1978).

EU issues show a certain degree of polarization across party constituencies: centre-left party constituencies (+EUR, PD, LEU) strongly support EU stances, whereas Lega's voters are on the opposite side, with M5S, FI and FDI voters somewhat in the middle (but with a prevalence of pro-EU positions). Hence, it seems that the parties actually could mobilize on EU issues: especially the centre-left parties. Indeed, EU issues were very salient for their voters (and quite salient for the whole electorate, as shown by Table 3). Moreover, there was a high level of agreement on pro-EU goals among electors of centre-left parties (ranging from 84 per cent of PD voters to 96 per cent of +EUR electors on the euro issue; see Figure 1) and a good level of agreement in the whole electorate (between 66 per cent on the euro issue and 61 per cent on the EU issue, see Table 3). Therefore, emphasizing such issues could have been a win-win strategy, which combined an expansion of votes with the preservation of party's usual constituency (see De Sio and Weber, 2014 De Sio et al. 2018).

However, only +EUR made use of this, as discussed above. Neither PD nor LEU dedicated considerable numbers of tweets to EU issues, contrary to the incentives considered above. Parties of the centre right and M5S adopted the same choice, but in this case their strategy was consistent with their issue opportunities. Indeed, as shown by Figure 1, EU issues for M5S, FI and FDI were highly divisive within their electorates and were less salient than other issues. Even among Lega voters there was a noticeable share of pro-EU positions (42 per cent for permanence in the EU and 38 per cent as regards the permanence in the eurozone). Furthermore, for Lega voters EU was less salient than for centre-left voters, and also compared with other issues (especially those related to immigration). Hence, the Lega's choice to focus more on immigration than on EU was in line with actual electoral incentives.

In a nutshell, in terms of economic and cultural issues most voters of Italian parties appear to converge on progressive economic issue goals, on progressive cultural goals related to civil rights and on conservative cultural goals related to immigration, in line with the previously mentioned preferences of the whole electorate. In particular, the data show that there is not a huge difference among the seven electorates on desiring a minimum hourly wage. A similar progressive agreement can be found on civil rights, although more relevant differences emerge and there is a clear exception of FDI voters who mostly oppose same-sex unions. Nevertheless, most party constituencies consider the economy to be more salient than civil rights.

In symmetry, conservative positions definitely prevail as regards the refugee issue: all electorates, except two small party constituencies (+EUR and LEU), favour the right-wing goal of reducing the number of refugees. However, the level of support here is much higher than on consensual left-wing economic goals: more than 80 per cent of M5S voters and 90 per cent or more of FI, the Lega and FDI voters support the anti-immigration position, which is shared by 56 per cent of PD voters. Also, slightly fewer than half voters for the left-wing party LEU want to reduce the number of refugees, as well as 42 per cent of +EUR voters. Moreover, there is much more variation in terms of salience: for centre-right voters (and Lega and FDI voters in particular), anti-immigrant goals are crucial;

while for M5S and PD voters, economic goals are more important. As far as access to citizenship for migrants' children is concerned, preferences are conversely more polarized between progressive positions on the left (PD, LEU and +EUR), and conservative positions on the right (FI, FDI and Lega) and among M5S voters.

To sum up, the success of challenger parties is not directly related to EU issues. Indeed, M5S emphasized EU issues neither in its manifesto nor during the electoral campaign on Twitter, reading correctly the issue opportunity configuration within its electorate, whose positions on issues were on average the closest to the median voter (and thus, more pro-EU than anti-EU). Hence, campaigning on anti-EU positions could have been a very risky choice. The Lega, while showing a strong positioning in its manifesto, did not campaign on Twitter against the EU (as it did in the 2014 European Parliament elections). This strategy allowed it to attract a divided (on the EU) electorate, while clearly occupying one camp of the positional issue. Both parties, indeed, had their best electoral opportunities on other issues: a mix of progressive issues on the economy and of conservative goals on immigration for the M5S, whereas the Lega was clearly the party of cultural demarcation on immigration. Although the EU issue does not explain the populist success, it might be one of the reasons behind the PD's failure. Focusing on pro-EU stances might have been a strategic choice for the main party of the centre left, with promising electoral opportunities according to our data. But this was not the case, as we have seen.

Concluding Remarks

The European dimension was not prominent during the electoral campaign on Twitter. Overall, out of roughly 1,300 policy tweets we collected and coded, less than 8 per cent concerned the EU, the euro, or EU economic policy, and less than 5 per cent the EU per se. For the M5S and the centre-right coalition the strategic decision to silence the EU dimension makes sense, given the internal clashes on the EU existing both in their electorate and in their political élites. On the centre right there was a coexistence of clearly pro-European figures (such as the former EU Commissioner and current European Parliament President, Antonio Tajani, who was FI's candidate for prime minister), with eurosceptic figures, including some who have an openly anti-EU stance (especially in the Lega). Ambiguity was also present within the M5S ranks. For the centre left, which is a clearly pro-EU actor, the choice of silencing the European dimension is less easily understandable. It probably has to do with the perceived growing unpopularity of the EU in the eyes of Italian voters, which made the party believe that campaigning on this issue would not be electorally beneficial.

All in all, based on the evidence of our analysis, it is hard to support the interpretation that euroscepticism was a main determinant of the election outcome. The (still minoritarian) negative views of the EU and the euro may have been fundamental for some voters, and may have indirectly affected the preferences of other voters on issues such as immigration and the economy (or the other way around); however, they did not play a direct role either in shaping the party's mobilization strategies or in structuring the voting choice of the electorate at large.

All this appears particularly interesting if we consider the post-electoral developments that resulted in the creation of a M5S-Lega government and in the relegation of both PD and FI to the opposition. Hence, eurosceptic parties are now in office on their own and Europhile parties are in opposition. The new government-opposition dynamics may be well interpreted as a sign of the emergence of the globalization (Kriesi *et al.,* 2006) or transnational cleavage (Hooghe and Marks, 2018), setting on the one side, eurosceptic, anti-immigrant and anti-globalization parties against, on the other side, Europhile, pro-multiculturalism and pro-globalization parties. However, as we have seen from our data, and also from the very first acts of the new government vis-à-vis the European authorities (for example, in reaching a compromise with the European Commission over its 2019 budget), the euroscepticism of M5S and the Lega has so far been limited to words and has not translated into action.

References

Bellucci, P. and Serricchio, F. (2016) 'Europeismo, Euroscetticismo e Crisi Economica'. In Pasquinucci, D. and Verzichelli, L. (eds) *Contro l'Europa? I diversi scetticismi verso l'integrazione europea* (Bologna: Il Mulino), pp. 215–32.

Carmines, E.G. and Stimson, J.A. (1980) 'The Two Faces of Issue Voting'. *American Political Science Review*, Vol. 74, No. 1, pp. 78–91.

Chiaramonte, A. and D'Alimonte, R. (2018) 'The New Italian Electoral System and its Effects on Strategic Coordination and Disproportionality'. *Italian Political Science*, Vol. 13, No. 1, pp. 8–18.

Conti, N. and Memoli, V. (2015) 'Show the Money First! Recent Public Attitudes towards the EU in Italy'. *Italian Political Science Review*, Vol. 45, No. 2, pp. 203–22.

De Sio, L. and Weber, T. (2014) 'Issue Yield: A Model of Party Strategy in Multidimensional Space'. *American Political Science Review*, Vol. 108, No. 4, pp. 870–85.

De Sio, L., De Angelis, A. and Emanuele, V. (2018) 'Issue Yield and Party Strategy in Multiparty Competition'. *Comparative Political Studies*, Vol. 51, No. 9, pp. 1208–38.

Emanuele, V., Maggini, N. and Marino, B. (2016) 'Gaining Votes in Europe against Europe? How National Contexts Shaped the Results of Eurosceptic Parties in 2014 European Parliament Elections'. *Journal of Contemporary European Research*, Vol. 12, No. 3, pp. 697–715.

Emanuele, V., Maggini, N., and Paparo, A. (2019) '"The Times They Are A-Changin"': Party Campaign Strategies in the 2018 Italian Election'. Accepted for publication in *West European Politics*.

Fleiss, J.L., Levin, B. and Cho Paik, M. (2013) *Statistical Methods for Rates and Proportions* (New York: John Wiley & Sons).

Green-Pedersen, C. (2007) 'The Growing Importance of Issue Competition: The Changing Nature of Party Competition in Western Europe'. *Political Studies*, Vol. 55, No. 3, pp. 607–28.

Hooghe, L. and Marks, G. (2018) 'Cleavage Theory Meets Europe's Crises: Lipset, Rokkan, and the Transnational Cleavage'. *Journal of European Public Policy*, Vol. 25, No. 1, pp. 109–35.

Kreiss, D. (2016) 'Seizing the Moment: The Presidential Campaigns' Use of Twitter during the 2012 Electoral Cycle'. *New Media & Society*, Vol. 18, No. 8, pp. 1473–90.

Kriesi, H., Grande, H., Lachat, R., Dolezal, M., Bornschier, S. and Frey, T. (2006) 'Globalization and the Transformation of the National Political Space: Six European Countries Compared'. *European Journal of Political Research*, Vol. 45, No. 6, pp. 921–56.

Lucarelli, S. (2015) 'Italy and the EU: From True Love to Disenchantment?' *JCMS*, Vol. 53, No. S1, pp. 40–60.

Massetti, E. and Farinelli, A. (2019) 'From the *Porcellum* to the *Rosatellum*: "Political Elite-Judicial Interaction" in the Italian Laboratory of Electoral Reforms'. *Contemporary Italian Politics*, Vol. 11, No. 2, pp. 137–57.

Middendorp, C.P. (1978) *Progressiveness and Conservatism: The Fundamentals of Ideological Controversy and their Relationship to Social Class* (The Hague: Mouton).

Parmelee, J.H. and Bichard, S.L. (2011) *Politics and the Twitter Revolution: How Tweets Influence the Relationship between Political Leaders and the Public* (Lanham, MD: Lexington Books).

Stokes, D.E. (1963) 'Spatial Models of Party Competition'. *American Political Science Review*, Vol. 57, No. 2, pp. 368–77.

JCMS 2019 Volume 57. Annual Review pp. 90–102   DOI: 10.1111/jcms.12920

"Don't Mention the War!" how Populist Right-Wing Radicalism Became (Almost) Normal in Germany

KAI ARZHEIMER
Johannes Gutenberg University, Mainz

Introduction

In the 1980s, the Populist Radical Right emerged as a new party family. Its members have a number of core characteristics in common: they are nativist, authoritarian, and usually also populist (Mudde, 2007). While their relationship with European integration is more complex than it would first seem, they are often also eurosceptic (Vasilopoulou, 2018).

By the early 2000s, electorally relevant populist radical right parties existed in many West European countries. The most prominent case was Austria, where in 1999 the FPÖ won 26.9 per cent of the votes and entered a coalition with the Christian Democrats, becoming the subject of EU sanctions. But other countries were similarly affected. Five years earlier, Berlusconi's Forza Italia (FI), a personal party with strong populist tendencies, had replaced the Christian Democrats as the dominant force in Italian politics. While FI itself was not normally seen as a populist *radical* right party, it formed a series of coalitions with the successor party of the neo-fascist MSI (with whom it later merged) and the populist and increasingly radical Lega (Nord). In France, the founder of the Front National progressed into the second round of the 2002 presidential election. In Belgium, the *cordon sanitaire* around the Vlaams Blok/Vlaams Belang forced mainstream politicians to form politically awkward coalitions. In the Netherlands, Pim Fortuyn, the "Pink Populist", created the blueprint for radical right parties that claimed to stand up for liberal democracy.

A decade later, only a handful of EU countries remained that had *no* radical right party, the most influential in terms of EU politics being Germany. But even this was about to change. The moderately eurosceptic "Alternative for Germany" (AfD) narrowly failed to win representation in the federal parliament in September 2013. Over the next two years, the party became progressively more radical and won seats in every single state-level election that it contested. By May 2017, it had delegations in 13 out of 16 state parliaments and in September of the same year, it won 12.6 per cent of the national vote, making it the strongest opposition party in the new parliament. The AfD was also successful in three further state elections held in 2017 and 2018. Even after a number of defections, it has 278 MPs at the federal and the state level at the time of writing and is expected to do well in the 2019 state elections in eastern Germany. Moreover, it holds seats in local and regional assemblies. As a result, the AfD now has a large cohort of professional politicians in its ranks, who have access to the media but also to considerable financial and organisational resources. Therefore, the AfD will continue to shape German politics, and in turn, European politics for years to come, even if their support may decline in the short-term.

2018 was a pivotal year for the AfD: the party had now existed for a full five-year electoral cycle and managed to enter the last two state parliaments (Bavaria and Hesse) in which it had *not* been represented, confirming the party's role as an integral yet isolated element of the German party system. Moreover, it was the year that their leaders in the federal parliament and their newly formed faction there emerged as a new power centre.

To put these events into perspective, I will address three related questions in this contribution. First, why has Germany finally succumbed to right-wing populism? Second, how is the AfD changing politics, and how has the party adapted to its new position within the party system? Third, what are the implications of the AfD's presence for Germany and the EU?

Why and How Did German Exceptionalism Come to an End?

The Extreme Right in (Western) Germany, 1949–2013

Right-wing extremism was deeply discredited in the Federal Republic. The young democracy outlawed the use of Nazi symbols and language and introduced legislation that made it possible to ban openly anti-democratic associations and parties. When the SRP, a thinly disguised NSDAP successor party, gained momentum in the early 1950s, it was quickly banned and disbanded. Any political group that came too close to right-wing extremist ideas potentially faced the same measures.

This does not mean that anti-semitism and authoritarian tendencies disappeared over night. However, openly extremist statements became increasingly stigmatised, which set in motion a virtuous cycle (Art, 2011): politically ambitious right-wingers had to moderate to pursue a career in the mainstream parties, whereas fringe parties could only attract politically inept extremists. In turn, these parties (most notably the NPD, which enjoyed a brief series of successes in state elections during the 1960s but rapidly declined after they failed to win representation in the 1969 federal election), were riddled with factionalism and became even more radical and isolated.

While there have been at least three waves of party-based right-wing mobilisation in the 1950s, 1960s and then again from the late 1980s onwards, these remained confined to the subnational level. History and political culture aside, there are two structural factors that help to explain this.

First, like other Christian Democratic parties (Kalyvas and van Kersbergen, 2010), Germany's CDU was programmatically vague and remained able to appeal to a very broad constituency. This appeal was further extended by the CDU's relationship with its "sister party", the Bavarian CSU. The CSU is more populist (Falkenhagen, 2013), more restrictive on immigration (Lubbers *et al.*, 2002), and also slightly more eurosceptic (Wimmel and Edwards, 2011) than the CDU. As the two parties do not compete and always form an electoral alliance at the national level, the CDU could still attract more radical voters (and the CSU more moderate voters) than it would have otherwise been the case.

Second, because of its lack of appeal to capable politicians and its fixation with toxic issues that increasingly fewer potential voters were interested in, the parties at the far right of the spectrum failed to modernise: they did not adopt the "new master frame" (Rydgren, 2005) of the radical right that avoids biological racism and explicit demands to abolish democracy. Only in the city state of Hamburg did parties emerge that promoted right-wing populist policies whilst avoiding references to Germany's traumatic past (Decker, 2008, 129–31). But these parties failed to establish a national presence. And so, for a long time, it seemed as if "Germany had executed containment [of the radical right] close to perfection" (Art, 2018, 79).

The AfD, 2013–2015

The AfD was founded just before the 2013 federal election by a group of third-tier politicians, journalists, academics, entrepreneurs and activists in protest over Germany's involvement in the bailout packages for Greece. Its very name - Alternative for Germany - was a reaction to Merkel's claim that there was *no* alternative to her policies.

Initially, the party's public ideology and perception, summarised in the nickname "professors' party", were dominated by members of the traditional elites. Many of them were close to or even former members of the Christian Democrats or the centre-right Free Democrats (FDP) party.[1] However, from its very beginning, the AfD also attracted less established and more radical right-wingers.

By the end of 2014, neither the party's manifesto for the EP elections nor their general demeanour showed evidence of radicalism or populism (Arzheimer, 2015a), but the tide was already turning. After some dithering, Bernd Lucke, the party's most prominent face at the time, decided to push back against eurosceptic, right-wing populist and even extremist factions within the AfD. When Lucke lost a protracted power struggle against co-leader Frauke Petry, who had no such qualms and was backed by even more radical forces, he left the party in July 2015, taking about 10 per cent of the members, some regional leaders and most of the AfD delegation in the EP with him.[2] Even before this quasi-split, the party had dropped below the critical five-percent threshold in national opinion polls and could easily have ended there and then.

The AfD 2015–2017

Two months later chancellor Merkel unexpectedly suspended the Dublin rules. The so-called "refugee crisis", i.e. the sometimes chaotic arrival of hundreds of thousands of refugees, provided a new lease of life to the party. Using social media data, Arzheimer and Berning (2019) show that from mid-2015, the AfD devoted less and less attention to European topics and instead turned to the signature issue of the radical right: immigration and the role of Muslims in European societies. Petry and other leading figures in the party stepped up their rhetoric, following a well-worn pattern: some outrageous statement guaranteed them the attention of the media but was quickly followed up by the claim that they had been misunderstood or misquoted. This repositioning proved highly successful. In five state elections that were held in 2016, the AfD garnered between 12.6 and 24.3 per cent of the vote, making it the strongest or second-strongest opposition party in some cases.

---

[1]Even after the party's radicalisation, 21 of its current MPs in the Bundestag are former members of the CDU/CSU and 10 were members of the FDP.
[2]Lucke went on to found a new, decisively moderate party that is of no political relevance.

Having established this impressive parliamentary presence, Petry came to the conclusion that tactical moderation was the AfD's future. She argued that in the medium term, the AfD should follow the example of the Austrian FPÖ and the Norwegian Progress Party and become available as a coalition partner for the centre right. In a bid to soften the image of the party while consolidating her own power base, like Lucke before her she tried but failed to expel Björn Höcke, party leader in Thuringia and, more importantly, the leader of a semi-official faction called "Der Flügel" (the "Wing" or "Tendency") that is particularly strong in eastern Germany.

In their manifesto, members of the "Wing" style themselves as defenders against the "united front of the old parties and the corrupt media" (Der Flügel, 2017). They see the AfD as a "resistance movement". Instead of conducting politics as usual by working with other parties, they want to turn the AfD itself into the political representation of a broad coalition of right-wing anti-establishment forces, including the islamophobic "Pegida" and similar groups (Der Flügel, 2015). The "Wing" quickly established a flurry of networking activities including an annual conference that is held near the Kyffhäuser monument, which has been a focus of right-wing extremist mobilisation since the 1890s.

Höcke is the most prominent face of the "Wing". Early on in the AfD's history, he had expressed sympathy for voters and rank-and-file members of the neo-Nazi NPD, to whom he offered a new political home. Later, he was recorded giving a racist speech on "Africans". He habitually uses language that is reminiscent of the Nazis and organises nightly assemblies in the streets of the state capital. Höcke's latest "gaffe" over which Petry wanted to expel him was a speech, delivered on the anniversary of the infamous Wannsee Conference, in which he called the Holocaust memorial in Berlin "a monument of shame" and demanded a "180-degree turnaround" in Germany's approach to its history (Höcke, 2017). Höcke apologised and claimed that he had been misunderstood (Spiegel Online, 2017).

Höcke has many influential supporters in the party. Moreover, many others were simply wary of Petry's ambitions, and so a rift began to grow between her supporters and her detractors. At the 2017 conference, the party refused to even discuss Petry's plan for the long-term strategic development of the AfD and denied her the role of the "Spitzenkandidat". Instead, Alexander Gauland and Alice Weidel led the AfD's national campaign. So far, Weidel had been counted as an ally of Petry and as a leading moderate, but given the top spot, she quickly adopted the inciting rhetoric the party base seems to demand.

After a long campaign and a last-minute spurt, the AfD won 12.6 per cent of the vote, making it the strongest of the four smaller parties now represented in parliament, although not by a large margin. The AfD did particularly well in the eastern Länder. In the south-eastern state of Saxony, they even became the strongest party, winning 27 per cent of the list vote. Results from a special count that is stratified by state, gender, and age bracket show that the AfD garnered 32 to 33 per cent of the vote amongst East German men aged 35–59. By way of contrast, only about 9 per cent of West German women in the same age group voted AfD, with support amongst western women younger than 25 or older than 69 being at about 5 per cent. The group showing the highest overall affinity are men aged 45–59 living in Saxony. About 39 per cent of them voted for the AfD.

What motivates these voters to support the AfD? Schmitt-Beck (2017), using data collected over the course of the 2013 campaign, demonstrates that the very first supporters of the party were primarily driven by euroscepticism. But even in 2013, anti-immigration attitudes were more important than euroscepticism for those who switched to the AfD during the last phase of the campaign. By late 2015, AfD voters were less welcoming towards refugees than other Germans, and by June 2016, these attitudes hard hardened (Hambauer and Mays, 2017). Welfare chauvinism, i.e. the wish to restrict welfare benefits to the native group was also important (Goerres *et al.,* 2018). Finally, Arzheimer and Berning (2019), using a very large data set spanning the whole 2013–2017 period, demonstrate that the effect of anti-immigration attitudes has become progressively stronger as the party radicalised and the saliency of the issue rose. By now, the AfD and their voters fit the somewhat stereotypical profile of a populist radical right party and its electorate.

How Has the AfD Changed German Politics?

The AfD's rise was facilitated by two structural changes in German Politics: partisan de-alignment (Arzheimer, 2017) one the one hand, and the CDU's move towards the political centre, mostly as a response to shifts in public opinion, on the other.[3] In turn, the AfD's emergence and establishment has an impact on German Politics in a multitude of ways. Here, I focus on three intertwined developments: changes to the way parliaments operate, problems of coalition formation, and changes to the public discourse and political agenda.

Parliaments and Policy Making

Policy making in Germany is characterised by a high degree of consensus, which is both required and supported by institutional arrangements. Opposition parties in parliament enjoy not just extensive rights of interpellation, but are also awarded committee leaderships in proportion to their strength and can sometimes affect policy in non-politicised matters. Under the 2005–2009 grand coalition government between the CDU/CSU and the SPD, about 22 per cent of all bills were passed unanimously after incorporating opposition views at the committee stage (Thränhardt, 2013).

The presence of the AfD's delegations in state parliaments and now also in the Bundestag has upset these often collegial procedures. To be sure, when new parties such as the Greens in the 1980s and the PDS/Left in the 1990s emerged, cultural and substantive conflicts were equally palpable. What sets the presence of the AfD apart from these earlier instances is the widespread perception amongst MPs that at least some of their new colleagues do not share the values of liberal democracy and will abuse their presence in parliament to undermine its institutions. The spectre of the Nazis' rise to power through free elections looms large. In this regard, parliamentary life with the AfD resembles the earlier tenures of the DVU and the NPD, which were ostracised in state parliaments as a matter of course.

These concerns are not entirely unfounded. Since 2014, a string of state MPs have been expelled or resigned from the AfD, citing the radicalisation of the party. In the

---

[3]Since 2005, CDU-led governments have abolished conscription and nuclear energy, introduced a national minimum wage and subsidies for young parents that are conditional on the man taking parental leave, legalised same-sex marriages and the right to adoption for same-sex couples, and relaxed the rules on dual citizenship and naturalisation.

Bundestag, the newly formed AfD faction harbours well-known anti-semites, islamophobes, and apologists for the annexation of Crimea. This does not only apply to the rank-and-file. Weidel, now one of the factions chairs, has become notorious for using inflammatory language on and off the floor and was formally reprimanded in parliament for defaming immigrants (Scally, 2018). Her co-leader, Alexander Gauland, declared they would "hunt down Angela Merkel" (Hanke, 2017), has claimed that the rule of the Nazis was but "a speck of bird shit in a 1000-year success story" (Deutsche Welle, 2018a) and appeared as keynote speaker at a "winter school" run by well-known right-wing extremists (Arzheimer, 2019). About 10 per cent of the AfD's nearly 300 staffers in the federal parliament alone are members or former employees of right-wing extremist organisations (Biermann *et al.*, 2019; Merker, 2019). One MP even gave a job to the German co-leader of the "Identitarian movement" (Biermann *et al.*, 2019), a group of young, internet-savvy far-right activists that operate in many European countries and have been linked to the Christchurch attacker (Wilson, 2019).

In response, the other parties have established a *cordon sanitaire*. Contact is restricted to a minimum, and the AfD's initiatives are routinely voted down. The *cordon* is most visible in the AfD's absence from the presidium comprised of the President and his deputies, who chair the plenary sessions. Under the current standing orders, each party nominates a deputy, who is then confirmed by the full house in a secret ballot. While there is rare precedent for rejecting a candidate deemed personally unsuitable, at the time of writing, the house has rejected *three* AfD nominees and it seems unlikely that they will confirm anyone from the AfD (FAZ, 2019). The party has encountered similar, if less high-profile resistance in state parliaments.

Coalition Building and Party Politics

In combination with the growing fragmentation of the party system, this exclusion has given the AfD what Sartori (1976) called "blackmail potential". Ideologically homogeneous two-party coalitions have been the norm since the 1990s, with the so-called grand coalition as a fall-back option. With the continuously strong position of Die Linke (the Left party) in the eastern states and the rise of the AfD, this pattern is not longer sustainable, and three-party-coalitions have become much more frequent. The most awkward so far was established in Saxony-Anhalt in 2016, when the AfD garnered 24.3 per cent of the vote and the FDP remained just below the electoral threshold. Because the CDU and the Left party would not work together and the heavy losses for the SPD meant that even a "grand" coalition was impossible, the only remaining option was to form a government that also involved the Greens and so consisted entirely of parties that had been punished at the ballot box.

After the 2017 federal election, the situation was complicated too. Moving the party to the left and leaving the coalition with the Christian Democrats behind had been the central plank of the SPD's campaign (Dostal, 2017). Similarly, Merkel was under intense internal pressure over her policies and was attacked in unprecedented ways by the CSU. But a centre-right coalition with the FDP was not viable because of the Christian Democrats' heavy losses, and so talks began with the FDP and the Greens about a "Jamaica" alliance, which would have been a first at the national level. Almost two months after the election, these talks collapsed, leaving Germany in turmoil (Chase, 2018b).

In the German context, swearing in a Christian Democratic minority government would have been read as a sign of defeat under the populist onslaught. Fresh elections would likely have resulted in further losses for the major parties and further gains for the AfD. And so, after an unusual intervention by the Federal President, Christian and Social Democrats began negotiations. In March 2018, six months after the election, a (much reduced) grand coalition was sworn in. Merkel, who was very much the focus of the AfD's mobilisation, would stay in office.

From the onset, this coalition was even more fraught with internal conflicts than its predecessors in 1966–69, 2005–09, and 2013–17. The CSU's attacks on Merkel and the CDU had ceased during the campaign, but with the likely loss of their absolute majority in the Bavarian state elections on October 14 in sight, the CSU desperately tried to win back voters from the AfD by relentlessly pushing the immigration/refugee issue back on the agenda. The CSU's insistence on new policy initiatives aimed at curbing the number of immigrants while upping the number of deportations paralysed and nearly brought down the new government during its first six months in office (Amann *et al.,* 2018).

Things came to a head late in the last week of August 2018, when a German man was killed in the eastern town of Chemnitz and the suspects turned out to be asylum seekers (Isenson, 2018). Thousands of right-wingers took to the streets and attacked people who looked like leftists or non-natives to them. For several nights, the police could not, or would not, uphold public order. Merkel and other coalition politicians decried the violence as racist man-hunts, but in an extraordinarily development, the chief of the domestic secret service, Hans-Georg Maaßen, publicly contradicted their assessment and claimed that a video showing a racist attack had been doctored. Although it quickly emerged that the video was genuine and that Maaßen and the service had no privileged information on the situation in Chemnitz whatsoever, Horst Seehofer, the Home Secretary and leader of the CSU backed Maaßen, who had previously argued that asylum seekers posed a security risk, and even tried to further promote him (Shelton, 2018).

Once more, this almost brought down the coalition, but the tide was now turning against Seehofer. Against the backdrop of declining numbers in the polls, Bavaria's Prime Minister Markus Söder made a last-ditch effort to soften his image and to shift attention to regional issues unrelated to immigration. He also set in motion a process through which he would succeed Seehofer as party leader in January 2019 (Brady, 2018).

Chemnitz was also a turning point for the AfD. Less than a year after they had entered parliament, one new MP justified the violence in streets as "self-defence". Gauland stood by this judgment and said the unrest was a "normal reaction" to a murder (FAZ, 2018). Höcke and other prominent members of the "Wing" even took part in a "silent march", alongside members of self-styled militias, Neo-Nazis and well-known right-wing extremists, which alerted a wider public to the many links between the AfD and the extreme right (Deutsche Welle, 2018c).

Six weeks later, the CSU lost its absolute majority in Bavaria but was able form a coalition with a smaller conservative party. Favourable conditions not withstanding, the AfD garnered just 10 per cent of the vote while the Greens won 17.5 per cent, more than twice their previous result. Exit polls suggested that at least some of their new strength was due to liberal-minded CSU voters deserting their former party over its hard line on immigration. The biggest loser of the election was the SPD, whose support dropped below ten per cent for the first time in Bavaria's post-war history (Mudge, 2018).

Agenda Setting and Public Discourses

Two weeks later, the state election in Hesse brought different but similar results: 13 per cent for the AfD, almost 20 per cent for the Greens, and double-digit losses for the CDU and the SPD. In response to these, Merkel announced that she would step down as party leader in December and would not run for parliament in 2021 (Deutsche Welle, 2018b). Her successor as leader (and potentially also as chancellor) is Annegret Kramp-Karrenbauer (Chase, 2018a). While Kramp-Karrenbauer was known as an ally of Merkel, she has since tried to re-establish the CDU's credentials as a socially conservative party. In a bid to heal the rifts within the CDU that Merkel's immigration policies have left, she has also organised a large-scale listening exercise. While it seems unlikely that Kramp-Karrenbauer will reverse all of Merkel's moves towards the centre of the socio-cultural dimension, she will most certainly push for some changes in style and content in the years to come.

The rise of the AfD has clearly rattled the CDU and the CSU, and it has contributed to the current popularity of the Greens. But it would be misleading to assume that the AfD and their inciting rhetoric have completely changed the public discourse of the Federal Republic. Arzheimer and Berning (2019) show that attitudes on immigration have hardly shifted since 2013 but became more salient, particularly in 2016. Since then, the importance of these issues has declined, although they still rank high on the public's agenda and will likely retain this position.

One of the AfD's biggest assets was the respectability of its first leader. Since 2015, the media have become much more cautious in their dealing with the AfD then they were in the past, journalists are very much aware of concepts such as agenda setting and the "Overton Window", and public reflection on the relationship between populists and the media has become almost a trope in the quality press.

The strong presence of the AfD on social media, particularly on Facebook, has therefore become a bigger concern. The AfD's central Facebook page has more likes than the ones of the CDU and the SPD combined and has become a focal node of the wider far-right online network in Germany (Arzheimer, 2015b; Stier *et al.,* 2017). More recently, the party has expanded into YouTube and Twitter and also seems to rely more and more on WhatsApp groups, which are not accessible to outsiders.[4]

Has German Politics Changed the AfD?

In European multi-party systems, challenger parties face a fundamental choice: they can retain their status as outsiders, appealing to core voters and members but affecting policy only indirectly, or they can tone down their message in a bid to appeal to more mainstream voters and potentially taking political office. During the last two decades, radical right parties in Europe have often opted for the latter. The "de-demonisation" of

---

[4]There have been repeated leaks of racist and defaming posts from closed AfD WhatsApp groups, see e.g. Der Westen (2018).

the National Rally in France (Mayer, 2013) and the transformation of the Sweden Democrats (Jungar, 2016) are two prominent cases in point.

The AfD, on the other hand, is the rare case where parliamentary representation has lead to further radicalisation. The party's many links to openly extremist actors have led to calls for closer scrutiny. In an extraordinary press conference held on January 15, 2019, the new head of the Office for the Protection of the Constitution presented the headline findings from a preliminary investigation (Euractiv, 2019). He declared that there was enough evidence of unconstitutional tendencies within both the "Wing" and the AfD's youth organisation to justify their covert observation, which could include wiretapping and email hacking, subject to strict legal constraints. This could, in principle, even apply to sitting MPs including Gauland, who has co-signed the "Wing's" founding manifesto and regularly attends their meetings. More generally, the office would continue to compile publicly accessible information on the party, with a view towards building a case for bringing the AfD as a whole under surveillance.

A couple of months later a donation scandal resurfaced. Meuthen, Weidel, and Guido Reil, all members of the national executive, have received a total of more than 130,000 Euros from Swiss businesses. German parties may only accept donations from EU citizens, so the AfD presented a list of alleged German donors, who then turned out to be straw men. The party was subsequently fined 403,000 Euros, and further investigations into their finances are under way (Henry, 2019).

Finally, in April 2019 the BBC published excerpts from a Russian strategy paper, calling for the Kremlin to support Markus Frohnmaier. In return, Frohnmaier, now an MP for the AfD, could be "absolutely controlled" after the election (Gatehouse, 2019). Frohnmaier denies any Russian involvement in his campaign, but the allegations chime with his controversial journeys to Crimea and the Donbass, the AfD's pro-Russian positions, and the Kremlin's entanglement with the West European Radical Right (Shekhovtsov, 2018).

In short, winning national representation has had no moderating effect on the AfD. Instead, the party has become even more of an outsider.

State of Play: What Is the Outlook for German Politics?

These developments have made co-operation between the AfD and the other parties even less likely. National voting intentions, however, have been largely unaffected so far, and still hover in the range of the AfD's result in 2017. The AfD's expected vote shares in three upcoming eastern state elections are considerably higher, and they might even become the strongest party in their stronghold of Saxony, although they are far from an outright majority. These survey data are also confirmed by the result of the European Parliamentary election on May 26, 2019. While the national result of 11 per cent was disappointing for the AfD, they became the strongest party in the states of Brandenburg (19.9 per cent) and Saxony (25.3 per cent) and scored between 17.7 and 22.5 per cent in the other eastern states.

The rapid rise of the AfD is not so much an expression of a change in national mood: by and large, public opinion data suggest that Germany is still a remarkably tolerant and overwhelmingly pro-European society. In line with international trends, it rather signifies a rise in party system fragmentation, segmentation, and polarisation.

Against the backdrop of the AfD's radicalisation, the centre right have not even contemplated the possibility of any future co-operation with the party. But this could change in the near future. It is likely that the CDU/SPD coalition in Saxony will lose its majority in the upcoming state elections, and that the AfD will become the second strongest or even the strongest party. Because the CDU in Saxony is particularly conservative, it is by no means a given that they would form a coalition that includes the Greens or the Left party. Instead, they may be tempted to negotiate a confidence-and-supply arrangement or even a formal coalition with the AfD, which in turn would give unprecedented legitimacy to the AfD and would change the coalition arithmetics in the eastern states (but probably not in the west or at the national level).

Either way, German politics is already much more unstable and unpredictable than it was five years ago and will remain that way as long as the AfD is a relevant player at the national and the state level. Paradoxically, in a system with as many veto points as the German, this means that the status quo will become even more entrenched. Therefore, my prediction is that as in other countries, the rise of a right-wing populist party will make Germany less flexible and more inward looking than it already is. This does not bode well for German and for European Politics.

REFERENCES

Amann, M., Clauß, A., Feldenkrichen, M., Neukirch, R. and Pfister, R. (2018) Inside the Battle that Almost Brought Down Merkel. Available at «https://www.spiegel.de/international/germany/the-cdu-csu-battle-that-almost-cost-merkel-her-job-a-1217115.html».

Art, D. (2011) *Inside the Radical Right. The Development of Anti-Immigrant Parties in Western Europe* (Cambridge: Cambridge University Press).

Art, D. (2018) 'The AfD and the End of Containment in Germany?' *German Politics and Society*, Vol. 36, No. 2, SI, pp. 76–86.

Arzheimer, K. (2015a) 'The Afd: Finally a Successful Right-Wing Populist Eurosceptic Party for Germany?' *West European Politics*, Vol. 38, pp. 535–56.

Arzheimer, K. (2015b) The AfD's Facebook Wall: A New Hub for Far-Right Mobilisation in Germany? Available at «https://www.kai-arzheimer.com/german-right-wing-internet.pdf».

Arzheimer, K. (2017) 'Another Dog That Didn't Bark? Less Dealignment and More Partisanship in the 2013 Bundestag Election'. *German Politics*, Vol. 26, No. 1, pp. 49–64.

Arzheimer, K. (2019) Schnellroda: AfD Leader Gauland Speaks at the New Right 'Winter School'. Available at «https://www.kai-arzheimer.com/schnellroda-afd-leader-gauland-speaks-at-the-newright-winter-school/».

Arzheimer, K. and Berning, C. (2019) 'How the Alternative for Germany (AfD) and Their Voters Veered to the Radical Right, 2013-2017'. *Electoral Studies*, forthcoming. https://doi.org/10.1016/j.electstud.2019.04.004.

Biermann, K., Geisler, A., Radke, J. and Steffen, T. (2018) 'AfD-Abgeordnete beschäftigen Rechtsextreme und Verfassungsfeinde'. Available at «https://www.zeit.de/politik/deutschland/2018-03/afd-bundestag-mitarbeiter-rechtsextreme-identitaere-bewegung/komplettansicht».

Biermann, K., Geisler, A. and Steffen, T. (2019) 'Identitären-Chef hat Job im Bundestag'. Available at «https://www.zeit.de/politik/deutschland/2019-04/rechtsextremismus-identitaerebewegung-afd-daniel-fiss-bundestag».

Brady, K. (2018) 'CSU's Horst Seehofer: Under Fire from Bavaria to Berlin'. Available at «https://www.dw.com/en/csus-horst-seehofer-under-fire-from-bavaria-to-berlin/a-45911270».

Chase, J. (2018a) 'Angela Merkel's Cdu Successor: Annegret Kramp-Karrenbauer'. Available at «https://www.dw.com/en/angela-merkels-cdu-successor-annegret-krampkarrenbauer/a-46622513».

Chase, J. (2018b) 'Germany's Jamaica Bombshell, One Year on'. Available at «https://www.dw.com/en/germanys-jamaica-bombshell-one-year-on/g-46364096».

Decker, F. (2008) 'Germany: Right-Wing Populist Failures and Left-Wing Successes'. In Albertazzi, D. and McDonnell, D. (eds) *Twenty-First Century Populism. The Spectre of Western European Democracy* (Houndmills: Palgrave Macmillan), pp. 119–34.

Der Flügel. (2015) Erfurter Resolution. Available at «http://www.derfluegel.de/erfurter-resolution/».

Der Flügel. (2017) Das Kyffhäusermanifest. Available at «https://www.derfluegel.de/2017/09/05/das-kyffhaeusermanifest/».

Der Westen. (2019) AfD in Nrw: Rechtsextreme Posts in Whatsapp-Chats Aufgetaucht – 'Entsetzlich, Unterirdisch, Widerlich'. Available at «https://www.derwesten.de/politik/afd-rechtsextreme-posts-in-whatsapp-chats-aufgetaucht-entsetzlich-unterirdisch-widerlich-id216578107.html».

Deutsche Welle. (2018a) AfD's Gauland Plays Down Nazi Era as a 'Bird Shit' in German History. Available at «https://www.dw.com/en/afds-gauland-plays-down-nazi-era-as-a-bird-shit-in-germanhistory/a-44055213».

Deutsche Welle. (2018b) Angela Merkel Will Not Run for CDU Party Chair Again. Available at «https://www.dw.com/en/angela-merkel-will-not-run-for-cdu-party-chair-again-live-updates/a-46068450».

Deutsche Welle. (2018c) Thuringia AfD Could Face Surveillance over Right-Wing Chemnitz Protests. Available at «https://www.dw.com/en/thuringia-afd-could-face-surveillance-over-right-wingchemnitz-protests/a-45386878».

Dostal, J.M. (2017) 'The German Federal Election of 2017: How the Wedge Issue of Refugees and Migration Took the Shine Off Chancellor Merkel and Transformed the Party System'. *The Political Quarterly*, Vol. 88, No. 4, pp. 589–602.

Euractiv. (2019) Germany Security Agency Steps up Watch of Far-Right AfD. Available at «https://www.euractiv.com/section/eu-elections-2019/news/germany-security-agency-steps-up-watch-of-farright-afd/».

Falkenhagen, F. (2013) 'The CSU as an Ethno-Regional Party'. *German Politics*, Vol. 22, No. 4, pp. 396–420.

FAZ. (2018) Gauland bezeichnet Krawalle als "Selbstverteidigung". Available at «https://www.faz.net/aktuell/politik/inland/afd-chef-gauland-nennt-krawalle-in-chemnitz-selbstverteidigung-15761753.html».

FAZ. (2019) Dritter AfD-Kandidat fällt durch. Available at «https://www.faz.net/aktuell/politik/inland/afdscheitert-auch-otten-bei-wahl-zum-bundestagsvize-16136364.html».

Gatehouse, G. (2019) German Far-Right MP 'Could Be Absolutely Controlled by Russia'. Available at «https://www.bbc.com/news/world-europe-47822835».

Goerres, A., Spies, D.C. and Kumlin, S. (2018) 'The Electoral Supporter Base of the Alternative for Germany'. *Swiss Political Science Review*, Vol. 24, No. 3, pp. 246–69.

Hambauer, V. and Mays, A. (2017) 'Wer wählt die Afd? - Ein Vergleich der Sozialstruktur, politischen Einstellungen und Einstellungen zu Flüchtlingen zwischen Afd-Wählerinnen und der Wählerinnen der anderen parteien." *Zeitschrift Für Vergleichende Politikwissenschaft'*. online first Vol. 12, No. 1, pp. 133–54. https://doi.org/10.1007/s12286-017-0369-2.

Hanke, J. (2017) German Far Right Will 'Hunt' Merkel from New Perch in Parliament. Available at «https://www.politico.eu/article/alexander-gauland-angela-merkel-afd-germany-far-rightleader-we-will-hunt-merkel/».

Henry, G. (2019) Germany's AfD Hit with Hefty Fine in Donations Scandal. Available at «www.politico.eu/article/germanys-afd-hit-with-hefty-fine-in-donations-scandal/».

Höcke, B. (2017) 'Gemütszustand eines total besiegten Volkes'. Available at «https://www.tagesspiegel.de/politik/hoecke-rede-im-wortlaut-gemuetszustand-eines-total-besiegten-volkes/19273518.html».

Isenson, N. (2018) 'Chemnitz, Saxony and Germany Grapple with Far Right'. Available at «https://www.dw.com/en/chemnitz-saxony-and-germany-grapple-with-far-right/a-45290983».

Jungar, A.-C. (2016) 'The Sweden Democrats'. In Heinisch, R. and Mazzoleni, O. (eds) *Understanding Populist Party Organisation. The Radical Right in Western Europe* (London: Palgrave Macmillan), pp. 189–219.

Kalyvas, S.N. and van Kersbergen, K. (2010) 'Christian Democracy'. *Annual Review of Political Science*, Vol. 13, No. 1, pp. 183–209.

Lubbers, M., Gijsberts, M. and Scheepers, P. (2002) 'Extreme Right-Wing Voting in Western Europe'. *European Journal of Political Research*, Vol. 41, pp. 345–78.

Mayer, N. (2013) 'From Jean-Marie to Marine Le Pen: Electoral Change on the Far Right'. *Parliamentary Affairs*, Vol. 66, No. 1, pp. 160–78.

Merker, H. (2019) 'AfD-Mitarbeiter am rechten Rand'. Available at «https://blog.zeit.de/stoerungsmelder/2019/02/05/afd-rechtsextreme-mitarbeiter-brandenburg-thueringen-verfassungsschutz_28014».

Mudde, C. (2007) *Populist Radical Right Parties in Europe* (Cambridge: Cambridge University Press).

Mudge, R. (2018) Germany at a Crossroads After Bavarian Poll Debacle. Available at «https://www.dw.com/en/germany-at-a-crossroads-after-bavarian-poll-debacle/a-45892514».

Spiegel Online. (2017) Wieso nicht in die NPD, Herr Höcke? Available at «https://www.spiegel.de/spiegel/bjoern-hoecke-droht-mit-spaltung-der-afd-falls-er-ausgeschlossen wird a 1135078.html».

Rydgren, J. (2005) 'Is Extreme Right-Wing Populism Contagious? Explaining the Emergence of a New Party Family'. *European Journal of Political Research*, Vol. 44, pp. 413–37.

Sartori, G. (1976) *Parties and Party Systems. A Framework for Analysis* (Cambridge: Cambridge University Press).

Scally, D. (2018) 'AfD Hijacks Berlin Budget Debate'. Available at «https://www.irishtimes.com/news/world/europe/afd-hijacks-berlin-budget-debate-1.3497750».

Schmitt-Beck, R. (2017) 'The 'Alternative Für Deutschland in the Electorate': Between Single-Issue and Right-Wing Populist Party'. *German Politics*, Vol. 26, No. 1, pp. 124–48.

Shekhovtsov, A. (2018) *Russia and the Western Far Right. Tango Noir. London* (New York: Routledge).

Shelton, J. (2018) 'Opinion: Spy Chief Row Exposes German Government's Cluelessness'. Available at «https://www.dw.com/en/opinion-spy-chief-row-exposes-german-governments-cluelessness/a-45495372».

Stier, S., Posch, L., Bleier, A. and Strohmaier, M. (2017) 'When Populists Become Popular: Comparing Facebook Use by the Right-Wing Movement Pegida and German Political Parties'. *Information Communication & Society*, Vol. 20, No. 9, pp. 1365–88.

Thränhardt, D. (2013) 'Gesetzgebung'. In Andersen, U. and Woyke, W. (eds) *Handwörterbuch Des Politischen Systems Der Bundesrepublik Deutschland* (7th edition) (Heidelberg: Springer VS), pp. 199–203.

Vasilopoulou, S. (2018) 'The Radical Right and Euroscepticism'. In Rydgren, J. (ed.) *The Oxford Handbook of the Radical Right* (Oxford University Press), pp. 122–40.

Wilson, J. (2019) Christchurch Shooter's Links to Austrian Far Right 'More Extensive Than Thought'. Available at «https://www.theguardian.com/world/2019/may/16/christchurch-shooters-links-to-austrian-far-right-more-extensive-than-thought».

Wimmel, A. and Edwards, E.E. (2011) 'The Return of 'Social Europe': Ideas and Positions of German Parties Towards the Future of European Integration'. *German Politics*, Vol. 20, No. 2, pp. 293–314.

JCMS 2019 Volume 57. Annual Review pp. 103–113   DOI: 10.1111/jcms.12932

The Geopoliticization of European Trade and Investment Policy

SOPHIE MEUNIER[1] and KALYPSO NICOLAIDIS[2]
[1]Princeton University, New Jersey [2]Oxford University, Oxford

Introduction

The academic debate about trade policy in the EU has been dominated of late by claims about the new politicization of trade. After many decades of insulation from domestic politics, trade policy has erupted into public discourse with the unprecedented mobilization against the Transatlantic Trade and Investment Partnership (TTIP) and Wallonia's coup in blocking the implementation of the Comprehensive Economic and Trade Agreement (CETA) between the EU and Canada. As a result, a body of academic scholarship has emerged that looks at the causes and implications of this politicization and variations across time and issue areas, as well as the nature of agreements and likely trends for future policies.

In this review contribution, we push back argue against this prevailing diagnosis on two counts. Firstly, internal politicization is nothing new. For decades trade agreements may not have had much public salience, nor played a role in creating political cleavages during electoral campaigns, but behind the scenes member states have been engaged in a hard political fight over competences and interests. Moreover, some salient and, arguably, successful public mobilization has happened before, notably in the late 1990s.

Second, it is our contention that, rather than simple politicization, the most important recent development has been the geopoliticization of trade and investment policy. Call it the China syndrome or the Trump effect, tariffs, retaliatory measures and counter-retaliation have featured prominently in the news in 2018, and the rhetoric of trade negotiations has given way to the language of economic battlefields and trade warfare. This geopoliticization of trade may pose a serious challenge to interdependence and multilateralism, which the EU has long safeguarded, but it is simply here to stay.

This diagnosis also has important implication for EU power *tout court*. Is the EU equipped institutionally and politically to respond to Trump's tit-for-tat threats and to resist attempts by China to divide and rule through targeted investments? By its very nature and its insistence on multilateralism, the EU may seem ill-equipped to thrive in this new world. But we argue that it is actually better positioned than common wisdom suggests and has become a major player in this geopoliticization game nonetheless. For the EU, the external politicization of trade is no longer about trying to change countries from within through trade power, as it tried to do in the previous two decades. Instead, it has become able to change the global balance of power through trade and to use economic statecraft to compete on a level playing field when the breakdown of multilateralism has fragmented the world into regions and rival powers. A series of policies adopted or discussed in the EU in 2018, ranging from concluding trade negotiations with Japan to launching them with Australia and to creating a novel framework for screening foreign investment, suggest as much.

The rest of this contribution is organized as follows. The first section introduces and challenges recent research on the politicization of European trade policy by arguing that politics has always been at its core. Section Two briefly recalls how, in the past, the EU has imposed domestic political and social conditions to third countries in exchange for preferential single market access and shows how this 'power through trade'– has waned in recent years. In Section Three we argue that trade has become geopoliticized of late and consider how the EU may fare in this context where regions deploy economic state-craft for geopolitical purposes. The last section focuses on the role played by Brexit in this new trade geopolitical strategy.

I. Politics in Trade: The New Politicization of Trade Policy?

Scholars of European integration have argued that the EU has become more politicized in the past decade, as evidenced by a growing polarization of opinions and public salience of policies (De Bruycker, 2017; De Wilde, 2011; Schimmelfennig *et al.,* 2015). Trade is no exception: the TTIP negotiations provoked unprecedented mobilization in several European countries, starting in Germany, followed by the politicization of the CETA negotiations between the EU and Canada (Bouza and Oleart, 2018; Chan and Crawford, 2017; De Bièvre and Poletti, 2017; De Ville and Siles-Brügge, 2017; Laursen and Roederer-Rynning, 2017; Magnette, 2017; Young, 2016, 2017). EU trade policy literature has been trying to unpack the causes and implications of this process (De Bievre and Poletti, 2019; Eliasson and Huet, 2019; Garcia-Duran *et al.,* 2019; Laursen and Roederer-Rynning, 2017; Young, 2017).

We challenge this characterization of the growing politicization of trade in three ways. Firstly, the degree of politicization of EU trade policy differs across member states and agreements. While hundreds of thousands of activists marched on the streets of Berlin and Barcelona to denounce chlorinated chickens and the investor–state dispute settlement process in 2016, few protested in Finland, Greece or even France, though it was a hotbed of anti-globalization activism in the late 1990s. Moreover, for all the media coverage of anti-TTIP and CETA mobilization, little attention has been paid to other trade and investment negotiations that have taken place before, during and after these contentious agreements, such as the EU–Japan Economic Partnership Agreement signed in December 2017 and entered into force in February 2019; the EU–Singapore Agreement negotiated between 2010 and 2014; and the EU–Vietnam free trade agreement negotiated mostly in 2015, concurrently with the TTIP.

Secondly, some contemporary trade and investment deals may be politicized today but it is not the first time that European publics pay attention to a policy area that has by design been mostly insulated from domestic politics (Meunier and Czesana, Forthcoming). Anti-globalization trade protests started in the 1990s, notably with the nongovernmental organization mobilization against the multilateral agreement on investment negotiated under the auspices of the Organisation for Economic Co-operation and Development in 1998 and against the launch of the new round of multilateral trade talks in Seattle in 1999. In both cases, this public mobilization was followed by the failure of the multilateral negotiations (Hopewell, 2015; Kobrin, 1998; Tieleman, 2000).

Thirdly, trade has always been a political issue, even if this has not been visible to the wider public. In the EU, member states have been in conflict on two fronts. On one hand, national governments have bargained at the intergovernmental level over the scope and context of EU trade mandates such as the cultural exception (Meunier, 2005). On the other hand, member states have fought back against the gradual transfer of trade and investment competences to the supranational level (Meunier, 2017; Meunier and Nicolaïdis, 1999). This inter-institutional politicization is more visible today because of the new role acquired by the European Parliament in making trade policy through the 2009 Lisbon Treaty (Meissner and Rosen, 2019; Rosen, 2017).

Thus, reports of the new politicization of trade policy in the EU may be overblown. Technology and recent institutional changes have certainly brought about more transparency in trade policy, making it easier to follow – and contest. But trade has always been politicized, as this policy area is fundamentally about altering the prevailing distribution of costs and benefits among individuals, among economic sectors and amond countries.

II. Politics through Trade: The Waning of Conditionality

In addition to the politicization of trade inside Europe, the EU has also politicized trade during the post-cold war era by using it as a tool of foreign policy – what we have called 'power through trade' (Meunier and Nicolaïdis, 2006). While trade became a means to transform the nature of the EU's partners, this form of power through trade has been waning in recent years.

Trade is the core instrument of the EU's civilian power and, therefore, of its political influence on the rest of the world (Damro, 2012; Meunier and Nicolaïdis, 2017; Moravcsik, 2017). The EU has long been a formidable trade negotiator because of the sheer size of the European single market, which can be used as a reward or as a threat to the outside world both for the possibilities it offers and from fear of being excluded. This market power has enabled the EU to expand its own regulatory practices to the rest of the world and therefore impose its values and politics, forged through its own internal compromises (Bradford, 2012; Egan and Nicolaidis, 2001; Newman and Posner, 2011; Young, 2015). Beyond what the World Trade Organization (WTO) calls product standards, the EU has leveraged its trade power to try to enforce changes in the domestic arena of its trading partners (akin to process standards writ large) throughout the 1990s and 2000s by generalizing the practice of linking access to the ever-expanding EU market to human rights, to labour and environmental standards, to development policies and to stands against the death penalty (Hafner-Burton, 2009; Smith, 1998).

While this political linkage has been a feature of EU trade agreements for the last three decades (albeit an unforced one), Article 207 of the 2009 Lisbon Treaty enshrined it into law by assigning for the first time non-commercial objectives to the common commercial policy, which 'shall be conducted in the context of the principles and objectives of the Union's external action' (European Union, 2009). As per Article 21 of the Treaty on European Union, these include, among others, the consolidation and support of democracy, the rule of law, and human rights, as well as efforts to improve the environment and promote multilateral cooperation (European Union, 2016).

This transnational politicization of trade, however, has been challenged by recent external and internal developments. Externally, the growth of emerging economies, notably

China, has provided the EU with new markets but also enhanced competition. Economically, the relative trade power of the EU has diminished as that of others has risen. Politically, alternative options are now available to the trading partners that used to be at the receiving end of EU trade conditionality and that interpreted it as neo-colonialism: they can afford to be less acquiescent to EU requests for changes to their domestic politics now that China is willing to provide trade and investment without political conditions attached – notably for countries that fall in the path of the Chinese Belt and Road Initiative. Local actors that accumulate unsustainable debt are starting to realize that conditionality is not only a constraint but may be a warrant of quality, but the shifts that may follow are still ahead of us.

Internally, the EU has suffered from a series of crises that have weakened its ability to give political lessons to the rest of the world. During the euro crisis, the EU forced austerity on its southern members even as they had been hit the hardest by the crisis. As seen from the rest of the world, is that an attractive, righteous EU? Moreover, the erosion of the rule of law in some member states, which continued to deepen in 2018, and more generally, increasing regime heterogeneity in the EU have weakened both member states' demands for good governance conditionality and the credibility of the EU externally, as accusation of double standards fly (Meunier and Vachudova, 2018). How can the EU tell its trade partners to respect the independence of the judiciary, for instance in light of Polish or Hungarian backsliding? And to top it all, the 2016 Brexit vote has showcased to the world the dramatic contestation from within of the European project – contestation that has expanded far beyond Britain, as the 2019 European parliamentary elections have attested. In short, in light of the Chinese trade and investment offensive, other countries have started to question the EU's position: 'do what I say, not what I do', especially as its own swerve towards greater illiberalism has further eroded its normative power.

III. The Geopoliticization of European Trade and Investment Policy

In 2018 the news was full of talk of trade warfare and strategic investment. Relative, rather than absolute, gains seemed to be the order of the day, as the American and Chinese governments engaged in a trade war that may be costly to the multilateral system but is also about enforcing the rules of this system (for example, procurement and intellectual property). In this context, trade and investment policies are becoming essential tools of geopolitics, partly as a result of the electoral success of populists in many advanced democracies advocating 'taking back control' and partly as a result of the growth of the Chinese economy under state management. We call this the geopoliticization of trade. While the EU may seem institutionally and politically ill-equipped to thrive in this new world of trade relations, we argue that it has already become a major player in this geopoliticization game.

From a hegemonic post-cold war world dominated by the USA, the world seems to be fragmenting into large regions, or at least spheres of influence, which determine alliances and rivalries that either emanate from economic competition or spill over from security concerns. Unlike in military power, where the USA may still reign supreme, when it comes to trade and investment patterns of codependence and structural rivalry are still in flux among three zones roughly equivalent in size – the USA, the EU and China. In other words, in a world of economically based geopolitical rivalry the EU is an equal player. The question continues to be how it exercises its trade power, no longer to change domestic politics but to affect global politics.

The term, geopoliticization of trade, could be deemed a tautology. After all, if geopolitics is global politics as influenced by geographical factors, we know from gravity models that trade patterns tend to be heavily influenced by geography. In this sense, trade is necessarily a component of global geopolitical configuration at a given point in time. Here, however, we use the idea of geopoliticization in a strategic sense, to characterize the external face of economic statecraft whereby trade policies come to be embedded in power rivalries. This is a policy space where geo-economics is both a product and a tool of security policies. In this sense, geopoliticization can designate the discursive construction of an issue as a geopolitical problem (Cadier, 2019), whereby policy instruments come to be used to win over allies, overcome foes and restructure the global balance of power.

Arguably, China, with its state management of the economy, has weaponized trade and investment strategies as instruments of geopolitics for a long time (Wong, 2019). Chinese efforts to deploy various tools of economic statecraft at the service of security goals have accelerated in the last decade. These include, among others; unfair trade practices, such as dumping and subsidies; the 'going out' strategy enjoining Chinese firms to invest abroad; an opaque review regime for inward foreign investments and obligations for foreign firms to partner with local firms, leading to forced transfers of know-how and technology; the signature of the Belt and Road Initiative, which may lead to debt traps; infrastructure investment in developing economies, notably through the Asian Infrastructure Investment Bank; industrial policy, most recently through the 'Made in China 2025' programme; and currency manipulation. Views in the West differ widely as to whether China should now be considered a foe. But most agree that it is at least a non-allied superpower with ambitious geopolitical goals that could put it at odds with at least some European countries that are wary of China's ultimate economic motives, including dual-use technology and strategic leverage. As a result, the EU is no longer earnestly trying to use its trade power to affect change within China, such as to improve the latter's human rights. Instead, its geopolitical goals focus on affecting the incentives China faces in remaining a responsible stakeholder in the multilateral trading system.

In 2018 the EU has also started to be concerned in earnest by the US administration's retreat from multilateralism and use of economic statecraft, including through the imposition of protectionist tariffs (for example, on steel and washing machines), tightened foreign direct investment review and the renegotiation of bilateral or regional agreements on a tit for tat basis. The concern is especially warranted if the EU interprets the election of Donald Trump not as a cause of these developments but as a symptom of the wider trend: 'My country first'. The President's very first action was to withdraw the USA from the Trans-Pacific Partnership (TPP), followed by more than a hundred threats to withdraw from the WTO. These developments are not only the result of the President's transactional and zero-sum vision of the world. Many in the USA – even beyond Trump's base – believe that their country has been duped by the promises of multilateralism, a perception that is bound to persist, and that it ought to fight back with whatever instruments at its disposal.

As trade wars became a fixture of the global landscape in 2018, Europeans have had to confront the question: what can we do to preserve multilateralism while addressing some of the underlying geopolitical issues, such as the national security and the economic implications of China catching up; and of the challenges by the USA to long-standing alliances and commitments? In the recent past, the EU would have sided with the USA and tried to balance China through the use of multilateral instruments. By 2018, however, facing a US president who has branded the EU as the 'greatest foe' (sic) of the USA, and two strongmen, Trump and Xi Jin Ping, neither of whom is ready to yield first (Wolf, 2019), the EU was looking after for itself and secondarily for the multilateral system.

One tool in the EU's geopolitical arsenal is to forge trade alliances that discriminate against non-members. To this end, the EU has accelerated the negotiation of trade agreements with a variety of partners in recent years. CETA has been provisionally applied since 2017. The EU has been active to secure partnerships in the Association of South-East Asian Nations region: it has signed trade and investment agreements with Singapore and Vietnam (neither of which have been ratified at the time of writing), has continued negotiations with Mexico and the Southern Common Market, MERCOSUR, and launched serious negotiations with Australia and New Zealand.

A telling example of this shift towards the geopoliticization of trade lies in the EU–Japan agreement. While these negotiations had lasted for many years (Ponjaert, 2015), they were suddenly concluded in 2018 and implemented in February 2019, while the issues that had hampered their conclusion were still clearly present. There is little doubt that both the EU and Japan saw this agreement as a geopolitical move following Trump's defection from the TPP, a project in which Japan had invested much hope and resources in its balancing strategy towards China. While Japan continues to hope that this is only a blip before Trump loses power, the US defection served as a catalyst for the agreement, trumping domestic consideration on both sides. The EU was clearly all too willing to oblige, given its own woes inflicted by the Trump administration. Hence the demise of the TPP ushered in a formal agreement in 2017 and significant concessions from both sides during the final legal clean up in 2018 to ensure the agreement passed. This would be the EU's Pacific trump card.

Most importantly, in this atmosphere of geopolitical urgency, Japan insisted on and obtained an agreement that the linkage between the two strategic and trade agreements be broken. In other words, political agreements over issues such as labour rights and the environment ceased to be formally linked to trade relations. It is important to note also that for the first time, Japan accepted the inclusion of mutual recognition in its agreements: Europe obtained phytosanitary mutual recognition and geographical appellations that in the end are in Japan's interest too – perhaps as the price to pay for this geopolitical prize.

Another novel tool of trade geopolitics for Europe involves inward foreign direct investment. In February 2019 the EU introduced a mechanism to scrutinize, and in some cases, reject incoming foreign direct investments deemed dangerous to national security and critical European interests through the adoption of the 'Framework for the Screening of Direct Investments into the Union' (European Union, 2019). This new European policy will facilitate the sharing of information on planned non-EU investment in critical technology and infrastructure (such as electric batteries and ports). It will allow any member state, and in some cases the Commission, to voice concerns about a proposed investment. Ultimately, however, the host country of foreign investment will make its own screening decision (Meunier, 2019). Though this new policy does not enable the EU to screen and block inward investment on its own, equally it does not force individual countries to screen at the national level (currently only 14 out of the 28 member states have some national screening legislation in place). It is a first step towards reining in investment with geostrategic motives – above all from China. Specific details of the new policy will be filled in during the implementation phase throughout 2019 and 2020.

Indeed, the new investment screening framework is included in the broader recent EU's Chinese strategy, a comprehensive 10-point action plan designed to improve reciprocity with China, labelled as a 'systemic rival', and to end European 'naivete' (European Commission, 2019). In addition to foreign direct investment, the strategy proposes new rules for European public procurement and industrial policies (which would enable the EU to create European giants able to compete with China's state-owned enterprises) This strategy also involves the negotiation of a comprehensive agreement on investment with China. These policies are all designed to restore a level playing field and force reciprocity, but they are highly controversial both inside and outside the EU and are likely to prompt some political and ideological fights in Europe in the coming years.

By the end of 2018, the EU's foray into the geopolitics of trade continued to be mitigated. For a start, it is less visible than that of its mega-rivals, China and the USA, and tends to be broadly reactive. Moreover, the EU is still, at least rhetorically, committed to safeguarding the multilateral system, in spite of the decline of the WTO's ability to deliver negotiated trade liberalization (De Bièvre and Poletti, 2017). Squaring the circle would mean for instance, convincing the Trump administration to frame its trade weapons as a means of enforcing existing multilateral rules. It could also mean imagining new multilateral mechanisms within which geopolitical considerations could be embedded and tamed – such as the creation of a multilateral investment court. In the meantime however, the EU's strategic acumen is being tested in its own patch.

IV. Brexit as a Test of the Geopoliticization Argument

While at the time of writing no-one knows whether the results of the 2018 negotiations over a withdrawal agreement will ever be implemented, the first phase of the Brexit negotiations forms a key part of our argument. For it can be argued that these negotiations provide the ultimate test for the emergence of this new geopoliticization of trade and the use of economic statecraft by the EU in dealing with the rest of the world. If the UK actually leaves with a so-called clean break, the EU will be amputated from one of its largest limbs (the fifth largest economy in the world) and will therefore have less leverage vis-à-vis third countries. Nevertheless, can the EU turn Brexit into a geopolitical advantage or at least minimize its geopolitical costs?

Two implicit geostrategic visions clash in the Brexit negotiations. On one hand, the EU – or at least, the Commission and some member states led by France – is determined to only put on offer a deal that makes visible the strategic value of EU membership. This in practice means that the EU has been ready to maintain a tough line on trade – willing to grant the UK a 'third country status' with few added privileges. On the other hand, the UK government has tried to promote the idea that the UK should remain a central strategic partner for the EU, which in practice means that the trade negotiations and the broader security relationship between the two sides cannot be delinked.

With hindsight, there is little doubt that ideological Brexiteers entered these negotiations with deeply flawed assumptions about the nature of trade deals with the EU, assumptions that were only partially corrected by the technocrats who conducted them. Above all, they held the misguided belief that agreeing to tariff-free trade between the EU and the UK (but with no other member of the WTO) was possible in the absence of an agreement that covers 'substantially all trade' (Article 24 of the General Agreement on Tariffs and Trade), while avoiding 'rules of origin' checks if its import from the rest of the world were to fall under an autonomous trade policy. Moreover, they had little sense of the core ecosystem of the EU single market predicated on the elimination of non-tariff barriers – safety standards, technical specifications and so on – as if these non-trade barriers were imposed by other countries and were easy to set aside, rather than being a simple product of regulatory differences. More generally, they failed to grasp the fact that the EU club is governed by a sense of diffuse reciprocity – the expectation that each country will gain over time, across issues and across trading partners. In such a world, little can be achieved unilaterally or bilaterally.

Nevertheless, the EU, too, has been found lacking until now in its approach to future EU–UK trade relations (Brexit 2.0). Arguably, as a country that has forged the managed mutual recognition regime that characterized the single market, and as a country whose sociopolitical constraints would preclude a deregulatory race to the bottom, the UK is best placed for a truly ambitious trade deal with the EU (Nicolaidis, 2018). Indeed, if we understand Brexit as a grand exercise in a translation between internal and external trade law, it would be strange for the EU to insist on trade deliberalization with the UK while continuing to present itself as the guardian of multilateral trade liberalization. Witness already the great concern prevalent in third countries with the prospect of having to choose between the EU and the UK when it comes to negotiating or renegotiating trade deals.

In short, both sides can be seen to be misguided: the EU for its strategic myopia, or the assumption that a bad outcome on the trade side would not hinder the broader strategic (both regional and bilateral) relation. And the UK for its strategic wishful thinking, epitomized by its alleged 'cakism' (having your cake and eating it), or the misconception that the EU would be ready to budge on its demands for a special relationship. Instead, a geostrategic vision of Brexit does require the conceptualization of a new and unique relationship between the EU and the UK, acknowledging the reality of a state which will become the first former EU member state (Nicolaidis, 2019). Time will show whether and how such a strategic understanding of the Brexit challenge comes to prevail in European capitals.

Conclusion

The geopoliticization of trade seems to be here to stay. At first sight, the EU may appear to be at a competitive disadvantage in a world where the management of trade and investment has become an instrument for competition among big powers rather than a force for moderation. We have argued, however, that the EU has started to adapt to this brave new world in order to maintain its power through trade. Nevertheless, the greatest danger for Europe in the longer term could reside within rather than outside its borders; namely, the risk of ideological contagion as its electoral base becomes receptive to the Trumpian argument that multilateralism has been a fool's bargain and should be abandoned. The challenge for the EU in the next few years will be to reconcile the rising geopoliticization of trade with its continued management under multilateral institutions.

References

Bouza, L. and Oleart, A. (2018) 'From the 2005 Constitution's 'Permissive Consensus' To TTIP's 'Empowering Dissensus': The EU as a Playing Field for Spanish Civil Society'. *Journal of Contemporary European Research*, Vol. 14, No. 2, pp. 87–104.

Bradford, A. (2012) 'The Brussels Effect'. *Northwestern University Law Review*, Vol. 107, p. 68.

Chan, A.T. and Crawford, B.K. (2017) 'The Puzzle of Public Opposition to TTIP in Germany'. *Business and Politics*, Vol. 19, No. 4, pp. 683–708.

Cadier, D. (2019) 'The Geopoliticisation of the EU's Eastern Partnership'. *Geopolitics*, Vol. 24, No. 1, pp. 71–99.

Damro, C. (2012) 'Market Power Europe'. *Journal of European Public Policy*, Vol. 19, No. 5, pp. 682–99.

De Bièvre, D. and Poletti, A. (2017) 'Why the Transatlantic Trade and Investment Partnership Is Not (So) New, and Why It Is Also Not (So) Bad'. *Journal of European Public Policy*, Vol. 24, No. 10, pp. 1506–21.

De Bievre, D. and Poletti, A. (2019) 'Explaining Varying Degrees of Politicization of EU Trade Agreement Negotiations: on Necessary and Sufficient Conditions, a Research Note'. Paper presented at the 2019 EUSA Conference, Denver, May.

De Bruycker, I. (2017) 'Politicization and the Public Interest: When Do the Elites in Brussels Address Public Interests in EU Policy Debates?' *European Union Politics*, Vol. 18, No. 4, pp. 603–19.

De Ville, F. and Siles-Brügge, G. (2017) 'Why TTIP Is a Game-Changer and Its Critics Have a Point'. *Journal of European Public Policy*, Vol. 24, No. 10, pp. 1491–505.

De Wilde, P. (2011) 'No Polity for Old Politics? A Framework for Analyzing the Politicization of European Integration'. *Journal of European Integration*, Vol. 33, No. 5, pp. 559–75.

Egan, M. and Nicolaidis, K. (2001) 'Regional Policy Externality and Market Governance: Why Recognize Foreign Standards?' *Journal of European Public Policy*, Vol. 8, No. 3, pp. 454–73.

Eliasson, L.J. and Huet, P.G.-D. (2019) *Civil Society, Rhetoric of Resistance, and Transatlantic Trade* (Cham: Springer).

European Commission (2019) 'EU-China Strategic Outlook: Commission Contribution to the European Council (21-22 March 2019)'. March 2019. Available online at: https://ec.europa.eu/commission/publications/eu-china-strategic-outlook-commission-contribution-european-council-21-22-march-2019_en. Last accessed 4 July 2019.

European Union (2009) 'Consolidated version of the Treaty on the Functioning of the European Union – Part Five: Article 207 (ex Article 133 TEC)'. Available online at: https://eur-lex.europa.eu/legal-content/EN/TXT/HTML/?uri=CELEX:12008E207&from=EN. Last accessed 4 July 2019.

European Union (2016) 'Consolidated Version of the Treaty on European Union'. Available online at: https://eur-lex.europa.eu/legal-content/EN/TXT/HTML/?uri=CELEX:12016M/TXT&from=EN. Last accessed 4 July 2019.

European Union (2019) 'Regulation of the European Parliament and of the Council Establishing a Framework for the Screening of Foreign Direct Investments into the Union'. 2017/0224(COD).

Available online at: https://eur-lex.europa.eu/legal-content/EN/TXT/?uri=CONSIL%3APE_72_2018_REV_1. Last accessed 4 July 2019.

Garcia-Duran, P., Costa, O. and Eliasson, L.J. (2019) 'Managed Globalization: The European Commission Response to EU Trade Policy Politicization?'. Paper presented at the 2019 EUSA Conference, Denver, May.

Hafner-Burton, E.M. (2009) 'The Power Politics of Regime Complexity: Human Rights Trade Conditionality in Europe'. *Perspectives on Politics*, Vol. 7, No. 1, pp. 33–7.

Hopewell, K. (2015) 'Multilateral Trade Governance as Social Field: Global Civil Society and the WTO'. *Review of International Political Economy*, Vol. 22, No. 6, pp. 1128–58.

Kobrin, S.J. (1998) 'The MAI and the Clash of Globalizations'. *Foreign Policy*, Vol. 112, pp. 97–109.

Laursen, F. and Roederer-Rynning, C. (2017) 'Introduction: The New EU FTAs as Contentious Market Regulation'. *Journal of European Integration*, Vol. 39, No. 7, pp. 763–79.

Magnette, P. (2017) *CETA: Quand l'Europe Deraille* (Waterloo: Luc Pire).

Meissner, K. and Rosen, G. (2019). 'Inter-parliamentary Alliances or Transnational Party Competition? Exploring Interaction between National Parliaments and the European Parliament in Trade Policy'. Paper presented at the 2019 EUSA Conference, Denver, May 2019.

Meunier, S. (2005) *Trading Voices: The European Union in International Commercial Negotiations* (Princeton, NJ: Princeton University Press).

Meunier, S. (2017) 'Integration by Stealth: How the European Union Gained Competence over Foreign Direct Investment'. *JCMS*, Vol. 55, No. 3, pp. 593–610.

Meunier, S. (2019) 'The EU Will Start Screening Foreign Investment'. *Washington Post*, April 10, 2019. Available online at: https://www.washingtonpost.com/politics/2019/04/10/eu-will-start-screening-foreign-investment-heres-full-story/. Last accessed 4 July 2019.

Meunier, S. and Czesana, R. Forthcoming "From Back Rooms to the Street? A Research Agenda for Explaining Variation in the Public Salience of Trade Policy-Making in Europe", *Journal of European Public Policy*.

Meunier, S. and Nicolaïdis, K. (1999) 'Who Speaks for Europe? The Delegation of Trade Authority in the EU'. *JCMS*, Vol. 37, No. 3, pp. 477–501.

Meunier, S. and Nicolaïdis, K. (2006) 'The European Union as a Conflicted Trade Power'. *Journal of European Public Policy*, Vol. 13, No. 6, pp. 906–25.

Meunier, S. and Nicolaïdis, K. (2017) 'The EU as a Trade Power'. In Hill, C., Smith, M. and Vanhoonacker, S. (eds) *International Relations and the European Union* (3rd editionNew European Union Series) (Oxford, New York: Oxford University Press), pp. 279–98.

Meunier, S. and Vachudova, M.A. (2018) 'Liberal Intergovernmentalism, Illiberalism and the Potential Superpower of the European Union'. *JCMS*, Vol. 56, No. 7, pp. 1631–47.

Moravcsik, A. (2017) 'Europe Is Still a Superpower'. *Foreign Policy,* Vol. 13. Available online at: https://foreignpolicy.com/2017/04/13/europe-is-still-a-superpower/' Last accessed 4 July 2019.

Newman, A.L. and Posner, E. (2011) 'International Interdependence and Regulatory Power: Authority, Mobility, and Markets'. *European Journal of International Relations*, Vol. 17, No. 4, pp. 589–610.

Nicolaidis (2018) 'Brexit and the Compatibility Paradigm A Guide for the Mutual Recognition Perplexed'. Available online at: https://ukandeu.ac.uk/wp-content/.../03/Brexit-and-the-compatibility-paradigm.pdf. Last accessed 4 July 2019.

Nicolaidis (2019) *Exodus, Reckoning, Sacrifice: Three Meanings of Brexit* (London: Unbound).

Ponjaert, F. (2015) 'The Political and Institutional Significance of an EU–Japan Trade and Partnership Agreement'. In Bacon, P., Mayer, H. and Nakamura, H. (eds) *The European Union and Japan: A New Chapter in Civilian Power Cooperation?* (Farnham: Ashgate) pp. 85–114.

Rosen, G. (2017) 'The Impact of Norms on Political Decision-making: How to Account for the European Parliament's Empowerment in EU External Trade Policy'. *Journal of European Public Policy*, Vol. 24, No. 10, pp. 1450–70.

Schimmelfennig, F., Leuffen, D. and Rittberger, B. (2015) 'The European Union as a System of Differentiated Integration: Interdependence, Politicization and Differentiation'. *Journal of European Public Policy*, Vol. 22, No. 6, pp. 764–82.

Smith, K.E. (1998) 'The Use of Political Conditionality in the EU's Relations with Third Countries: How Effective?' *European Foreign Affairs Review*, Vol. 3, No. 2, pp. 253–74.

Tieleman, K. (2000) 'The Failure of the Multilateral Agreement on Investment (MAI) and the Absence of a Global Public Policy Network'. Case Study for the UN Vision Project on Global Public Policy Networks. Available online at: https://www.google.com/search?client=firefox-b-d&channel=crow&q=The+Failure+of+the+Multilateral+Agreement+on+Investment+%28MAI%29+and+the+Absence+of+a+Global+Public+Policy+Network#. Last accessed 4 July 2019.

Wolf, M. (2019) 'The US-China Conflict Challenges the World'. *Financial Times*. 21 May. Available online at: https://www.ft.com/content/870c895c-7b11-11e9-81d2-f785092ab560. Last accessed 4 July 2019.

Wong, A. (2019) 'China's Economic Statecraft under Xi Jinping'. (Blog). Brookings, 22 January. Available online at: https://www.brookings.edu/articles/chinas-economic-statecraft-under-xi-jinping/. Last accessed 4 July 2019.

Young, A.R. (2015) 'The European Union as a Global Regulator? Context and Comparison'. *Journal of European Public Policy*, Vol. 22, No. 9, pp. 1233–52.

Young, A.R. (2016) 'Not Your Parents' Trade Politics: The Transatlantic Trade and Investment Partnership Negotiations'. *Review of International Political Economy*, Vol. 23, No. 3, pp. 345–78.

Young, A.R. (2017) *The New Politics of Trade: Lessons from TTIP* (Newcastle upon Tyne: Agenda).

JCMS 2019 Volume 57. Annual Review pp. 114–127   DOI: 10.1111/jcms.12948

Double Trouble: Trump, Transatlantic Relations and European Strategic Autonomy

LISBETH AGGESTAM and ADRIAN HYDE-PRICE
University of Gothenburg, Gothenburg

Introduction

Transatlantic relations were already fractious and fraught at the start of 2018 and the divisions subsequently deepened further. This trend was seen as symptomatic of the general decline of the liberal world order (Ikenberry, 2018) which was accentuated by the unexpected and unwelcome defection of its founder and prime mover, the USA, from many of its core principles and key multilateral agreements. In the words of the European Council President Donald Tusk (2018), 'the rules-based international order is being challenged [...] by its main architect and guarantor, the US'.

This move had a profound impact on the EU, which is inextricably bound by the transatlantic relationship within a stable multilateral order. But are the current travails of transatlantic relations a passing storm or the harbinger of full-blown climate change? How serious is this crisis, given the dire catalogue of disputes and controversies on a range of policies, and to what extent is this the doing of the 45th President of the USA Donald Trump? And what, effectively, are the implications of this deterioration for the EU's foreign and security policy?

Although it is tempting to attribute the deterioration in transatlantic relations to one specific factor; the personality and style of President Donald Trump, we argue in this contribution that the problems besetting transatlantic relations are deeper and more multifaceted than that, and go beyond the influence of the current occupant of the Oval Office. Europe and the USA have been drifting apart for nearly three decades, as the glue provided by US existential security guarantees to Europe disappeared with the end of the cold war. This brought to the fore pre-existing and underlying differences over a range of policy domains – from the Balkans and the Middle East, to trade and security cooperation, which have steadily weakened transatlantic ties.

The aim of this contribution is to shed light on some crucial developments in transatlantic relations that took place during 2018, and to assess their significance for EU foreign and security policy. President Trump's unilateralist 'America First' policy and his transactional approach to multilateral institutions continued unabated during 2018, accompanied by a questioning of many of the core principles that define the EU's approach to global governance and effective multilateralism. In 2018 the US government withdrew its support for several international agreements, including the Treaty on Intermediate Range Nuclear Forces in October. In May it withdrew from the Iran nuclear deal (the Joint Comprehensive Plan of Action, JCPOA), which Trump claimed 'was one of the worst and most one-sided transactions the United States has ever entered into' (White

House, 2018b). In response, the EU's chief architect to the deal, the EU's High Representative Federica Mogherini (2018a), replied that 'the nuclear deal is not a bilateral agreement and it is not in the hands of any single country to terminate it unilaterally'.

Later in May the USA moved its Embassy in Israel to Jerusalem, heightening concerns of further destabilization of Arab countries across the Middle East. In the same month the fractious G7 summit in Charlevoix (Canada) was followed by the Brussels Nato summit (11–12 July), which did little to smooth over differences in the troubled transatlantic relationship. Instead, it witnessed Trump's attack on 'delinquent' Nato allies, berating them for not paying their fair share of the European defence burden within Nato, and attacking European ambitions to enhance EU military capabilities in the context of a Defence Union as 'insulting' and driven by the self-interests of France. Throughout the year Germany remained a primary focus of the President's ire, although many other European leaders found themselves the target of one of Trump's tirades or tweets (*The New York Times*, 2018).

Thus, rather than celebrating their shared liberal democratic values within the transatlantic security community, the two sides found themselves in dispute over a broad range of key policy issues. Relations were further worsened by a series of personnel changes in the Trump administration. Secretary of State Jim Mattis, Secretary of State Rex Tillerson and National Security Advisor Herbert McMasters (widely regarded as the 'adults in the room') all resigned, and took the opportunity to air their frustrations about the direction of Trump's policies. Trump took the opportunity to appoint a more hawkish Secretary of State, Michael Pompeo, and an ultra-hawkish National Security Advisor, Stephen Bolton. Trade fell firmly under the control of Peter Navarro, another 'America First' enthusiast, while Gordon Sondland was appointed US Ambassador to the EU – a post that had remained vacant after Trump came to power.

All the new appointees share Trump's disdain for international institutions, including the EU, which they see as bureaucratic, unrepresentative and constraining, and as serving the interests of global cosmopolitan elites rather than ordinary citizens. Hence, the EU is seen as a 'foe set up to take advantage of the United States' and for this reason, Trump celebrated the Brexit vote, called on the UK to appoint Nigel Farage as its ambassador to the USA and criticized Prime Minister Theresa May for negotiating a 'soft' Brexit (*The Guardian*, 2018). Secretary of State Pompeo (2018a) made clear his broad scepticism of multilateral institutions in a speech delivered in Brussels: 'Multilateralism has too often become viewed as an end unto itself', he argued.

> Brexit – if nothing else – was a political wake-up call. Is the EU ensuring that the interests of countries and their citizens are placed before those of bureaucrats here in Brussels? [...] Every nation [...] must honestly acknowledge its responsibilities to its citizens and ask if the current international order serves the good of its people as well as it could. (Pompeo, 2018a)

These disruptive and disconcerting developments in transatlantic relations constitute both a challenge and an opportunity for the EU as a global security actor. On the one hand, they mean that the EU faces opposition to its regional and global foreign policy ambitions from the USA, the most powerful actor in the international system. They have also brought to the surface underlying divisions among EU member states over foreign and security policy, further weakening EU cohesion and contributing to new patterns of more informal European foreign policy practices (Aggestam and Bicchi, 2019). On the other hand, however, the events of 2018 can be viewed as constituting a European moment that can galvanize EU action in foreign, security and defence policy. Thus, as the transatlantic allies have differed over important foreign policy issues and Trump has cast into question the sanctity of Nato security guarantees precisely when Europe faces a deteriorating external security environment, key European states have felt compelled to work towards the ambition of European strategic autonomy.

Consequently, at present the EU's legitimacy and credibility as a multilateral actor in the international system is being questioned by its former American patron and challenged from within by eurosceptic and populist forces, and from the outside by global competitors, a resurgent Russia and a turbulent neighbourhood. Furthermore, the EU's legitimacy as a global actor is intrinsically linked to a functioning global governance system that is now beginning to unravel. Hence, we argue that the events of 2018 may constitute part of a critical juncture in transatlantic relations, in which the EU will be compelled to assume greater responsibility for regional and global security in order to preserve the multilateral, rules-based order within which it so embedded, and to which its fate is so closely tied (Laatikainen, 2013).

The article is organized in three main parts. The first underlines the need for a multilevel analysis to capture the centripetal and centrifugal forces at play within transatlantic relations, and an evaluation of the agency-structure dynamic. The second and third parts explore some critical developments in transatlantic relations during 2018, focusing on differences over Middle East policy and European security and defence cooperation. We argue that these events have triggered different dynamics and processes in EU foreign policy and revealed new patterns of foreign policy cooperation among EU member states. They have also reinforced the EU's central role conception as a 'defender of international multilateralism', and stimulated concrete steps towards deeper security and defence cooperation.

I. Understanding Transatlantic Relations: A Multilevel Analysis

It would be a mistake to attribute transatlantic divisions primarily to Trump's abrasive style of personalized diplomacy and his unpredictable behaviour. Certainly, his emphasis on 'America First', his transactional approach to foreign policy, his disdain for protocol and his sympathy for strongmen and autocrats have soured transatlantic relations. Trump has attacked virtually all the key multilateral institutions and liberal values that most EU member states hold dear, and demonstrated clear disdain for the EU and all it represents (Peterson, 2018, p. 641). Yet he is not the first US president to criticize European pusillanimity, weakness and ambiguity, and not the first US president that Europeans have criticized for being unilateral, self-serving and heavy-handed. Transatlantic discord preceded Trump, and is likely to continue after he leaves office (Polyakova and Haddad, 2019). Europeans generally held President Barack Obama in high regard, but many European allies were highly critical of his failure to uphold the US's clear red lines in Syria. Conversely, Obama was scathing in his criticism of European military weakness and impotence during the Libya operation in 2011, which demonstrated the gulf between European ambitions to be a security provider and its military and political weakness (Peterson, 2018, p. 647). Trump downgraded the official status of the EU's diplomatic representation in the White House in November 2018, meaning that fewer representatives could attend high-level briefings. However, it should not be forgotten that it was President Obama who put a stop to the biannual summits between the US president and cabinet with their counterparts in the EU Commission and the Council of the European Union in 2014, deciding that they were largely set piece, symbolic affairs holding little value.

Burden sharing and European unwillingness to invest in their own security and defence is another of Trump's bugbears. 'Nato members must finally contribute their fair share and meet their financial obligations, for 23 of the 28 member nations are still not paying what they should be paying and what they're supposed to be paying for their defence', Trump argued in May 2017. He highlighted this issue again during the 2018 Brussels Nato summit, but burden sharing is not new. Virtually all US administrations have called on their Europeans allies to share the burden of their own defence. Obama's Secretary of Defence Robert Gates, for example, warned the Europeans in his farewell speech to Nato allies in 2011 that:

> the blunt reality is that there will be dwindling appetite and patience in the US Congress – and in the American body politic writ large – to expend increasingly precious funds on behalf of nations that are apparently unwilling to devote the necessary resources or make the necessary changes to be serious and capable partners in their own defence (Gates, 2011).

Deep cuts in defence expenditure in the decade preceding the Ukraine crisis left most European militaries parlously underfunded and unable to undertake even limited operations. Most were left with what Mölling (2011) has termed bonsai armies'. Germany has been a notable laggard here, failing to invest adequately in its military capabilities and unwilling to share responsibility for European security and defence. Although European defence budgets have been steadily rising since Russia's illegal annexation of Crimea – prior to Trump's election – improvement has been slow and uneven.

Tensions in transatlantic relations therefore reflect more deep-seated structural factors going back to the end of the cold war. Europe is now no longer as reliant on US security guarantees as it was during the East–West conflict, and the USA is now more focused on China and East Asia than it is on Russia and Europe. The EU and its member states have grown in confidence and self-assurance over recent decades, and have proven increasingly willing both to define their own foreign policy preferences (in Africa, the Middle East and Asia), and to criticize US foreign policy when it takes a direction that Europeans dislike (such as the 2003 Iraq war and the wider global war on terror). Conversely, the USA increasingly sees Europe as rich and prosperous but unwilling either to support the USA in its global ambitions or to provide for their own security (Brooks and Wohlforth, 2016). More generally in terms of the international system, the EU consists of small or medium-sized status-quo-oriented states, who benefit from a rules-based multilateral system that can constrain challenges from revisionist states and allow them to focus on trade, welfare and democracy promotion. The USA, on the other hand, is a global superpower with a sense of responsibility for global peace and security, and which therefore resists having its freedom of action restrained by multilateral institutions or cautious allies. Indeed, when it comes to unilateral action and the use of coercive military power, Europeans are from Venus and the Americans are from Mars, as Robert Kagan (2003) famously argued.

Hence, a combination of both agential factors and deeper structural trends in the international system have emerged, bringing about a profound crisis in transatlantic relations. Yet another important driver of transatlantic relations is at work at a lower, and perhaps more fundamental level than institutional, strategic or personal: domestic politics. Europe and the USA are both embedded in the same global socioeconomic system characterized by liberal market capitalism. For both there are growing social cleavages in terms of income differentials, class inequalities and growing social fragmentation; this has contributed to what has been termed the 'hollowing out' of liberal democracy (Mair, 2013). This is contributing to a growing disconnect between public and mainstream politicians on both sides of the Atlantic, and is reflected in rising populism. In Europe, nationalist and eurosceptic populist political forces have challenged the permissive consensus on globalization, European integration and liberal internationalism. This has weakened the political cohesion of the EU and, most dramatically, contributed to the shock outcome of the UK's Brexit referendum. Populism has also led to clear trends towards democratic backsliding in parts of central and eastern Europe, most notably in Hungary and Poland. EU attempts to exert leverage on these two countries is impeded by the ideological affinity between them and the Trump administration.

In the USA, similar populist, anti-globalist and conservative nationalist forces brought Trump to power. US congressional elections in 2018 demonstrated deep and enduring divisions in the US body politic: Trump consistently enjoys 45–46 per cent of support in polls and votes, but faces strong opposition from young, urban and educated voters – especially college-educated suburban women (Nato Parliamentary Assembly, 2019, p. 10). Domestic politics are thus shaping the course of transatlantic relations in a way never seen before. This adds a new element of unpredictability and concern. Demographic trends also appear to be eroding the traditional, postwar societal foundations of the transatlantic relationship, with the increase in Latin American and Asian groups in the USA, and Middle Eastern, African and Balkan populations in Europe. In this changed domestic political context, some now fear that Trump will further politicize the issue of Nato and transatlantic relations, leading to a fracturing of the broad bipartisan consensus of the value of the link that has existed since World War II.

At the same time the transatlantic relationship is still characterized by multiple bonds, linkages and affinities. Politically, there is still considerable support for a more constructive and mutually beneficial transatlantic relationship among US elites, which is clearly evident in Congress, the quality press, academic debate and the think-tank community. The USA and the EU have more in common in terms of liberal democratic values, institutions and norms than they do with any other major external partner. Above all, trade relations are extensive and significant, and the USA–European economic relationship remains the largest and most integrated in the global economy (Lewis *et al.,* 2018, p. 6). The USA–EU trading relationship is the most important global trading corridor in the international economy, valued at 1 trillion dollars. The USA remains the main importer of EU goods, as well as the main source of EU imports. The two account for 46 per cent of the global gross domestic product, half of the world's foreign direct investment (FDI) and a third of the world's trade flows (Nato Parliamentary Assembly, 2019, p. 5). Although trade disputes are growing and the Trump administration is seeking to change the terms of trade with Europe, the strength of the economic bond between the EU and the USA gives an underlying material foundation to the multifaceted transatlantic relationship.

II. Iran and the Middle East

One of the long-standing areas of disagreement in transatlantic relations for over four decades has been policy towards the Middle East and North Africa. During 2018 these differences were manifested in multiple policy disagreements: the Israel–Palestine conflict; Saudi Arabia and the murder of the dissident journalist Jamal Khashoggi; and Syria, when Trump made a surprise announcement in December 2018 that he was withdrawing US troops from the country without any prior consultation with his European allies. However, no dispute was as significant and potentially game changing as his decision to cease compliance with the Iran nuclear deal (the JCPOA) in May 2018.

Transatlantic differences over policy towards the Middle East reflect the same structural asymmetries in the relationship identified above. As the world's only superpower, the USA has been the dominant external influence in the Middle East and North Africa for many decades. Although it is now less reliant on oil from the Middle East because of the shale gas revolution, it still has major strategic and economic interests in the region – not least, its commitment to the survival of the State of Israel. For Europe, on the other hand, the Middle East and North Africa is a region of critical importance because of its geopolitical proximity. It is part of Europe's neighbourhood and has featured centrally in EU external relations strategies, notably through the European neighbourhood policy. Yet European political and strategic influence has long been marginal to the affairs of the region. This has created an asymmetry in transatlantic relations in a key policy domain: the USA has a decisive influence on the Middle East and North Africa but it is geographically insulated from the region's negative externalities; Europe has much less influence but it is very exposed to these negative externalities, including nuclear proliferation nuclear, terrorism, migration and regional conflicts.

These asymmetries were evident in the dispute over the JCPOA Iran nuclear deal, which was originally agreed in July 2015 by Iran and the five permanent members of the UN Security Council (China, France, Russia, the UK and the USA), along with Germany (also known as the P5+1 group). The JCPOA was the fruit of years of patient diplomacy by the EU3 (the UK, France and Germany), supported by the EU High Representative. Indeed, in the latter stages of the negotiations, the P5+1 group was represented by EU High Representative/Vice President (HRVP) Federica Mogherini, who played a crucial role in the final stages of the negotiations leading to the successful conclusion of the JCPOA. Consequently, for the EU, the deal constitutes a major affirmation of its policy emphasizing effective multilateralism and gives credence to EU claims as a global security actor.

HRVP Mogherini and the EU as a whole thus has a lot of political capital invested in this agreement (Cronberg, 2018). The HRVP formally coordinates the executive body of the nuclear agreement and the EU is accepted as a primus inter pares in the Joint Commission among the five permanent members of the Security Council, Germany and Iran. Its role is not just to convene and facilitate discussions about the implementation of the nuclear deal but also to mediate disputes among any of the participants. Given its role in the JCPOA, the EU sees the preservation of this treaty as a crucial test case for its ambitions to be a diplomatic actor on the global stage (Cronberg, 2017).

President Trump, on the other hand, has long regarded the JCPOA as 'the worst deal ever negotiated' (White House, 2018a). His administration has consistently denounced Iran as a state sponsor of terror, a radical regime exporting its divisive ideolog and a corrupt dictatorship sowing chaos, discord and destruction. On 8 May 2018 President Trump announced the withdrawal of the USA from the agreement:

> The Iran deal is defective at its core. If we do nothing, we know exactly what will happen. In just a short period of time, the world's leading state sponsor of terror will be on the cusp of acquiring the world's most dangerous weapons (White House, 2018a).

Trump's opposition to the JCPOA – beyond the fact that it was one of the significant achievements of his predecessor, Barack Obama – was justified on grounds that it did not curb Iran's nuclear programme, did not address its missile arsenal and did not prevent Iran from undertaking destabilizing activities across the region. Consequently, the USA ramped up pressure against Iran with a tough sanctions regime and by deploying additional US military assets to the region. President Trump also proposed bilateral negotiations with Iran to hammer out a new, more comprehensive deal, pointedly excluding any role for the EU or France, Germany and the UK.

These actions created a deepening, albeit slow-burning crisis, as Iran responded with growing belligerency. It also led to a major rift in the transatlantic relationship and reinforced the determination of a core group of EU member states to carve a distinct leadership role for Europe on this key foreign policy issue. France, Germany and the UK (as the three European partners to the agreement) took the lead and issued a joint statement signalling strong support for the deal. Mogherini was also central in defining the EU's collective stance, arguing:

> Our position as Europeans has not changed. On the contrary, we have seen the reasons why this agreement was a good agreement. We remain committed to the full and effective implementation of the nuclear deal with Iran. Our determination to preserve the deal is also in the interest of the United States, because preserving the nuclear deal is essential to our common security – both for Europe and the United States – and for the entire Middle East, that might otherwise fall into a spiral of nuclear proliferation and of an even more dangerous level of conflictuality (Mogherini, 2018b).

The EU position was based on the assumption that nuclear proliferation posed an existential threat to peace and security in the Middle East – with dire implications for Europe, given its geographical proximity. Despite the Iranian regime's autocratic character and its role as a state sponsor of terrorism, giving it incentives for not developing nuclear weapons was an overriding priority. The EU maintained that the JCPOA was technically sound and had constrained Iran's nuclear enrichment (as the International Atomic Energy Agency (IAEA) inspections confirmed). Terminating the JCPOA would decrease the credibility of similar multilateral agreements and diplomatic engagement, further radicalize Iran (weakening President Rouhani and strengthening the Revolutionary Guard) and push it towards more assertive action. Moreover, sanctions would hurt the Iranian people and would probably not be effective. Iran borders nine countries, which makes it easy to evade sanctions, and many Russian, Chinese and Kazakh firms would continue to trade with Iran. The EU feared that US actions would also push Iran further into the arms of China and Russia. It was argued as well that Iran could acquire a nuclear weapon within a year after abandoning the JCPOA (Nato Parliamentary Assembly, 2019, p. 4).

Despite the JCPOA's limitations, many EU countries saw it as part of a process of building trust and cooperation (Cronberg, 2017). They hoped that its success would make possible discussions on other, more problematic, aspects of Iran's foreign and domestic policy – including its support for terrorist groups, its domestic repression and its foreign assassination plots. In a joint statement by Mogherini and the UK, Germany and France, they regret the reimposition of US sanctions. For the EU, the JCPOA remains a key element in the global non-proliferation architecture, described by Mogherini (2018b) as 'the biggest achievement diplomacy has ever delivered', pointing out its approval by UN Security Council Resolution 2231.

In order to keep the JCPOA alive, the EU promised to protect EU firms who wished 'to pursue legitimate business with Iran' and started to draw up an instrument in support of trade exchanges in November 2018 as a system to help European businesses circumvent unilateral US sanctions on humanitarian trade. This system involves a barter trade arrangement in order to avoid direct payments to Iran; however, its impact was primarily symbolic and implementing it has proven to be slow and limited in scope.

The dispute over the JCPOA has been the most serious rift in transatlantic relations during the Trump presidency. The EU has done all it can to preserve the deal, as a vindication of its commitment to effective multilateralism and a demonstration of its abilities as a global security actor. Nonetheless, the dispute shows the limits of EU diplomacy, given the asymmetric power relations between the USA and the EU when it comes to policy towards the Middle East. The transatlantic rift over the JCPOA demonstrates the EU's ability to define its interests and its policies in ways that diverge significantly from those of the USA. But it also clearly demonstrates the limits of European power, and the 'expectations-capabilities gap' (Hill, 1993) that continues to limit the EU's ability to function as an autonomous strategic actor.

III. Transatlantic Relations and European Security

Central to deepening European concerns about the parlous state of transatlantic relations in 2018 were growing doubts about Trump's commitment to Nato and European security. Whatever aspirations some European leaders harbour about a more robust and effective EU security and defence policy, virtually all recognize that the Alliance remains the bedrock of peace, security and stability on the European continent. During the presidential campaign Trump repeatedly questioned the utility of Nato and the sanctity of the Alliance's Article V security guarantee. On coming to power he continued to cast doubt over the value of Nato to the USA, and suggested that Article V security guarantees were conditional on the European allies honouring their commitment to spend 2 per cent of their gross domestic product on defence. He berated the Europeans for free riding and argued that they were taking advantage of US generosity. Given his unpredictability and his penchant for disrupting multilateral gatherings (for example, the G7 in Charlevoix, Canada, in May), it was with growing trepidation that the European allies viewed the approach of the Brussels Nato summit on 11–12 July 2018.

Just prior to the summit, President Trump sent letters to European and Canadian government leaders outlining his administration's grievances about free riding and insisting they spend more on defence. He wrote to Chancellor Merkel that '[c]ontinued German underspending on defence undermines the security of the alliance and provides validation for other allies that also do not plan to meet their military spending commitments' (Atlantic Council, 2018). This set the stage for his outspoken attack at the summit itself on the USA's 'delinquent allies' for not spending enough on defence, with his vitriol being directed – once again – primarily at Germany, which he accused of being 'controlled by Russia' through the Nord Stream II pipeline deal. 'What good is Nato if Germany is paying Russia billions of dollars for gas and energy?' he tweeted (quoted in Petersson, 2019, p. 32).

Yet despite such outbursts, the summit was in many respects a success. President Trump signed up to a robust common statement reaffirming Article V and criticizing Russia for illegally annexing Crimea, fermenting conflict in eastern Ukraine, using a nerve agent in Salisbury, consistently violating allies' airspace, holding large military exercises without warning and using 'irresponsible and aggressive nuclear rhetoric'. The summit took important steps to enhance Nato's deterrence and defence posture, including creating two new Nato commands, deepening cooperation with enhanced partners, developing new cyber capacities, strengthening the enhanced forward presence in Poland and the three Baltic states and agreeing a series of exercises and training. In addition, Nato agreed to begin negotiations on accession by North Macedonia, to extend funding for the mission in Afghanistan and create a larger training mission in Iraq (Nato, 2018).

The Nato alliance remains the lynchpin and key institutional buckle of the transatlantic relationship and in many respects it appears to be in rude health. Across Europe and Canada, defence expenditure is rising, with a larger share going to equipment purchases and research and development rather than salaries and pensions. Despite Trump's personal antipathy to Nato, transatlantic security cooperation functions smoothly and effectively at the working level on issues such as terrorism, nuclear proliferation and intelligence sharing. This has been facilitated by senior officials in the Trump administration, who have gone out of their way to reaffirm the US commitment to Nato and Article V. During his first visit to Nato headquarters in April 2018, Secretary Pompeo emphasized that the alliance had been 'an essential pillar of American security interests for decades', and that the US 'commitment to the collective defence under Article V of the Washington Treaty remains ironclad' (Pompeo, 2018b). Moreover, the alliance enjoys strong bipartisan support in the US Congress and in American public opinion, and it is evident that if Trump were to propose withdrawing from Nato the Senate would have broad bipartisan support to block this.

Nonetheless, the combination of Russia's resurgence and revisionist approaches and Trump's unpredictability and deep euroscepticism have galvanized renewed European efforts to deepen security and defence cooperation. After the bitter transatlantic divisions at the G7 summit in May 2018, Chancellor Merkel, voicing the fears of many European leaders, noted that 'it is not the case that the United States of America will simply protect us. Instead, Europe must take its destiny in its own hands. That is our job for the future' (Merkel, 2018). This task has been formulated in terms of an aspiration for European strategic autonomy, which has emerged as the unifying concept for a series of steps to enhance European military capabilities, deepen defence cooperation and forge a common European strategic culture. The term remains somewhat ambiguous and contested, but both German and French leaders, who are driving the project, with support from Spain and Italy, have insisted that it is aimed at strengthening the European pillar of the transatlantic alliance, and is a complement to Nato, not an alternative.

The EU affirmed its commitment to greater defence cooperation at the EU summit in June 2018: 'Europe must take greater responsibility for its own security and underpin its role as a credible and reliable actor and partner in the area of security and defence'

(European External Action Service, 2018). Central to EU defence cooperation are three linked initiatives: PESCO (permanent structured cooperation), CARD (coordinated annual review on defence) and the European defence fund. PESCO is the centrepiece of this project to forge a European defence union and achieve strategic autonomy, and has been described as a 'game changer for European cooperation' (Fiott *et al.*, 2017, p. 5). The first meeting of EU defence ministers in the PESCO format took place on 6 March 2018, when it approved the first 17 projects (of which four were led by Germany). Another set of projects was agreed in November 2018, and included a European medical command, a logistical hubs network, a training mission competence centre, a crisis response operational core to speed up the deployment of troops to emergency situations and a Belgium-led effort to develop submarine drones to tackle mines at sea (Zandee, 2018). When PESCO was first launched President Tusk stressed that

> [f]or many years the strongest argument against PESCO had been the fear that it would lead to the weakening of Nato. But it is quite the opposite – strong European defence naturally strengthens Nato. This is why PESCO is not only good news for us, but it is also good news for our allies (Tusk, 2017).

It is therefore plain that tensions in transatlantic relations have given renewed emphasis to the long-held aspiration for European strategic autonomy. This aspiration was restrained because of the absence of a 'clear and present danger', the US commitment to European security and opposition from Atlanticists within the EU led by the UK. But by 2018 it was clear that a critical juncture had been reached: the EU faced a deteriorating external security environment, with a clear threat from Russia; the USA was no longer a reliable guarantor of European security and Brexit removed a key opponent of deepened European defence cooperation. The result has been a great leap forward in strengthening European military capabilities and creating the preconditions for European strategic autonomy. As President Macron noted in June 2018: 'On European defence, things are advancing at an unprecedented rate compared to past decades; it is becoming reality' (Brzozowski, 2018).

The progress made in strengthening European defence is still patchy and uneven. Differences remain between France and Germany, particularly over how inclusive the PESCO process should be and how defence cooperation in EU relates to other initiatives, such as the French-led European intervention initiative, the UK-led joint expeditionary force and the Anglo-French joint combined expeditionary force, developed as part of the 2011 Lancaster House agreement. President Macron's aspirations are bold and ambitious. During his visit to Finland on 30 August 2018 he called for Europe to work for strategic autonomy in defence, adding that the EU should adopt 'a kind of reinforced article 5' within the EU to build collective defence. He proposed that 'cooperation [should be] reinforced almost automatically, which will mean that, for member states who agreed with the reform, we could have a real solidarity of intervention if one state was attacked' (Euractiv, 2018). One important source of potential friction is the relationship between PESCO and third parties, specifically, the UK. The UK is seeking a 'deep and special' security relationship with the EU and is keen to be involved in PESCO projects (Mills, 2019). The informal meeting of EU defence ministers in Vienna (29–30 August 2018) exposed significant divisions between EU member states over the future of PESCO. The Netherlands led a bloc of 13 member states favouring a more inclusive approach to the UK, the USA and third parties. On the other hand, France, Germany, Spain and Italy were in favour of promoting EU strategic autonomy by strengthening EU member states defence industrial collaboration, thereby reducing reliance on the USA (Zandee, 2018).

Although the French have emphasized that PESCO is not designed to replace Nato, and that the alliance remains the key to European territorial defence, questions remain. Poland and the Baltic states, for example, worry that PESCO may divert from Nato and territorial defence and that it is primarily designed to develop expeditionary capabilities to implement French strategic priorities (in the Sahel, the Mediterranean and North Africa). Talk of a European army or Europeans acting against the USA is both unrealistic and divisive; PESCO provides a means for strengthening the Alliance by increasing European defence capabilities. Indeed, Nato Secretary-General Jens Stoltenberg made his support clear: 'I welcome the initiative to strengthen European defence because I believe that will be good for the European Union, for Europe and for Nato'. But he also warned about potential conflicts with Nato commitments and called for non-EU allies (that is, the UK and Norway) to be fully involved: 'We cannot risk ending up with conflicting requirements from EU and from Nato to the same nations' (Stoltenberg, 2017). The signing of a joint declaration on EU–Nato cooperation on 10 July 2018 was intended to allay fears of competition, exclusion and duplication (European Council, 2018).

Conclusions

Ahead of the EU Summit in June 2018, Donald Tusk warned EU leaders that 'despite our tireless efforts to keep the unity of the West, transatlantic relations are under immense pressure due to the policies of President Trump. It is my belief that, while hoping for the best, we must be ready to prepare our Union for worst-case scenarios' (Deutsche Welle, 2018). In a relationship that has long had to weather the buffeting of disputes and differences (Ikenberry, 2018, p. 3), it is no understatement to conclude that transatlantic relations during 2018 were experiencing a uniquely troubled time. Under Trump the relationship appears to be more fragile and fragmented than ever. He has starkly brought out the differences that exist between the USA and Europeans over interests, preferences, identities and perceptions (Nye, 2019). The two continents face different geopolitical challenges, different strategic concerns, widening differences on values and norms and differences over trade and economic relations. The USA and EU, it has been argued, 'are engaged in a form of structural competition' and as 'geo-economic competitors' (Sbragia, 2010, pp. 368, 396). Moreover, there are policy differences across a range of issues, particularly regarding the Middle East.

Despite these growing differences, however, there is also a great deal that binds the two: history and culture; trade and economic compatibility, based on liberal markets and open trade; security interests and liberal democratic norms and values. Certainly from the global South's point of view, as well as in Russia and China, the USA and Europeans still constitute a distinctive Western liberal-democratic community. As many have argued, there are no two regions so closely bound together than Europe and the USA (Ikenberry, 2018; Nye, 2019; Peterson, 2018).

Thus, although the transatlantic relationship may be in severe crisis, it is not necessarily in terminal decline. If it is to survive, it will need nuanced and sustained diplomatic engagement from both sides. The relationship still has underlying strengths and is based on shared interests and values. But it now requires careful nurturing, cultivation and encouragement. Trump is not simply the cause of transatlantic travails, but a symptom of underlying problems. The Europeans must play a long game, diversifying transatlantic bonds by cultivating new links with Congress, the US foreign policy community and civil society groups. At present it is important for Europeans to avoid being provoked by Trump and to focus on pragmatic cooperation at the working level – as it currently does with Nato.

Yet, the relationship needs to be rebalanced and reforged, with a clear commitment and willingness on the part of Europeans to take on greater responsibility for their own security and defence, and in responding robustly to threats and challenges to the liberal world order. A more coherent and effective Europe is thus a precondition for a healthy and balanced transatlantic relationship. This may require the emergence of a more cohesive inner core committed to effective defence cooperation (in the context of a multi-speed Europe of concentric circles), and certainly demands a willingness to engage with third parties – above all, the UK after Brexit. Therefore, the future of the transatlantic relationship lies in the hands of Europeans themselves more extensively than in the vagaries of the 45th President.

References

Aggestam, L. and Bicchi, F. (2019) 'New Directions in EU Foreign Policy Governance: Cross-loading, Leadership and Informal Groupings'. *Journal of Common Market Studies*, Vol. 57, No. 3, pp. 515–32.

Atlantic Council (2018) Trump Sends Disturbing Letters to Nine Nato Leaders Before Key Summit, 2 July. Available online at: https://www.atlanticcouncil.org/blogs/natosource/trump-sends-disturbing-letter-to-trudeau-and-eight-european-leaders-ahead-of-nato-summit Last accessed 20 May 2019.

Brooks, S. and Wohlforth, W. (2016) *America Abroad: Why the Sole Superpower Should Not Pull Back from the World* (Oxford: Oxford University Press).

Brzozowski, A. (2018) 'Europe Aims for Greater 'Strategic Autonomy' from US on Defence'. 29 June. Available online at: https://www.euractiv.com/section/defence-and-security/news/europe-aims-for-greater-strategic-autonomy-from-us-on-defence/1252497/. Last accessed 22 May 2019.

Cronberg, T. (2018) *Nuclear Multilateralism and Iran: Inside EU Negotiations* (London: Routledge).

Cronberg, T. (2017) 'No EU, No Iran Deal: The EU's Choice Between Multilateralism and the Transatlantic Link'. *The Nonproliferation Review*, Vol. 24, No. 3–4, pp. 243–59.

Deutsche Welle (2018) 'Donald Tusk Warns EU Leaders to 'Prepare for the Worst' in EU-US relations'. Available online at: https://www.dw.com/en/donald-tusk-warns-eu-leaders-to-prepare-for-the-worst-in-eu-us-relations/a-44429145. Last accessed 20 May 2019.

Euractiv (2018) 'Macron Proposes EU Collective Defence Plan'. 30 August. Available online at:. Available online at: https://www.euractiv.com/section/defence-and-security/news/frances-macron-proposes-eu-collective-defence-plan/. Last accessed 22 May 2019.

European External Action Service (2018) 'Europe Must Take Greater Responsibility for Its Own Security'. 29 June. Available online at: https://eeas.europa.eu/topics/common-security-and-defence-policy-csdp/47738/europe-must-take-greater-responsibility-its-own-security-eu-heads-states-and-government-agree_en. Last accessed 22 May 2019.

European Council (2018) 'Joint Declaration on EU-Nato Cooperation'. 10 July. Available online at: https://www.consilium.europa.eu/sv/press/press-releases/2018/07/10/eu-nato-joint-declaration/. Last accessed 1 August 2018.

Fiott, D., Missiroli, A. and Tardy, T. (2017) 'Permanent Structured Cooperation: What's in a Name?'. Chaillot Paper No. 142 (Paris: EU Institute for Security Studies).

Gates, R.M. (2011) 'Reflections on the Status and Future of the Transatlantic Alliance'. *The Atlantic Council*. 10 June. Available online at: https://www.atlanticcouncil.org/blogs/natosource/text-of-speech-by-robert-gates-on-the-future-of-nato. Last accessed 15 May 2018.

Hill, C. (1993) 'The Capability–Expectations Gap, or Conceptualizing Europe's International Role'. *JCMS*, Vol. 31, No. 3, pp. 305–28.

Ikenberry, J. (2018) 'The End of the Liberal International Order?' *International Affairs*, Vol. 94, No. 1, pp. 7–24.

Kagan, R. (2003) *Of Paradise and Power: America and Europe in the New World Order* (New York: Alfred A. Knopf).

Laatikainen, K.V. (2013) 'EU Multilateralism in a Multipolar World'. In Jørgensen, K.E. and Laatikainen, K.V. (eds) *Routledge Handbook on the European Union and International Institutions* (London: Routledge), pp. 472–87.

Lewis, P., Parakilas, J., Schneider-Petsinger, M., Smart, C., Rathke, J. and Ruy, D. (2018) 'The Future of the United States and Europe: An Irreplaceable Partnership'. London: Chatham House Research Paper. Available online at: https://www.chathamhouse.org/publication/future-united-states-and-europe-irreplaceable-partnership. Last accessed 22 May 2018.

Mair, P. (2013) *Ruling the Void: The Hollowing Out of Western Democracy* (London: Verso).

Merkel, A. (2018) 'Speech by Federal Chancellor Dr Angela Merkel at the Ceremony Awarding the International Charlemagne Prize to French President Emmanuel Macron'. Aachen, 10 May 2018. Available online at: https://www.bundesregierung.de/breg-en/chancellor/speech-by-federal-chancellor-dr-angela-merkel-at-the-ceremony-awarding-the-international-charlemagne-prize-to-french-president-emmanuel-macron-in-aachen-on-10-may-2018-1008554. Last accessed 27 July 2019.

Mills, C. (2019) 'EU Defence: The Realisation of Permanent Structured Cooperation (PESCO)'. Briefing Paper No. 8149, House of Commons Library. Available online at: https://researchbriefings.parliament.uk/ResearchBriefing/Summary/CBP-8149. Last accessed 20 June 2019.

Mogherini, F. (2018a) 'Remarks by HR/VP Mogherini on the statement by US President Trump regarding the nuclear deal (JCPOA)'. 8 May. Available online at: https://eeas.europa.eu/headquarters/headquarters-homepage/44238/remarks-hrvp-mogherini-statement-us-president-trump-regarding-iran-nuclear-deal-jcpoa_en. Last accessed 25 May 2019.

Mogherini, F. (2018b) 'Speech by HR/VP Mogherini on the Iran Nuclear Agreement at the European Parliament Plenary Session'. Brussels, 12 June. Available online at: https://eeas.europa.eu/headquarters/headquarters-homepage/46380/speech-high-representativevice-president-federica-mogherini-iran-nuclear-agreement-european_en. Last accessed 1 September 2018.

Mölling, C. (2011) 'Europe without Defence'. *SWP Comments 38*, Berlin, November. Available online at: https://www.swp-berlin.org/fileadmin/contents/products/comments/2011C38_mlg_ks.pdf. Last accessed 27 July 2019.

Nato (2018) 'Brussels Summit Declaration'. 11–12 July 2018. Available online at: https://www.nato.int/cps/en/natohq/official_texts_156624.htm. Last accessed 23 July 2018.

Nato Parliamentary Assembly (2019) '18[th]Annual Parliamentary Transatlantic Forum Report'. 10–12 December 2018, Washington: D.C. Available online at: https://www.nato-pa.int/document/2018-transatlantic-forum-report-256-18-e. Last accessed 20 May 2019.

Nye, J. (2019) 'The Rise and Fall of American Hegemony from Wilson to Trump'. *International Affairs*, Vol. 95, No. 1, pp. 63–80.

Peterson, J. (2018) 'Structure, Agency and Transatlantic Relations in the Trump Era'. *Journal of European Integration*, Vol. 40, No. 5, pp. 637–52.

Petersson, M. (2019) *Nato and the Crisis in the International Order: the Atlantic Alliance and its Enemies* (London: Routledge).

Polyakova, A. and Haddad, B. (2019) 'Europe Alone: What Comes after the Transatlantic Alliance'. *Foreign Affairs,* 11 June. Available online at: https://www.foreignaffairs.com/articles/europe/2019-06-11/europe-alone?utm_medium=promo_email&utm_source=promo_2&utm_campaign=jun19-camp3-newsltr-panel-a&utm_content=20190626&utm_term=jun19-camp3-newsltr-panel-a. Last accessed 20 June 2019.

Pompeo, M. (2018a) 'US Secretary of State, Remarks at the German Marshall Fund'. Brussels. Available online at: https://ua.usembassy.gov/remarks-by-secretary-pompeo-at-the-german-marshall-fund/. Last accessed 22 May 2019.

Pompeo, M. (2018b) 'Remarks by Secretary of State Mike Pompeo at Nato Headquarters'. U.S. Department of State. Available online at: https://www.state.gov/remarks-at-a-press-availability-3/. Last accessed 20 September 2019.

Sbragia, A. (2010) 'The EU, the US, and Trade Policy: Competitive Interdependence in the Management of Globalization'. *Journal of European Public Policy*, Vol. 17, No. 3, pp. 368–82.

Stoltenberg, J. (2017) 'Doorstep Statement by Nato Secretary General Jens Stoltenberg at the Start of the European Council. Available online at: https://www.nato.int/cps/en/natohq/opinions_150001.htm'. 14 December. Available online at: https://www.nato.int/cps/en/natohq/opinions_150001.htm. Last accessed 5 January 2018.

The Guardian (2018) 'Trump calls European Union a 'foe' – ahead of Russia and China'.15 July. Available online at: https://www.theguardian.com/us-news/2018/jul/15/donald-trump-vladimir-putin-helsinki-russia-indictments. Last accessed 1 August 2018.

The New York Times (2018) 'Nato Summit Live Updates'. 11 July. Available online at: https://www.nytimes.com/2018/07/11/world/europe/trump-nato-live-updates.html. Last accessed 12 July 2018.

Tusk, D. (2018) 'Remarks by President Donald Tusk before the G7 Summit in Charlevoix, Canada'. Available online at: https://www.consilium.europa.eu/sv/press/press-releases/2018/06/08/remarks-by-president-donald-tusk-before-the-g7-summit-in-charlevoix-canada/. Last accessed 1 June 2019.

Tusk, D. (2017) 'Reinforcing European Defence: Remarks by President Donald Tusk at the Event of PESCO'. 14 December. Available online at: https://www.consilium.europa.eu/en/press/press-releases/2017/12/14/reinforcing-european-defence-remarks-by-president-donald-tusk-at-the-pesco-event/. Last accessed 20 February 2018.

White House (2018a) 'Remarks by President Trump and Nato Secretary General Jens Stoltenberg at Bilateral Breakfast'. Available online at: https://www.whitehouse.gov/briefings-statements/remarks-president-trump-nato-secretary-general-jens-stoltenberg-bilateral-breakfast/. Last accessed 20 September 2018.

White House (2018b) 'President Donald J. Trump Is Cutting Off Funds the Iranian Regime Uses to Support Its Destructive Activities Around the World'. 8 May. Available online at: https://www.whitehouse.gov/briefings-statements/president-donald-j-trump-cutting-off-funds-iranian-regime-uses-support-destructive-activities-around-world/. Last accessed 20 September 2018.

Zandee, D. (2018) 'PESCO Implementation: The Next Challenge'. Policy Report. (Clingendael: The Netherlands Institute of International Relations). Available online at: https://www.clingendael.org/sites/default/files/2018-09/PB_Pesco_Sept2018.pdf. Last accessed 1 March 2019.

JCMS 2019 Volume 57. Annual Review pp. 128–140   DOI: 10.1111/jcms.12931

The EU in Russia's House of Mirrors

MAXINE DAVID[1] and TATIANA ROMANOVA[2,3]
[1]Leiden University, Leiden [2]St. Petersburg State University, Saint Petersburg [3]Higher School of Economics, Moscow

Introduction

2018 offered little hope to those still waiting for the potential of the EU–Russia relationship to be realized. If anything, relations continued on their downward descent, aided by Russia, some of the EU member states themselves and their 'ally' across the water, the USA. The stagnating relationship was punctuated by moments of high drama, even farce. However, both sides continued to polish their established positions, as signified by the remarks of the EU's High Representative for Foreign Affairs Federica Mogherini (2018), following a session of the Foreign Affairs Council and by the Russian Foreign Minister Sergei Lavrov (2018a) at the Russian-German Forum. For the EU, it boiled down to the five guiding principles on Russia (Mogherini, 2016), whereas Russia insisted that it had not been integrated properly and on equal terms into the post-Cold War architecture, while remaining open to deep, primarily economic, relations with the EU.

For the most part, the year contributed to a feeling that the key actors were waiting, but it is not precisely clear for what. Russia's hosting of the World Cup helped to legitimate Putin's regime in the manner that such a spectacle is designed to achieve (Koch, 2017), going some way, at least in the public mind, to offset the negative publicity garnered as a result of a number of its activities. Yet Russians themselves grew increasingly unhappy about their declining standards of living, which affected their support for the government's course (Levada, 2019) but not their support of Putin. Meanwhile, the EU looked like an organization under pressure from a number of internal problems, notably growing populism and nativism in member states and narratives of disintegration fuelled by Brexit, which help to crystallize the ambitions of Putin's Russia.

As in other years, in 2018 Russia functioned as a house of mirrors for the EU and its member states, often distorting their image, sometimes reflecting them accurately, at other times making them look better than they were in reality. In this respect, five points deserve particular attention: the EU's unity and solidarity; its values and identity; its long-term goals and selective engagement; the EU's and Russia's damage limitation by encouraging multilevel relationships; and the EU–US–Russia triangle.

I. EU Unity and Solidarity

To begin with the relatively positive features, the continued solidarity shown in relation to Russian actions in Ukraine should not go unremarked. Here, the institutional backbone of the EU has to be credited. Few commentators were unsurprised by the early agreement to impose sanctions on Russia and few have been unsurprised about their rollover in the years since then, given member states' exposure to the Russian market and therefore the price paid in relation to EU sanctions and the Russian tit-for-tat sanctions imposed on European agriculture and other products. In 2018, the EU extended sanctions six times and added new names to various black lists on three occasions (the presidential elections in Crimea, the construction of the Kerch bridge and the so-called elections in the breakaway regions of Ukraine). Amid pressure to maintain coherence and in the absence of a consensus to lift the sanctions, the choice has been to maintain them, a choice aided, admittedly, by the fact that the sanctions are linked to the Minsk agreement, for which there is a lack of political support in Kyiv.

Any surprise at the solidarity on sanctions stems from a wider and justifiable view that the member states are divided on Russia. Nevertheless, 2018 offered evidence that differences in the EU should not be overstated and that there is much that glues the member states together. Greece, often seen as the weak point here, serves as a good example. In June, the controversy between Greece and the Former Yugoslav Republic of Macedonia over the latter's name was resolved, with both parties agreeing to a renaming, resulting in the emergence of the Republic of Northern Macedonia in February 2019. Russia's objection to the deal struck between Athens and Skopje was well known. In October 2018, the Russian Ministry of Foreign Affairs (MFA) reacted publicly to the Republic's referendum, understandably referring to the low turnout that invalidated the vote, as well as to how 'leading politicians from NATO and EU member states participated in this large-scale propaganda campaign directly, freely interfering in the internal affairs of this Balkan state' (Ministry of Foreign Affairs of the Russian Federation, 2018). This did not stop Greece playing its part in removing an obstacle to North Macedonia's membership of NATO. Moreover, the support that the Greek Orthodox Church provided to the Ukrainian Orthodox Church autocephaly led to a further deterioration of relations between Moscow and Athens.

The Skripal poisonings that occurred in England in March 2018 (alleged to have been committed by Russian military intelligence officers) were for many a sign that Russia was no longer playing by any rulebook that the West could accept. Although Russia argued that the accusations were unfounded, the event prompted a strong show of solidarity from the EU and led to a mass expulsion of Russian diplomats from most EU member states (and others, including the USA). The June European Council called for measures to prevent further similar incidents and in October, the Council adopted a new mechanism allowing the introduction of restrictive measures to prevent proliferation and chemical weapons usage. The feeling that an EU member state was under attack contributed to the speed and intensity of the EU's reaction.

Nevertheless, member states pursued their own agenda in certain areas, probably the most prominent example being the Nord Stream II gas pipeline, intended to enlarge the direct link between Russia and Germany. Various national politicians advocated the improvement of relations with Russia and argued that sanctions were not fulfilling their function. Italian and Hungarian leaders were particularly noticeable in this regard. Moreover, Austrian, French and Greek leaders visited Russia to explore ways to engage with it but also to use their bilateral dialogues to negotiate leverage in the EU.

In sum, the Russian house of mirrors reflected an overly flattering image of EU solidarity and unity in the context of an uncooperative and assertive Russia. In that sense, Russia continued to function as the 'Other' against which the EU's unity and solidarity was reaffirmed. Significantly and unfortunately, no member state managed to turn its more positive relationship with Russia towards improving the EU-Russian relationship; nor did that unity deliver any constructive, long-term solution of how to deal with Russia.

II. Values, Identity and Soft Power

Recent events have therefore seen Russia functioning for many member states and Brussels itself as the 'Other', against which not only its unity but also its very identity is asserted. The April 2018 Council on Russia highlighted the idea that the 2016 'five guiding principles […] provide a flexible framework for EU relations with Russia, allowing firmness on EU values and selective engagement where there is a clear EU interest' (Council of the European Union, 2018). Hence, for the EU, values continued to figure prominently, despite its efforts to instil more pragmatism in its external relations, as illustrated by the 2016 Global Strategy (EU, 2016). The EU continued to criticize Russia both for the attack on the rules-based international order, notably in Ukraine, and for the 'decrease of respect for human rights and the rule of law' in Russian internal politics (Mogherini, 2018). Hence, EU soft power logics with their promotion of liberal values were preserved.

Russia was continually reproached for interfering in the EU's political life, including through its contacts with and support of populist, Eurosceptic and frequently extreme right political forces. Those political activists visited Russia, advocated the lifting of sanctions and the recognition of Russia's 'repatriation' of the Crimea. Moscow widely publicized their visits, especially domestically, to demonstrate that its position on Ukraine had some support in the EU and the West. At the same time, far-right political activists' attention to Putin as a charismatic leader and their praise for Russia's embrace of conservative values form, for some, elements of Russia's nascent soft power (Keating and Kaczmarska, 2019). This serves various purposes for Putin, assisting in Russia's identity-building project, connecting to like-minded actors elsewhere in Europe, and undermining the EU's attempts to consolidate its values-based identity (Stepanova, 2015).

Russian perception of the EU's soft power remained ambiguous. Russian officials tend to emphasize that the EU is Russia's key economic partner, omitting mention of most of the EU's political and any (possible) normative influence (see Lavrov, 2018a, for example). Yet, the publicity given to the visits by any EU politician to Russia is easily interpreted as a search for the EU's approval and hence the EU's legitimation of Russian policies (Morozov, 2015).

The EU's promotion of values is universal but becomes stronger when Brussels talks to European countries. Russia's claims to be a European country have therefore always reinforced the legitimacy of EU's demands. Elsewhere, analysis may have pivoted to neo-Eurasianism in Russia and the seeming rejection of its European identity, yet, as Shekhovtsov (2008) persuasively argues, even the most conservative of Russian neo-Eurasianist authors, Alexander Dugin, draws on a body of European intellectuals to develop his concepts. The Kremlin has also continued to support the charge against perceived attempts to conflate Europeanness with EU membership; challenging the EU's right to speak on behalf of Europe and to monopolize the idea of Europe. At the same time, Russia itself sometimes reinforces the notions that it rejects. An analysis of official MFA statements reveals that Russian officials themselves increasingly use the adjective 'European' to refer to the EU; moreover, in 2018 Russia again participated in Asia–Europe (EU) Meetings (ASEM) as an Asian state. On top of this, the EU's Partnership Instrument classified Russia as a part of Wider Asia. Hence, both sides give the impression they have drifted away from the straightforward recognition of Russia as a European country (without necessarily implying the EU's authority to set the norms).

Developments in 2018 in EU member states continued to challenge the EU's normative authority and soft power, such that attributing all negative developments there to Russia would be a distortion of the reality. One of the ongoing challenges for the EU, a challenge fast approaching crisis point, is how to increase the salience of 'Europe' for its citizens and defend 'European' values against the assertion of nativism. In December 2017, the EU instituted Article 7 proceedings against Poland for breaching the rule of law; a fundamental value of the EU, following up in 2018 with the decision to take a similar route with Hungary. Orbán's appeal to traditional, Christian values (Orbán, 2018) are consistent with Putin's now familiar invocation of religion, tradition and conservatism in political life.

Perhaps most worryingly, profound questions have been asked of the European Parliament's centre-right grouping, the European People's Party, for its failure to expel Hungary's Fidesz party from its bloc. Both sets of Article 7 proceedings look unlikely to be resolved any time soon (de la Baume and Bayer, 2018) and the 2019 European Parliament elections show that the consequences for the European People's Party have, like chickens, come home to roost. Those consequences will be felt far more widely than the single grouping or the European Parliament itself, given the latter's central role in much EU decision-making today. Long the (only) voice of conscience for the EU on its relations with Russia, the European Parliament's failure to defend European values robustly is significant and undermines its extensive and intensive litany of complaints against Russia (see especially European Parliament, 2019). If power in the European Parliament swings more towards the political groupings whose grievances are directed at the EU and not Russia, this will both play into Kremlin narratives and potentially be the catalyst that breaks EU solidarity on sanctions against Russia and hinder more recent decisions to prepare a Magnitsky Act for the EU (European Parliament, 2019).

Russian funding of extreme right and left parties and the amplification of their messages through Russian media such as Sputnik and RT has been the subject of much attention (Klapsis, 2015; Laruelle and Rivera, 2019; Shekhovtsov, 2008, 2017). The extent of Russian influence continues to be disputed, although Klapsis speaks of the 'astonishingly similar stance towards Putin's Russia' in these political parties in Austria, Bulgaria, France, Greece, Hungary, Italy and the UK (2015, p. 13). However, as with other issues, we should be cautious in attributing too much agency to the Kremlin; states today are exposed to the same structures, policies and consequences as each other, that they give rise to similar political groups and politics is unsurprising. This is particularly the case in the context in which Russia does not have the same significance for all member states, as highlighted by the varying extents to which EU member states consider Russia a threat or a friend (see Liik, 2018). For Mediterranean states, the bigger perception of threat comes from the south in the form of refugees from conflict zones and migrants, for some of those further to the east, it is Russia's activities in Ukraine. Thus, geography, history and events determine whether arguments for pragmatic dialogue and engagement preside over arguments for punishment as deterrence.

Even while the EU is open to criticism for its failure to mount a swift and robust defence of its values, the dilemma it has faced has not been its alone, as debates about Russian membership in the Council of Europe show (see, for example, House of Commons,

2018). Liberal democracies and their organizations, of course, are required to balance competing demands from competing levels of politics and society. Yet those debates challenge the EU's normative authority and, if anything, Russia's house of mirrors magnifies the contradictions in this normative authority.

III. The Long-Term Agenda versus Selective Engagement

Both Russia and the EU continued to believe in 2018 that time was on their side. Any, even emergent, proposal for a long-term solution was entirely absent. Rather, the reiteration of the five guiding principles emphasized that any rebooting of EU–Russian relations would require the full implementation of the Minsk agreement (Mogherini, 2016, 2018). Further signs of entrenchment came with the continued reliance on the existing international institutions, most importantly with twin controversial - for Moscow - facts still unacknowledged: NATO remaining as the key for the continent's security; and the (crucial for Moscow) asymmetry of today's international (security) arrangements, highly Western and Euro-centric in form as they are. Lavrov gave a clue to Russian thinking, when speaking of living in 'a post-Western world' one 'still […] in the process of formation' (Lavrov, 2018b). Hence, Moscow concluded it has only to wait until the collective West (including the EU) collapses and a new world order that is fair to Russia will be established. Nevertheless, Russia voiced no substantial alternative, remaining loyal, at least rhetorically, to the principles of market economy and democracy.

In the absence of any long-term concept of cooperation, the EU had to cling to another of Mogherini's guiding principles, that of selective engagement. The High Representative cited a fairly long list of issues that were 'strategically important for Europeans' (Mogherini, 2018): the nuclear deal with Iran, the Middle East peace process, Afghanistan and North Korea, as well as the environment, migration and the fight against terrorism. 'Selective engagement' on 'strategically important' issues in itself seems a contradiction in terms, betraying the EU's perception of it as engagement out of necessity. Russia for its part believed that it was a step towards more pragmatic, interest-based cooperation.

Both the long-term agenda and the choice of areas for selective engagement are dependent on threat perceptions. The EU continued to view Russia as a source of various threats, against which it had to be resilient. Before 2018, these threats were related to energy supply, hybrid threats in the cyberspace and strategic communication. In 2018, the EU added to the list the disproportionate activity of Russia's security services as well as potential chemical, biological, radiological and nuclear-related risks, following incidents in Salisbury and The Hague. The EU had proclaimed in its 2016 Global Strategy that in a connected world the 'Union cannot pull up a drawbridge to ward off external threats' and promised to 'manage interdependence' (EU, 2016). Yet, as energy relations and the information war demonstrated, this was easier said than done.

In energy, the European Commission ended an anti-monopoly investigation against Gazprom, and Germany defended Nord Stream, using loopholes in the third liberalization package, in line with the kind of market logics and interdependence traditionally promoted by the EU. Nevertheless, Nord Stream attracted severe criticism from many other member states. Moreover, the EU continued to look for ways to diversify its energy supply or to rely more on domestic sources and therefore to disengage with Russia. The transit of gas through Ukraine, especially after 2019, remained a contentious issue, leading to numerous bilateral (EU–Russia) and trilateral (also involving Ukraine) consultations. Hence, geopolitics continued to compete with market logics, dividing rather than uniting EU member states.

Similarly, in the information space, a liberal approach granting the free circulation of information and the freedom of speech, competed with geopolitics. The first presupposed a free flow of information but also increased the responsibility of information agencies and the mass media as well as advocating better education of citizens. The second is a more paternalistic strategy, of identifying what is 'fake' (which can lead to the stigmatization of some media), or even limiting access to such information. Both approaches found their way into the 2018 EU Action Plan against Disinformation (EU, 2018). The European Commission favoured the liberal approach while the European External Action Service (EEAS) with StratCom, charged with fighting Russian disinformation, tends to incorporate the more paternalistic approach. A greater variety of positions exists among member states, divided between those that favour complete freedom and those that believe that blocking some media is justified (Kremlin Watch Team, 2018).

Russian disinformation was not specifically named in the Action Plan, a sign perhaps of a realization that any Russian activities in this regard can find traction only in a polity and society that has been left vulnerable to such tactics. In this sense, Russia might be said to function, entirely unintentionally, as a critical friend that shines a light on the susceptibilities within the EU member states, as well as the institutions of the EU; Russia therefore is an aggregator of discontent. In the coming years, we might reasonably hope also that the EU will show signs of realizing that such dangers emerge from within and implement measures to combat them. Such a realization will be vital for the improvement of EU–Russia relations.

Treatments of historical events are a further case in point. In an editorial in October 2018, amid preparations across Europe to commemorate key anniversaries of the Second World War, the Russian Ambassador to the EU Vladimir Chizhov chose to sow division rather than accord, referring to the anniversary of the partition of Czechoslovakia. Questioning the motivations of France, Italy and the UK, Chizhov cast the partition as an attempt to make the USSR the target for 'Nazi aggression', comparing it with the exclusionary nature of the European security system today (Chizhov, 2018). Such rhetoric is apiece with other attempts by the Russian leadership to harness history for contemporary political purposes. It can also be seen as a preemptive attack against EU discussions of the 1939 Molotov–Ribbentrop Pact.

In sum, Russia's house of mirrors revealed the EU's self-centrism and inability to begin the search for a long-term solution. EU–Russian relations also demonstrated the vital necessity of selective engagement, although this is conceptualized in different ways by Moscow and Brussels, as well as the difficulty the EU faces when preserving an open and liberal approach in the context of numerous real or perceived Russian threats in the energy and information spaces.

In the face of this rather depressing state of EU–Russia relations, this account now argues for the necessity of drilling down beyond the political relationships, which, no matter how important in political terms can also be superficial and twist perceptions. It is the case that the relationship has continued to function at multiple levels, something rarely reflected in wider accounts and narratives; for this, both actors should be credited. The next section addresses this plurality, even while acknowledging that problems continue to beset the relationship. Nor is it optimistic about the prospects for overcoming these problems and achieving more fruitful engagement and cooperation. Nevertheless, the fact of the multiple levels should not be disregarded.

IV. Damage Limitation: Multilevel Relationships

Most intergovernmental relations between the EU and Russia have remained frozen since 2014, but in 2018 the top leaders met on the margins of various international events (like the UN, the G20 or ASEM). Meetings between top figures of the EEAS and the Russian MFA were also regular. Trans-governmental relations continued to stall. No EU–Russian dialogues (including on energy) were resumed and just a few meetings of EU and Russian officials (on energy, veterinary, migration, science and technology and the prevention of drug trafficking) were arranged on an ad hoc basis. The EU provided sparse information on those meetings while the Russian Mission to the EU carefully documented all the meetings to demonstrate that various contacts with the EU are preserved. Small EU projects on counterfeiting, piracy and technical barriers to trade were continued. The EEAS engaged with Russian partners more actively than the Commission (normally reputed to be more technical and less political), perhaps best understood as being the result of the areas chosen for selective engagement. Contacts among Russian MPs and their peers in the European Parliament were not restored in 2018, which did not prevent the European Parliament being the EU institution most critical of Russia.

Russia's calls to establish relations between the EU and the Eurasian Economic Union (EAEU) continued to fall on deaf ears, although the EU's Delegation in Russia maintained unofficial contacts with EAEU officials, mostly relating to the approximation of standards and technical regulations. The nature of that engagement confirmed both the remaining importance of the EU as Russia's key economic partner and the EU's wider market power.

The EU continued to demonstrate its interest in the Arctic region (governed by the Arctic states, none of which is an EU member, although EU member states are susceptible, particularly low-lying states like the Netherlands, to the effects of climate change there) on the basis of the 2016 communication that stresses the EU's expertise in the environment to justify its involvement in the governance of the Arctic. The allocation of the EU's Partnership Instrument to Russia was even renamed as Russia/Arctic to signify the EU's interest and involvement. The Arctic remains one of the few issue areas where Russia has something to offer to the EU to relaunch the relationship. Yet, neither Russia nor other Arctic states are ready at the moment to incorporate a new player into the governance of that region.

The EU and Russia preserved cross-border cooperation (that is, involving sub-state actors in different bordering states in the EU and Russia and covering a range of sectors, including, cultural, scientific, educational and commercial) and their funding of related projects has continued. Five projects continued to function at the Russian border with Finland, Estonia and Latvia. The Russian MFA paid much closer attention to those remaining islands of cooperation. Yarovoy (forthcoming) rightly conceptualizes them as playing 'an important stabilising role ensuring the continuation of regional cooperation'. Moreover, the Northern Dimension cooperation that brings together the north-west of Russia and the Nordic and Baltic states as well as parts of Poland and Germany bordering the Baltic Sea, was also preserved. Here, as elsewhere, of course, the existence of subnational networks alone are no guarantee of success. One of the things we know is that funding matters and, as Yarovoy points out, to a large extent, future cross-border cooperation (CBC) will depend on the allocation of money from the top downwards.

Business to business transnational relations have suffered far more than other transnational relations as a result of the declining relations between the EU and Russia, largely because of sanctions (Romanova, 2016) but also due to non-tariff barriers to trade that have survived Russia's accession to the World Trade Organization. Russia put its policy of import substitution firmly in place in 2018, which will ultimately make the deepening of economic relations more difficult. Finally, US secondary sanctions make EU businesses extremely cautious when engaging with Russian partners.

In looking for reasons for optimism, transnational civil society's and educational contacts provide some traction. In education, for instance, the story is one of continued EU funding of higher education projects through the Erasmus+ programme. The number of Jean Monnet projects in Russia passed the 100 mark in the period 2015–18, compared with 22 in 2007–14 (Deriglazova and Makinen, forthcoming). The extent to which academic cooperation contributed to the emergence of a transnational academic community remains contested (Romanova, 2019). The EU also carried out a project on public diplomacy, which involved experts' dialogue on EU–Russian relations as well as support for various academic exchanges and study visits to Brussels. Although the exposure of the project to Russian civil society gradually grew, its role in increasing the visibility of the EU and its image in Russia remains to be explored.

Finally, the EU continued to support, both administratively and financially, the EU–Russian civil society forum, on which Russia has been lukewarm since its launch in 2011. Moscow at the same time promoted cooperation between the more institutionalized civil society structures: the Civic Chamber of the Russian Federation and the EU's Economic and Social Committee. Their regular meeting took place in September 2018 and was publicized by the Russian MFA. Hence, Moscow attempted to assert supervision over the civil society dialogue (including by way of selecting participants) by suggesting an alternative to the forum. The EU for its part supported both lines of civil society engagement. The EU also remained sensitive to Russian societal demands, responding, in particular, to the growing criticism of gender inequality in Russia by preparing a less politicized project, the National Action Strategy for Women.

Less positive contact continues in the form of relations between parties of the extreme right and left in EU member states and Russia, supported by the latter (including by funding). These parties provoked all sorts of suspicions in the EU. It remains to be seen whether anything comes from the establishment of groups such as that in April 2018 of the People's Council of Russian Germans (Volksrat der Russlanddeutschen), headed by an MP from Alternative für Deutschland, a German nationalist party (Klapsis, 2015). United more by their opposition to the EU, the global financial system and other manifestations of the liberal world order than anything else, these groups may be willing to draw on the anti-European and anti-Western sentiments of some in Russia (Polyakova, 2014) but the longevity and effectiveness of any contacts are very questionable.

Public opinion polls underline the message that pluralism does not automatically result in an improvement in perceptions or relations. In December 2018, the Pew Research Centre's poll of 25 countries, including 10 EU member states, was revealing of a negative view of Russia. Of the EU states, only Greece expressed a favourable view (52 per cent favourable, 48 per cent unfavourable) (Letterman, 2018). Polls in Russia reveal that the proportion of those who have a positive opinion of the EU decreased from 76 per cent in 2004 to 19 per cent in 2014 but bounced back to 36 per cent in 2018 (Levada, 2018). Although the dynamics seem to be relatively positive on the Russian side, their attitude to the EU remains very critical, aided by both sanctions and Russian official narratives that characterize the EU as subordinate to the USA. Such polls are, of course, snapshots in time. They matter, however, because they speak of how attitudes are being framed within each of the areas and therefore are indicators of the challenge that will be faced by policymakers of the future seeking to return relations to a more positive footing.

In sum, the Russian house of mirrors reflected the downslide of traditional EU-fostered transgovernmental and business links, although the EU tried to compensate for this by fostering civil society contacts, educational exchanges and cross-border cooperation. Russia responded positively to most of these initiatives, yet with efforts to put them all (including civil society dialogues) on a more institutionalized and better supervised basis and to imitate the EU's activities in its own territory, promoting Moscow's version of soft power.

V. The EU–Russia–US Triangle

2018 contained remarkable moments in the dynamics between the EU, Russia and USA, especially with President Trump's tour of Europe that was tornado-like in its effects. It is difficult to remember a greater boon to critics of the rational decision-making model than President Trump placing the EU at the top of the US's list of 'foes', ahead of both Russia and China. Helsinki was then the scene for a far from ordinary press conference, starring the presidents of Russia and the USA, Trump's performance so startling that the former Central Intelligence Agency director John O'Brennan was moved to call it 'treasonous'. Extraordinary in the particularities, the year was nonetheless ordinary in its consistency with the more long-term triangle of relations in which the EU and the USA have not always seen eye to eye over how to deal with Russia and in which the USA has often been critical of Europe's lack of self-sufficiency.

President Trump's relationship with Russia continued, of course, to be the subject of multiple investigations in the USA, most notably Mueller's, even while for many in Washington it was Russia that was the object of suspicion, for some a pariah. Trump continued to criticize European NATO members for not fulfilling their budgetary obligations, leading to much speculation about the USA's commitment to Europe. Meanwhile, the EU moved ahead with developing 34 projects under Permanent Structured Cooperation (PESCO), including in relation to training, maritime, cyber joint enabling and space. Developments here will be closely watched from Moscow but ultimately it should be remembered that Trump is not the first US president to level such criticisms at the Europeans or to try and pivot away from Europe. Nor is PESCO the first manifestation of an EU intention to develop its own security architecture and, by its very nature, it is as much a signifier of the reluctance of some in the EU to move ahead here as it is of the enthusiasm of others to do so.

Despite the unpredictability of the present incumbent of the White House, cooperation between the EU and the USA on Russia remained strong and coherent, which is mostly the result of the institutionalized politics on both sides and the power of bureaucracy. Russia's favourite idea of playing the nineteenth-century game of triangles (in this case, EU–US–Russia) and balancing one against the other, predictably failed one more time. It is for this reason that Russia continued to argue that the EU is not ready for any independence from US decision-making and readily incurred economic losses as a result of US-inspired sanctions (Lavrov, 2018b). Yet, the picture remained more nuanced than Russia portrayed when palpable interests were on the table. For example, the EU (under German pressure) managed to negotiate exceptions from US secondary sanctions for the companies that construct Nord Stream II and remained determined to complete that very project despite the ever-intensifying pressure from Washington to decrease dependence on Russian oil and gas.

That being said, the development of US sanctions legislation, when the same and additional sanctions are supported by new pieces of legislation and – more importantly – by additional motivation (Russian interference in elections, weapons proliferation, human rights' violations, illicit trade with North Korea and support to Syria), meant that US sanctions were cast in stone, and made it impossible to lift them in the near future. That contrasted vividly with the EU's present strategy of linking sectoral sanctions against Russia with the Minsk agreement as well as with the political rationale of using sanctions as an instrument to change policy. The US sanctions strategy (coupled with its secondary sanctions that threaten any company wishing to operate in the US market and violating US sanctions) effectively deprives the EU of its most powerful foreign policy instrument, sanctions. It also means that, in Russia's eyes, the attractiveness of the EU as an economic partner and independent player has plummeted as a result of the rush of sanctions in Washington.

At the same time, the Trump Administration's decision to abandon the deal on Iran enhanced the importance of Brussels' selective engagement with Russia on the Joint Comprehensive Plan of Action. Moreover, the EU's decision (realized in February 2019) to set up a financial mechanism to bypass US sanctions is watched with great interest in Moscow – although at present it does not lead to any illusion that EU-Russian relations will greatly improve.

In sum, despite some reasons to be nervous about the extent to which today's USA can be relied upon and reasons also to be frustrated by some unhelpful developments, the EU–US relationship offered few opportunities for Russia to exploit divisions. Nor have Russian activities given cause for the USA to make good on its threats to leave the security of Europe to the Europeans, quite the contrary.

Concluding Remarks

The EU–Russia relationship matters for a number of significant reasons. It is the EU's largest neighbour, the state with which it has the longest ground border and is, as such, a key security actor. But it is also *the* test case for the EU, a test from which the EU once again has not emerged well. Russia evades any attempts to fit it into the EU's existing pattern of relations and the EU has still not managed to develop – or even imagine – a new one.

The future of the EU–Russia relationship is naturally dependent on a range of factors. However, it is perhaps most dependent on each actor acting in a manner consistent with its own self-interest. First and foremost, each needs to acknowledge certain problems as homegrown. The divisions increasingly evident in the EU are the product of internal (to the EU as well as the member states individually) differences. Russia may seek to exploit them, to sow further division and dissent but it has not created the original problem. Equally, Russia's problems are not the result of EU interference, they reflect certain growing authoritarian tendencies, disappointment with the international engagements of the 1990s and the slow development of civil society. In blaming the other, each actor is indirectly pointing to its own vulnerabilities. That vulnerability would exist even in the absence of the other actor. Yet, at the moment, Russia acts as a powerful house of mirrors for the EU, amplifying its drawbacks and current problems, doing little justice to its achievements or contributing to them along negative lines alone.

References

Baume, M. de la and Bayer, L. (2018) 'After Parliament SLAPS Hungary, What Next?' *Politico*. Available online at: https://www.politico.eu/article/hungary-article-7-viktor-orban-after-european-parliament-slaps-what-next/. 13 September, updated 19 April 2019. Last accessed: 5 May 2019.

Chizhov, V. (2018) '80th Anniversary of the Great Treachery in Europe'. Euractiv. 1 October 2018. Available online at: https://www.euractiv.com/section/global-europe/opinion/80th-anniversary-of-the-great-treachery-in-europe/. Last accessed: 5 May 2019.

Council of the European Union (2018) 'Outcome of the Council Meeting 3613rd Council Meeting. Foreign Affairs'. Luxembourg, 16 April. 7997/1. Available online at: https://www.consilium.europa.eu/media/33743/st07997-en18.pdf. Last accessed: 28 May 2019.

Deriglazova, L. and Makinen, S. (forthcoming) 'Academic Cooperation'. In Romanova, T. and David, M. (eds) *Handbook on EU–Russian Relations: Structures, Actors, Issues* (London: Routledge).

EU (2016) 'Shared Vision, Common Action: A Stronger Europe. A Global Strategy for the European Union's Foreign and Security Policy', Brussels, Available online at: https://eeas.europa.eu/archives/docs/top_stories/pdf/eugs_review_web.pdf. Last accessed: 12 May 2019.

EU (2018) 'Action Plan against Disinformation'. Available online at: https://ec.europa.eu/commission/sites/beta-political/files/eu-communication-disinformation-euco-05122018_en.pdf. Last accessed: 29 May 2019.

European Parliament (2019) 'Report on the State of EU-Russian Political Relations' (2018/2158(INI)). Available online at: http://www.europarl.europa.eu/doceo/document/A-8-2019-0073_EN.html. Last accessed: 5 May 2019.

House of Commons (2018) 'Russia and the Council of Europe'. Available online at: https://researchbriefings.parliament.uk/ResearchBriefing/Summary/CDP-2018-0179#fullreport. Last accessed: 29 May 2019.

Keating, V.C. and Kaczmarska, K. (2019) 'Conservative Soft Power: Liberal Soft Power Bias and the "Hidden" Attraction of Russia'. *Journal of International Relations and Development*, Vol. 22, No. 2, pp. 1–27.

Klapsis, A. (2015) *Unholy Alliance: The European Far Right and Putin's Russia* (Brussels: Wilfrid Martens Centre for European Studies).

Koch, N. (2017) *Critical Geographies of Sport, Space, Power, and Sport in Global Perspective* (London: Routledge).

Kremlin Watch Team (2018) *2018 Ranking of Countermeasures by the EU28 to the Kremlin's Subversion Operations*. Prague: European Values Protecting Freedom. Available online at: https://www.kremlinwatch.eu/userfiles/2018-ranking-of-countermeasures-by-the-eu28-to-the-kremlin-s-subversion-operations.pdf. Last accessed: 2 November 2018.

Laruelle, M. and Rivera, E. (2019) *Collusion or Homegrown Collaboration? Connections between German Far Right and Russia* (Hungary: Political Capital). Available online at: https://www.politicalcapital.hu/news.php?article_read=1&article_id=2393. Last accessed: 5 May 2019.

Lavrov, S. (2018a) 'Vystuplenie i otvety na voprosy Ministra inostrannyh del Rossii S.V. Lavrova na Germano-Rossiiskom forume, Berlin'. 14 September. Available online at: http://www.mid.ru/web/guest/meropriyatiya_s_uchastiem_ministra/-/asset_publisher/xK1BhB2bUjd3/content/id/3344050#sel=34:53:DG9,34:100:hfh;33:50:5Tp,33:114:0yw;47:46:haq,47:85:VaV.   Last accessed: 28 May 2019.

Lavrov, S. (2018b) 'Interview ministra inostrannyh del Rossii S.V. Lavrova britanskomu kanalu "Kanal 4"'. Moscow, 29 June. Available online at: http://www.mid.ru/web/guest/meropriyatiya_s_uchastiem_ministra/-/asset_publisher/xK1BhB2bUjd3/content/id/3285972 Last accessed: 29 May 2019.

Letterman, C. (2018). Pew Research Center. Global Attitudes and Trends. 6 December 2018. Available online at: https://www.pewresearch.org/global/2018/12/06/image-of-putin-russia-suffers-internationally/. Last accessed: May 5 2019.

Levada (2018) 'Otnoshenie k ES'. 11 March. Available online at: https://www.levada.ru/indikatory/otnoshenie-k-stranam/. Last accessed: 21 March 2019.

Levada (2019) 'Otsenka tekuschego polozheniya del v strane'. Available online at: https://www.levada.ru/indikatory/polozhenie-del-v-strane/. Last accessed: June 3 2019.

Liik, K. (2018). 'Winning the Normative War with Russia: An EU–Russia Power Audit'. European Council on Foreign Relations. 21 May. Available online at: https://www.ecfr.eu/publications/summary/winning_the_normative_war_with_russia_an_eu_russia_power_audit#.   Last accessed: 4 June 2019.

Ministry of Foreign Affairs of the Russian Federation (2018) 'Comment by the Information and Press Department on the Results of Macedonia's Referendum'. 1 October 2018. Available online at: http://www.mid.ru/en/foreign_policy/news/-/asset_publisher/cKNonkJE02Bw/content/id/3363368. Last accessed: 5 May 2019.

Mogherini, F. (2016) 'Remarks by High Representative/Vice-President Federica Mogherini at the Press Conference Following the Foreign Affairs Council'. Brussels, 14 March. ID: 160314_02. Available online at: https://eeas.europa.eu/headquarters/headquarters-homepage/5490/remarks-by-high-representativevice-president-federica-mogherini-at-the-press-conference-following-the-foreign-affairs-council_en. Last accessed: 29 May 2019.

Mogherini, F. (2018) 'Remarks by HR/VP Mogherini at the Press Conference Following the Foreign Affairs Council'. Luxembourg, 16 April. Available online at: https://eeas.europa.eu/diplomatic-network/european-neighbourhood-policy-enp/42996/remarks-hrvp-mogherini-press-conference-following-foreign-affairs-council_en. Last accessed: 28 May 2019.

Morozov, V. (2015) *Russia's Postcolonial Identity: A Subaltern Empire in a Eurocentric World* (Basingstoke: Palgrave).

Orbán, V. (2018) 'Viktor Orbán Denounces the Blackmail of the EU – Full Speech'. *V Post*, September 11. Available online at: https://visegradpost.com/en/2018/09/11/viktor-orban-denounces-the-blackmail-of-the-eu-full-speech/. Last accessed: 5 May 2019.

Polyakova, A. (2014) 'Strange Bedfellows: Putin and Europe's Far Right'. *World Affairs*, Vol. 177, No. 3, pp. 36–40.

Romanova, T. (2016) 'Sanctions and the Future of EU–Russian Economic Relations'. *Europe-Asia Studies*, Vol. 68, No. 4, pp. 774–96.

Romanova, T. (2019) 'Studying EU-Russian Relations: An Overview in Search for an Epistemic Community'. *Journal of Contemporary European Studies*, Vol. 27, No. 2, pp. 135–46.

Shekhovtsov, A. (2008) 'The Palingenetic Thrust of Russian Neo-Eurasianism: Ideas of Rebirth in Aleksandr Dugin's Worldview'. *Totalitarian Movements and Political Religions*, Vol. 9, No. 4, pp. 491–506.

Shekhovtsov, A. (2017) *Russia and the Western Far Right. Tango Noir* (London: Routledge).

Stepanova, E. (2015) 'The Spiritual and Moral Foundation of Civilisation in Every Nation for Thousands of Years: The Traditional Values Discourse in Russia'. *Politics, Religion and Ideology*, Vol. 16, No. 2–3, pp. 119–36.

Yarovoy, G. (forthcoming) 'EU-Russian Cross-border Cooperation, its Instruments and Programmes'. In Romanova, T. and David, M. (eds) *Handbook on EU-Russian Relations: Structures, Actors, Issues* (London: Routledge).

JCMS 2019 Volume 57. Annual Review pp. 141–151   DOI: 10.1111/jcms.12933

The Calm after the Storm: Plurilateral Challenges to the Post-2020 EU–ACP Partnership

MAURIZIO CARBONE
University of Glasgow, Glasgow

Introduction

The Cotonou agreement governing relations between the EU and the group of African, Caribbean and Pacific States (hereafter the ACP group), will expire in February 2020. Preparations somehow proceeded smoothly until early 2018, when both sides were hit by a storm, which lasted for a good part of the year before calm eventually returned. This contribution, accordingly, investigates different types of challenges posed to the renegotiation of the EU–ACP partnership. Firstly, it sketches the rationale behind the proposal made by the European Commission (EC) in December 2017 for an innovative framework consisting of a general section that is applicable to all ACP countries, and three regional pillars applicable to countries in Africa, the Caribbean and the Pacific, respectively. Secondly, it delves into the process resulting in the adoption of the EU negotiating mandate in June 2018, including the rows between EU member states over the duration of the future agreement, the institutional organization and the issue of migration. Thirdly, it examines the preparatory process in the ACP group, particularly the adoption of its negotiating mandate in May 2018, but also the problems generated by some contradictory pronouncements made by the African Union (AU), first entailing the abolishment of the ACP group and then recommending a two-track process, one for EU–ACP relations and the other for EU–AU relations. Fourthly, it touches upon the initial phases of the EU–ACP negotiations, characterized by delays and complications, which are attributable to the form rather than the substance of the future agreement.

I. To Renew, or Not to Renew: The Proposal of the European Commission

The adoption of the Cotonou agreement in June 2000, which succeeded the Lomé Convention (1975–2000), was hailed as the last step before the full normalization of relations between the EU and its former colonies. Broader in scope than its predecessor – a third pillar on political dialogue was added to development and trade cooperation – it was meant to deliver on the fight against poverty and contribute to the integration of ACP countries into the world economy, while reflecting the politicization of the EU's external action with a new or stronger emphasis on democracy, human rights and good governance, as well as security and migration. Over the course of its implementation, however, these expectations were met only in part. Importantly, relations between the two sides became strained because of the controversial negotiations of the economic partnership agreement, intended to replace the trade regime resting on non-reciprocity applied across all ACP countries with a new system based on free trade agreements to be concluded with different subregions. The adoption of the Joint Africa–EU Strategy (JAES) in 2007, which brought together countries in both North Africa and sub-Saharan Africa, with the AU playing a leading role, and of the Joint Caribbean–EU Partnership Strategy in 2012, added concerns over whether the EU–ACP cooperation framework was fit for purpose (Bossuyt *et al.,* 2016; Carbone, 2013; Montoute and Virk, 2017).

With negotiations between the EU and the ACP group due to start by the end of August 2018, the European Commission, together with the High Representative of the Union for Foreign Affairs and Security Policy, engaged in an extensive preparatory process instigated by the adoption of a discussion paper (October, 2015) and followed by consultations with different stakeholders (October–December 2015) and an impact assessment evaluating several scenarios, resulting in a communication that presented the building blocks of the future EC proposal (November, 2016). The starting point was whether the EU–ACP partnership should be preserved in its entirety or for the most part, given its contractual and comprehensive nature. Linked to this was the idea of anchoring future relations with the ACP group in a legally binding framework, in line with the EU's approach of adopting broad framework agreements with third countries. The alternative was to adopt three separate agreements, one per region: Africa, the Caribbean and the Pacific. In the case of Africa, one point of contention concerned the role of North African countries in the new framework, considering that each of them had signed association agreements with the EU under the European Neighbourhood Policy (ENP) (Carbone, 2019; Keijzer and Schulting, 2018; Kühnhardt, 2016).

The culmination of this preparatory process was the recommendation adopted by the EC on 12 December 2017. The EC proposed to have a single agreement with unlimited duration, consisting of a general part applicable to all ACP countries complemented by three distinct regional compacts in the form of protocols. The EC proposal stipulated that the general part of the future agreement would list overarching objectives, principles and priorities, and streamline the institutional system: the EU–ACP Summit and the EU–ACP Council of Ministers would take place on ad hoc basis and the Joint Parliamentary Assembly would be replaced by a joint meeting of the three regional assemblies to be held only if necessary. The regional protocols, governed by more regular summits, councils of ministers and parliamentary assemblies, would become the centre of gravity for action, reflecting the growing importance of regionalism and regional actors as well as the increased differentiation in challenges and needs among the three regions. The EC also proposed to deliver finally on the one Africa approach, somehow involving countries in North Africa, possibly by granting them the status of observers (EC, 2017).

In terms of substance, the EC reaffirmed its ambition to promote political norms in relation to peace and security, human rights, democracy and good governance, or to integrate into the future agreement the relevant goals on human development and environmental sustainability of the 2030 Sustainable Development Agenda and the Paris agreement on climate change. Importantly, the EC was much bolder than it has been on previous occasions about the promotion of EU economic interests, specifically over the generation of business opportunities for European entrepreneurs and investors. Furthermore, it placed strong emphasis on preventing and fighting against irregular migration, including the adoption of an effective mechanism aimed at strengthening the legal obligation of countries of origin to readmit and reintegrate irregular migrants. The addition of a new part on international cooperation, building on the decisive contribution of the EU–ACP alliance for the adoption of the Paris agreement, was an absolute novelty. The aim was that of joining forces to tackle global challenges, thus boosting EU (and ACP) diplomatic clout in international settings, considering that the two sides represent over 1.5 billion people and more than half of UN membership (Carbone, 2018; EC, 2017). A potentially controversial aspect of the EC proposal – vis-à-vis the demands of the ACP group – was the short section devoted to means of cooperation. The motivation lied in the attempt to depart finally from donor–recipient dynamics, replacing the attention previously paid mostly to development cooperation by the new slogan of a comprehensive political partnership. Moreover, the future of EU external assistance was being discussed in a different forum, in the context of the negotiations for the upcoming multiannual financial framework (2021–2027). The plan to incorporate the European Development Fund into the EU budget and to allocate resources separately for sub-Saharan Africa, the Americas and the Caribbean, and for Asia and the Pacific, rather than for the ACP group as a whole (EC, 2018).

II. The Bumpy Road to the EU Negotiating Mandate

The EC proposal was the subject of numerous sessions of the ACP Working Party of the EU Council starting from mid-January 2018 and a few meetings of the Committee of Permanent Representatives in the EU in May and June before the negotiating mandate was adopted in June 2018. The initial aim of the Bulgarian presidency was to finalize the EU negotiating mandate in time for the EU–ACP Council of Ministers of May 2018 and entrust the EC with starting negotiations soon afterwards. Plurilateral Challenges to the Post 2020 EU-ACP Partnership[1]. However, this scenario did not materialize, largely because of disagreements over migration and other issues.

The first bone of contention concerned the architecture of the future agreement. There was broad convergence among EU member states on the fact that the centre of gravity should move to the three regions, whereas positions on the merit of the EU–ACP dimension diverged. In this regard, two distinct matters, the duration of the future agreement and the EU–ACP institutional system, were dealt with together, with the aim of striking a compromise between competing pressures. A group of member states led by France (and supported by countries in southern Europe) endorsed the EC proposal: an unlimited duration of the agreement and the preservation of the EU–ACP institutional system. Another group, led by Germany (and with all Nordic countries being very vocal), insisted on limiting the duration of the agreement by introducing a sunset clause[2] and proposing to abolish the EU–ACP Summit and the Joint Parliamentary Assembly and to reduce the periodicity of the EU–ACP Council of Ministers to ad hoc meetings. Clearly, their intention was to dismantle the EU–ACP framework at the earliest opportunity. Following intense consultations, some taking place between representatives of the two camps beyond the negotiation table, a compromise was found: the duration of the agreement would be 20 years, with a possible extension of 5 years and a midterm review to take place in

---

[1] Note that the ACP working party as well as the working party on development cooperation continue to be chaired by the presidency despite the entry into force of the Treaty of Lisbon, which entailed that that role should have been taken up by the European External Action Service.

[2] The duration of the future agreement would range from 7 years (linked to the upcoming multiannual financial framework) to 20 or 25 years (in line with previous EU–ACP partnerships).

2030 at the expiry of the Sustainable Development Agenda. The EU–ACP Summit and
the Joint Parliamentary Assembly would be abolished and the meeting of the EU–ACP
Council of Ministers would take place every three years or when needed (EU, 2018,
Agence Europe, 19 May 2018; *Euractiv*, 28 May 2018; Keijzer and Schulting, 2018).

A second controversial matter concerned the EU's relations with Africa; specifically the
link between the EU–Africa Protocol of the post-Cotonou agreement and the JAES. The
EC proposal was not very specific, as a result of divergences between different stakeholders within the EC. Some wanted the EU–Africa Protocol to replace the JAES and give
a prominent role to the AU; others cast doubts upon the involvement of North African
countries. Similar divisions arose among the EU member states. On the one side there were
those (primarily Germany) who supported the one-Africa approach and saw the legally
binding nature of the EU–Africa Protocol as a straightjacket, preventing the full involvement of countries in North Africa. On the other side there were those who perceived the
EC proposal as a threat to the European Neighbourhood Policy. Some (among whom
Spain and Portugal were very vocal) were cautious about its implications for the EU's
privileged relations with North Africa; others (specifically the Baltic states and some countries in Eastern Europe) were concerned about the consequences for the eastern dimension
of the European Neighbourhood Policy. These divergences, however, did not significantly
affect the EC proposal, not least because the AU and the 48 African members of the ACP
group had yet to consolidate their position, as explained in the following section. Thus, the
final text indicated that the EU–Africa Protocol would not 'replace and upgrade' the JAES,
as envisaged by the EC proposal, but instead would 'build on, reinforce and upgrade' it
(De Groof and Medinilla, 2019; *Euractiv*, 28 May 2018; Keijzer and Schulting, 2018).

A third divisive issue was migration. The Bulgarian presidency opted first to address all
other parts of the EU negotiating mandate and then concentrate on the migration chapter,
which did not turn out to be a wise choice. The starting point was the balanced and comprehensive approach proposed by the EC, which was endorsed, with some marginal
changes, by all EU member states except Hungary. The government led by Viktor Orbán
sought to downplay the benefits of legal migration and to give more emphasis to the fight
against irregular migration, which in its view was not adequately signalled as a security
threat to Europe (*Agence Europe*, 19 May 2018). The adoption of the EU negotiating mandate planned for the end of May 2018 was delayed as no agreement could be reached in
various meetings of the Committee of Permanent Representatives in the European Union
that could accommodate the demands of Hungary and be acceptable to all (*Agence Europe*,
29 May 2018). A compromise was brokered only after some tense negotiations beyond the
official negotiating table took place, involving the Cabinet of Commissioner Mimica, the
Bulgarian presidency, and a small group of EU member states belonging to the two camps
(Hungary was somehow supported by Poland). The final text strengthened the language on
irregular migration (one of the objectives of the future agreement became that of 'stem-
ming migration'), deleted references to the benefit of migration, and introduced a clear sep-
aration between national and supranational competences. This new approach, reluctantly
accepted by the rest of EU member states, was the price paid to Hungary for the sake of
launching the negotiations on time (*Agence Europe*, 23 June 2018; *Euractiv*, 28 May
2018; Keijzer and Schulting, 2018).

A few additional changes were made to address the specific concerns of some EU
member states but did not alter the substance of the EC proposal – showing that, lacking

experience and a clear vision on EU–ACP relations, the main concern of the Bulgarian presidency was to act as an honest broker and achieve a workable compromise before the end of its term at the helm of the EU. A new section on sexual reproductive health and rights (SRHR) was added as the result of a prolonged discussion between those (mostly in northern Europe) who sought to expand women rights and those (notably Hungary, Malta and Poland) who manifested concerns about the link between SRHR and abortion – which led Poland to place a last-minute reservation on the EU negotiating mandate, that was eventually lifted thanks to the inclusion of a unilateral declaration in the official minutes stating that any measure on SRHR would not impact on national legislation (*Agence Europe*, 21 June 2018). More emphasis, in response to pressure from France and the Netherlands, was given to the EU's Overseas Countries and Territories, foreseeing their greater involvement in political and implementation processes and the possible granting of the status of observers. The same treatment could be reserved, in a post-Brexit scenario, to the UK, whose departure from the EU did not obstruct the EU's preparation for the post-Cotonou agreement (*Agence Europe*, 25 May 2018; EU, 2018; *Euractiv*, 26 March 2018).

The adoption of the EU negotiating mandate on 22 June 2018 attracted limited public attention.[3] More generally, its preparation involved a small circle of senior officials and policy experts in the taskforce set up by the EC, the European External Action Service and the ACP Working Party of the EU Council of Ministers. European non-governmental organizations (NGOs) were invited to periodic consultations with the EU taskforce, organized some public events, and produced a few policy papers, which had a very limited impact, if any, on the EU's position.[4] One of their key concerns, which they shared with the European Parliament, was the approach to migration, in which too much attention was paid to return and readmit migrants compared with establishing the legal pathways for regular migration. As expected, the NGOs complained that, from being the main objective of the Cotonou agreement, development had become just one of the six strategic objectives of the post-Cotonou agreement. The European Parliament and the NGOs also joined forces in seeking to preserve the Joint Parliamentary Assembly, that had played a crucial role over the years not only in enhancing accountability in the EU–ACP partnership but also in cultivating democratic practices across ACP countries (*Agence Europe*, 28 April 2018; *Euractiv*, 26 March 2018, 17 June 2018).

III. The EU's Interlocutors: Clashes between the ACP Group and the AU

The adoption of the ACP negotiating mandate by the ACP Council of Ministers in Lomé, Togo, on 30 May 2018 was the result of a lengthy preparatory process, including two summits of heads of state and government, several meetings of the ACP Council of Ministers, and numerous sessions of the ACP Committee of Ambassadors.[5] The general view was that the EU–ACP partnership had produced significant results, yet some changes

---

[3]The rush to adopt the EU mandate on the fringe of the Economic and Financial Affairs Council of 22 June, rather than in the context of the General Affairs Council of 26 June, should be seen against the risks presented by the AU summit in Mauritania starting on 25 June, which may have made the EU adoption of a negotiating mandate redundant.
[4]Position papers on the post-Cotonou Agreement were also presented by the business community and the trade unions, but also in this case their impact was limited.
[5]The summits were held in Equatorial Guinea in December 2012 adopting the Sipopo Declaration and in Papua New Guinea in May–June 2016 adopting the Waigani Communiqué.

were deemed essential, specifically to ensure that equality between the parties, the achievement of sustainable development goals and the promotion of inclusive growth in ACP countries would be enshrined in the future agreement (Gomes, 2013; Montoute and Virk, 2017). Moreover, ACP representatives consistently reaffirmed their intention to negotiate as one bloc, secure a legally binding agreement and build on the positive experiences of the Cotonou agreement. These guiding principles did inform the ACP negotiating mandate, which also stipulated that in line with the Cotonou agreement, the future agreement should consist of three pillars: trade, investment, industrialization and services; development, technology, science and research; and political dialogue and advocacy, including peace, security and migration. Surprisingly, there was limited reference, if any, to aspects of human development and environmental sustainability apart from health, the oceans and the seas, and climate change. Of particular significance – which led some observers to criticize the rather conservative approach taken by the ACP group – were the sections on institutions and development cooperation. The recommendation was to maintain the existing institutional architecture, acknowledging some differences between the three regions; to preserve the European Development Fund or create a dedicated multi-annual financial instrument reserved to only ACP countries; and to increase intra-ACP funding as a way to strengthen the role of the ACP Secretariat and the ACP Committee of Ambassadors, both based in Brussels (ACP, 2018; Carbone, 2018).

The renegotiation of the post-Cotonou agreement was also discussed in the AU context, where the ACP group was perceived as an obstacle to the AU's supranational aspirations and more generally to pan-Africanism, whereas the AU was seen as the only voice that could legitimately represent African instances to global powers. The uncertainty in the EC proposal that the JAES – seen by the AU, perhaps instrumentally, as a genuine partnership based on the respect of African unity and the promotion of continent-to-continent dialogue – be subsumed by the post-Cotonou agreement generated apprehension in some African capitals and certainly within the AU Commission (Carbone, 2018). Nevertheless, the decision adopted in March 2018 by the AU stipulating that Africa's relations with the EU should be governed by 'a single framework for cooperation from Union to Union/continent to continent, independently of the ACP–EU framework' (AU, 2018), caught many by surprise. Interestingly, it eventually emerged that its consequences had not been fully appreciated by all AU member states. Indeed, one powerful minority, consisting of the then AU Chair Paul Kagame and the AU Commission Chair Moussa Faki Mahamat, their countries of origin Rwanda and Chad, and few others – had managed to impose its preferences on the rest. Their claim was that Africa's bargaining power is in its unity and to achieve more favourable outcomes it was necessary to strengthen the role of AU supranational institutions. By contrast, a vast majority of AU member states were cautious about the risk of pulling national sovereignty and instead felt more comfortable operating within the ACP context (*Africa Confidential*, 26 October 2018; De Groof and Medinilla, 2019).[6]

---

[6]Interestingly, in the same context, 44 countries signed the African Continental Free Trade Agreement, set to become the world's largest free trade area and boost intra-African trade by more than 50 per cent. This was a further signal, together with the ambitious plans to reform the AU's institutional architecture and ensure its financial sustainability proposed by Paul Kagame (President of Rwanda) and Donald Kaberuka (former President of the African Development Bank) respectively, that Africa wanted to become a stronger and more effective actor in the international arena (Carbone, 2018).

The intention of the AU, or specifically the AU Commission, was to discuss the AU decision in the context of the ACP Council of Ministers of May 2018 in Lomé. The request to allow Faki Mahamat to present it formally before the ACP ministers was denied; the legalistic reason being that the Georgetown agreement governing the ACP group did not entrust the AU with any official role in the EU–ACP partnership. Thus, the AU decision was presented by the AU Commissioner for Economic Affairs Victor Harison in a consultation session organized on the fringe of the ACP Council of Ministers to enable all regional organizations to express their position. In this venue, as admitted by Faki Mahamat (2018), some African states took the floor recommending adherence to the ACP structure, which 'demonstrated lack of unity on the African side'. The scenario in front of the EU was unprecedented, having two groups of ministers representing the same countries taken two decisions that seemed difficult to reconcile: in March, the AU ministers of foreign affairs proposed to abolish the EU–ACP framework and instead have the AU negotiate a new AU–EU agreement; in May, the ACP ministers of finance adopted a negotiating mandate for a renewed ACP–EU agreement. The EU opted to take a wait-and-see approach, yet it sought to convey the message that the AU decision was compatible with the EC proposal for strong regional pillars of the future EU–ACP agreement, with the AU playing a leading role in managing the EU–Africa protocol (Carbone, 2018). A solution to this impasse, it was hoped, could come only from the meeting of AU heads of state and government scheduled in Mauritania in early July 2018. Surprisingly, the AU summit was inconclusive and instead returned the issue to the ministerial level, that is, a meeting of the AU executive council, this time enlarged to include ministers in charge of ACP matters. It also asked the EU and the ACP group to postpone the start of the negotiations until all African states and the AU had time to consolidate their position (De Groof and Medinilla, 2019; *Euractiv*, 7 February 2019).

IV. Negotiating at Last

The extraordinary AU ministerial meeting of September 2018 did not produce an outcome document, yet it emerged informally (via the tweets of some African ambassadors) that the EU–ACP framework would not be abolished, and that the AU would have to play a prominent role in a future EU–AU partnership. This resolution, backtracking from the decision taken 6 months earlier, was made public at the AU extraordinary summit of November 2018, where it was specified that the post-2020 negotiations with the EU would follow a two-track process: one through the AU, for continent-to-continent relations; the other through the ACP group, focusing mostly on development aspects. The AU resolve for a two-track process ran counter the one-Africa approach proposed by the EU, whose aim was to streamline different, and often competing, processes.[7] Yet some commentators claimed that 'ironically, much of the lobbying for the ACP to represent Africa was done by the European Commission' (*Africa Confidential*, 26 October 2018).

---

[7]It should be noted that the EU was accused of sending potentially mixed messages about the future of the EU–ACP framework and the role of the AU. In May 2018 an AU–EU Memorandum of Understanding on Peace, Security and Governance was signed, reinforcing existing cooperation with the AU with the objective of African solutions to African problems. In September 2018 President Juncker launched the Africa–Europe Alliance for Sustainable Investment and Jobs with the aim of boosting trade and investment in the whole African continent (De Groof and Medinilla, 2019).

Similarly, Carlos Lopes, appointed AU High Representative for AU–EU negotiations, indirectly blamed the EU: 'my view is that the Africans got confused because they were taking the European mandate as the basis for discussion […] the moment this was clarified there was no problem' (*Euractiv*, 21 December 2018).[8]

Having adopted their negotiating mandates, in August 2018 the EU and the ACP group agreed to launch negotiations through an exchange of letters, but to comply only with the deadline set by the Cotonou agreement (*Agence Europe*, 30 August 2018). Meanwhile, negotiations had been publicly opened in New York on 28 September 2018, in the margins of the UN General Assembly, by the two chief negotiators: the European Commissioner in charge of international cooperation and development Neven Mimica and the Minister of Foreign Affairs of Togo Robert Dussey. In this context it was agreed to structure negotiations into two main rounds: focusing first on the general part of the agreement, to be concluded by the end of 2018, before attention would shift in early 2019 to the three regional protocols. It was also decided that negotiations would be conducted mostly at a technical level in Brussels, with political meetings of the chief negotiators taking place alternatively in Brussels or in an ACP country to resolve outstanding issues (*Agence Europe*, 17 October 2018). The ambition of both sides was to conclude negotiations by the summer of 2019, not just to ensure that the new EU–ACP agreement could enter into force by the deadline of 1 March 2020 but, more importantly, to avoid any potential negative consequence linked to the elections of the European Parliament of May 2019 (*Agence Europe*, 2 October 2018).

Technical negotiations started in mid-October 2018, with a significant amount of time spent on the skeleton of the general part of the future agreement; specifically the titles of the various articles associated to the six strategic priorities: sustainable and inclusive economic development; human and social development; human rights, democracy and governance; peace and security; migration and mobility; environment and climate change.[9] By the first political meeting in December 2018, less progress than expected was achieved, with the chief negotiators being able to note only broad convergence on the structure of the future agreement and agreeing on the need to intensify talks in the new year (*IDN News*, 26 December 2018). At the second political meeting held in April 2019 in Ndjamena, Chad, the first round of negotiations was (declared) to have been concluded. In fact, various issues remained outstanding. Furthermore, the technical teams were tasked to start engaging on the regional protocols. Some high-level consultations were conducted in early 2019 in Samoa and Jamaica, showing significant alignment between the EU and the Pacific and Caribbean regions on the needs and priorities to be addressed in the next decade or less. Similar broad convergence between the EU and Africa was apparently recorded in the consultations conducted in May 2019 in eSwatini, yet in this case the process promised to be less smooth (*Euractiv*, 19 May 2019).

---

[8]It was agreed that the AU Commission would extend technical support to the African members of the ACP negotiating team for their negotiations with the EU (*Euractiv*, 21 December 2018).
[9]The technical experts of the ACP Group were led by ambassadors with the ACP secretariat in a supporting role, whereas for the EU it was a joint effort between the EC (with the Directorate-General for International Cooperation and Development in the lead) and the European External Action Service.

Conclusion

This contribution has identified three phases in the preparation for the renewal of the partnership between the EU and the ACP group. At the beginning of 2018 all seemed on track to conclude negotiations for a successor to the Cotonou agreement on time. The EC proposal for an innovative framework consisting of one general part and three distinct regional pillars was accepted by all EU member states, albeit reluctantly by some. The ACP group, on its part, had agreed on a number of general principles and priorities to guide the drafting of its negotiating mandate. By mid-2018 matters had become complicated. The EU faced an impasse over the issue of migration, which delayed the adoption of its negotiating mandate and risked compromising its credibility. Even more dramatically, the ACP group suffered a major blow: African ministers meeting in the AU context adopted a very controversial decision that implied the dismantlement of the EU–ACP framework, yet soon afterwards the ACP Council of Ministers rushed to adopt unanimously an unfinished ACP negotiating mandate. Towards the end of 2018 calm returned after these storms. The EU was eager to start negotiations, yet it was not clear who its interlocutors would be, at least in relation to Africa. A solution was eventually found, with the AU agreeing on a two-track process, one for EU–ACP relations and the other for EU–AU relations, and the ACP group accepting the idea of action-oriented regional pillars in which the AU could take a prominent role.

These preparatory phases revealed a number of tensions, within rather than between the two sides. In the EU camp, there was the traditional cleavage between the regionalists that sought to preserve the EU–ACP partnership as a unique and comprehensive framework in the EU external action, and the globalists that sought to dismantle it, either by opening it to all developing countries or proposing to concentrate on Africa as a whole. Interestingly, the EU was held hostage over the issue of migration by one of its member states, which had little stake in ACP countries and provided small amounts of foreign aid, exposing the increased politicization of EU–ACP relations. In the ACP camp there was a battle over survival and visibility between the ACP group and the AU, with the EU caught in between. The ACP group and the AU, projecting alternative views on the nature and achievements of the EU–ACP partnership, competed over who would best represent the interests of Africa when engaging with the EU. The AU sought to use the post-Cotonou process to boost its profile as an international actor and its credibility vis-à-vis its member states, in line with its supranational aspirations. The ACP group reacted effectively to threats to its existence, capitalizing on its intergovernmental nature and the experience gained in negotiations with the EU, and eventually succeeded.

These tensions affected both the start and the pace of the EU–ACP negotiations. Though the official launch took place through an exchange of letters in August 2018 and in a public ceremony in September 2018, negotiations on the substance of the post-Cotonou agreement effectively started only at the end of October 2018, much later than expected. Moreover, the unfinished ACP negotiating mandate entailed extending preparatory rounds before ACP representatives could sit at the negotiating table. As for the substance, no significant disagreements could be anticipated over the general principles covered in the chapters on environment and climate change, human and social development, peace and security, and democracy and human rights. By contrast, the chapters on economic development (specifically, investment and trade cooperation) and migration (particularly the issue of irregular migration and readmission measures), looking at the two mandates as well as clashes emerging from various fora, promised to be contentious. The talks on the institutional framework could be expected to be even more divisive, with the ACP group seeking to preserve a major role for all-ACP institutions (for example, the ACP Secretariat, the ACP Council of Ministers and the Joint Parliamentary Assembly) and the EU emphasizing the devolution of responsibility to actors in the three regions, and on the means of cooperation, whereby the ACP group consistently stressed the need to keep a financial mechanism devoted only to EU–ACP relations and sought reassurance on the level of financial commitments from the EU. A similar degree of uncertainty surrounded the talks on the regional pillars, not least because the ACP negotiating mandate did not contain any discussion on the priorities for the three regions – in fact, initial consultations revealed broad a convergence between the EU and the Pacific and Caribbean regions, whereas some hard negotiations on the operationalization of the commitments on migration and on human rights and democracy could be expected for the EU–Africa protocol. All this, ultimately, meant that not only was the ambitious goal to conclude the future agreement by October 2019 impracticable, but even the possibility of having a new treaty by the expiration of the Cotonou agreement did not sound realistic.

References

African, Caribbean, and Pacific group of States [ACP group] (2018). *ACP Negotiating Mandate for a Post-Cotonou Partnership agreement with the European Union*, ACP/00/011/18 Final. 107th Session of the ACP Council of Ministers, Lomé, 30 May.

African Union [AU] (2018). *Decision on the African Common Position for Negotiations for a New Cooperation agreement with the European Union*. Ext/EX.CL/Dec.1 & 2(XVIII), Kigali, 19 March.

Bossuyt, J., Keijzer, N., Medinilla, A. and De Tollenaere, M. (2016). *The Future of ACP–EU Relations: A Political Economy Analysis*. Policy and Management Report 21. Maastricht: ECDPM. Available online at https://ecdpm.org/wp-content/uploads/PMR21-Future-ACP-EU-Relations-PEA-January-2016.pdf. Last accessed 7 July 2019.

Carbone, M. (2013). 'Rethinking ACP–EU Relations after Cotonou: Tensions, Contradictions, Prospects'. *Journal of International Development*, Vol. 25, No. 5, pp. 742–56.

Carbone, M. (2018). 'Caught between the ACP and the AU: Africa's Relations with the European Union in a post-Cotonou agreement Context'. *South African Journal of International Affairs*, Vol. 25, No. 4, pp. 481–96.

Carbone, M. (2019). 'Purposefully Triggering Unintended Consequences: The European Commission and the Uncertain Future of the EU–ACP Partnership'. *International Spectator*, Vol. 54, No. 1, pp. 45–59.

De Groof, E. and Medinilla, A. (2019). Mixed Messages from Europe and Africa Stand in the way of an Intercontinental Deal. Discussion Paper No. 239, September. Maastricht: ECDPM.

European Commission [EC] (2017). *Recommendation for a Council Decision Authorising the Opening of Negotiations on a Partnership agreement between the European Union and Countries of the African, Caribbean and Pacific group of States*. COM(2017) 763 Final. Strasbourg, 12 December.

European Commission [EC] (2018). *Proposal for a Regulation of the European Parliament and the Council establishing the Neighbourhood, Development and International Cooperation Instrument*. COM(2018) 460 final, Brussels, 14 June.

European Union [EU] (2018). *Negotiating Directives for a Partnership agreement between the European Union and its Member States of the One Part, and with Countries of the African, Caribbean and Pacific group of States of the Other part*. ST 8094 2018 ADD 1. Brussels, 21 June.

Gomes, P.I. (2013). 'Reshaping an Asymmetrical Partnership: ACP-EU Relations from an ACP Perspective'. *Journal of International Development*, Vol. 25, pp. 714–26.

Keijzer, N. and Schulting, G. (2018) 'What Role for the Rotating Presidency in European Development Policy? The Case of ACP–EU Relations'. *Journal of European Integration*. https://doi.org/10.1080/07036337.2018.1546303.

Kühnhardt, L. (2016). 'Maturing beyond Cotonou: An EU–ACP Association Treaty for Development A Proposal for Reinventing EU Relations with the African, Caribbean and Pacific (ACP) group of States'. ZEI Discussion Paper C235 2016, Bonn: Universität Bonn.

Montoute, A. and Virk, K. (eds) (2017). *The ACP group and the EU Development Partnership: Beyond the North–South Debate* (London: Palgrave Macmillan).

Index

Note: Italicised page references indicate information contained in tables.

Democratic Party (PD) 77, 78, 80, *81*, 82, 83, *85*, 86, 87, 88
economic issues 83, *85*, 86
election results *82*, 82–83
electoral law 78
EU-related issues *85*, 86, 87
European budget 88
euroscepticism 10, 77–89
Five Star Movement (M5S) 8, 10, 77, 78, 79, 80, *81*, 81–82, 83, *85*, 86, 88
Forza Italia (FI) 77, 78, 79, 80, *81*, 82, 83, *85*, 86, 87, 88
Fratelli d'Italia (FDI) 78, 79, *81*, *85*, 86, 87, 90
immigration 86, 87
Insieme 78
Italian Social Movement (MSI) 90
Lega 78, 79, 80, *81*, 82, 83, 86, 87, 88, 90
Liberi e Ugauli (LEU) 78, 80, *81, 85*, 86, 87
Noi con l'Italia–Unione di Centro (NCI-UDC) 78
Northern League 8, 10, 77, 78, 90
parliamentary elections 6, 8, 10, 77–89
party manifestos 78–79, 80, *81*, 87
Più Europa (+EUR) 78, 79, 80, *81, 85*, 86, 87
Popular Civic List (CP) 78
public opinion 83, *84*
social issues 85
Twitter electoral campaign 79–82, 83, 87
Johnson, Boris 28
Joint Comprehensive Plan of Action (Iran Nuclear Deal)
US withdrawal 114–115, 119–121, 137
Juncker, Jean-Claude 6, 16, 18, 19, 35, 50, 55, 59, 147
'political Commission' 49–61
presidency 49–61
Juncker Fund 56
Kaberuka, Donald 146
Kagame, Paul 146
Khashoggi, Jamal 119
Kramp-Karrenbauer, Annegret 97

Latvia
parliamentary elections 8
Who Owns the State? (KPV) 8
Lavrov, Sergei 128, 132
Lopes, Carlos 148
Lucke, Bernd 92
Luxembourg
BRI agreement with China 7
parliamentary elections 8
Maasen, Hans-Georg 96
Macron, Emmanuel 5, 6, 34, 47, 70, 123
Mahamat, Moussa Faki 146, 147
masculinity 65, 72
Mattis, Jim 115
May, Theresa 9, 16, 21, 23, 24, 28, 29, 34, 115
McMasters, Herbert 115
Meloni, Georgia 80
Merkel, Angela 50, 92, 95, 96, 97, 121, 122
Meuthen, Jörg 98
Middle East 114, 115, 119–121, 124
peace process 132
migration 10, 54, 71, 77, 86, 87, 91, 94, 119, 131, 132, 141, 144, 148, 149–150
Mimica, Neven 148
Mogherini, Federica 115, 119, 121, 128, 132
Monti, Mario 77
multilateralism 103, 107, 108, 111, 114, 116, 119, 121
NATO 10, 115, 117, 118, 121–122, 132, 136
Navarro, Peter 7, 115
neo-nationalism 70
Netherlands 34, *44, 45*, 123, 134, 145
populism 90
New Hanseatic League 34
non-governmental organizations (NGOs) 145
Nord Stream II gas pipeline 122, 129, 132, 137
North Africa 119–121
North Korea 132, 137
North Macedonia 122, 129
Northern Ireland